WITH LOVE

WITH LOVE

by *Maurice Chevalier*

I
The
Music
of
Love

II
Love
in
a
Golden
Bowl

III
In
Sad
or
Singing
Weather

IV
Love
and
Thought
and
Joy

as told to
EILEEN and
ROBERT MASON POLLOCK

Little, Brown and Company
BOSTON   TORONTO

Part of this book
first appeared in *McCall's*.

The lines on page 257 are from
"A Match" by A. C. Swinburne,
Oxford Dictionary of Quotations.

Published simultaneously in Canada
by Little, Brown & Company (Canada) Limited

PRINTED IN THE UNITED STATES OF AMERICA

Illustrations appear at pages 122 and 314.

It is the little rift within the lute,
That by and by will make the music mute,
And ever widening slowly silence all.
                    —ALFRED, LORD TENNYSON

I

The
Music
of
Love

. . . Un

T HE PARIS SKY was gray that hot summer afternoon in
1896. A group of laborers, their clothes grimed with
the plaster they handled all day in the factory beyond the
hill, huddled on the sidewalk around a packing box they
used for a table. They frowned or smiled or scowled over
the cards in their game of *belotte*.

The eight-year-old boy whose head was too large for his
short little body (I'd fought like a demon the day in school
they'd called me "Big Head") stared fascinated at the gam-
blers. Let the other kids play and run in the streets of Ménilmontant — this workingman's section on the right bank of
the Seine west and north of the grand cathedral of Notre
Dame. For me the greater thrill was to feel a part of these

3

men who gambled with real money, centimes enough to buy an armful of the sugared almonds I adored or forbidden cigarettes.

I fingered the coin in my pocket as I'd done a thousand times today. One sou, five whole centimes — a penny — earned for delivering a note to the lady in the apartment house across the street. Perhaps if I prayed for more such windfalls?

Someone was tugging at my sleeve, and though I hated to miss the game even for a second I turned. It could be Mama, tired of waiting supper for me in our shabby two-room flat a block away. But no, it was the man with the note. This morning I had climbed the six flights to the lady's room, given her his note and waited for the hopeful answer. Angrily she had torn it to shreds. I'd brought the pieces back and watched this man's face crumple to the point of tears before he walked away without a word. Now — pale skin with freckles, thin brown listless hair, blue eyes that seemed forever on the edge of watering — he looked twice as miserable and unhappy as before.

My heart sank. I knew he wanted his money back, for I had failed in my errand. "But it wasn't my fault," I blurted and wished I had already spent the sou.

Wordlessly he handed me a new note, and as if my prayer had been miraculously answered, another sou. This was too much to hope for.

"Which apartment this time, m'sieur?"

"The same."

My miracle was premature. The same apartment? I couldn't take his money under false pretenses. I had seen the lady's anger, and I was sure this note would meet a similar fate. But when I told him so, he pleaded with such misery that I felt my conscience was clear. I pocketed my new riches and scurried up the winding stairs. Then, timidly, I knocked. Perhaps I had been too forward before and helped to make her angry. This time I would be a proper little man and earn my fee.

4

I needn't have worried. The lady wasn't angry at all. In fact, she had been crying. Her cheeks were stained with dried tears, and she looked at me blankly till I proffered the paper. Her eyes lit up as she read it and then she blew her nose on her apron and smiled a fluttery smile. I responded with a hopeful grin which disappeared when the lady suddenly moved away. Was there to be no answer at all this time?

But abruptly she was back. In her hands was a flower. A single rose. Not quite red, not quite fresh. But it was her reply, and she patted my cheek gently when she gave it to me for the man who waited outside.

The man himself did more than that. His face transformed from despair to ecstasy, he thrust an extra sou into my hand and ran deliriously into the building. I remember I stood there not exactly comprehending for a moment. Then finally I looked up to the sixth-floor window and I saw them, locked in each other's arms in a long, long kiss.

So now I understood. A lovers' quarrel. I had heard Mama speak of such things. I shrugged and turned back to the game of *belotte*. But a strange thing had happened to me. An amazing thing. Call it an accident — a miracle — what you will. There was something in my heart I had never known before. I found myself distracted, glancing up constantly to that window hoping to see that kiss again. That tenderness — happiness — it suddenly meant more than cards or centimes or even sugared almonds. You see? I was eight years old, and I had been blessed with a priceless moment of living — I had been a witness to the joy of love.

In the sixty-odd eventful years which have passed since that day of awakening, I have come to know those joys of love so intimately. And the pains? Well — like Byron, "I have tasted the sweets and the bitters of love." I have known the heaven and hell of it, the delight and the torment. It has played a starring part in the story of my life, and I'm glad. For to have loved, even if it goes wrong, is to have lived — and these many, many decades I have thankfully been very much alive.

That year when I was eight I also met the pain of love, and this time it crossed my own doorstep. It was Mama who suffered. There were five of us crowded into our cramped apartment — Mama, my father, my brother Charles, who was almost twenty, Paul, who was fifteen, and I.

I had never exactly understood my father. A house painter — and a good worker, they said in the neighborhood — he was sometimes gentle with Mama and us boys, then as quickly as the carrousels of the traveling carnivals that set up nearby he would whirl and become another man. Mean, loud, sometimes even vicious. The reason was simple, though not to a little boy; when my father was sober, he was good — drunk, he was bad. And unfortunately, much of the time he was drunk.

Mama loved him, I knew that. I could read it in her wistful good-by when he left for work in the morning, and preparing supper for his homecoming she used to hum a little tune, an almost eager little tune. Then, as the hour of his appearance passed with no familiar footsteps on the stairs, she would force a smile and feed her boys and begin the wait that always ended in the same way. The door would burst open finally and he would lurch inside. The man who had left so sweetly at the beginning of the day had stopped at *bistros* the whole way home, and now was charged up for his tirade.

I watched Mama silently accept his ill-tempered abuse, never revealing the strain she felt inside. But long after my father had fallen into a drunken sleep and my brothers were breathing softly beside me, I would awake to the sound of weeping to find Mama in the other room, her features twisted with the heartbreak she could hide from everyone but herself.

Once she saw me standing there in the doorway, and she must

6

have seen the bewilderment and fright in my face. Swiftly she put a warning finger to her lips.

"But you're crying, Mama," I whispered.

"Only because my eyes hurt from the bad light all day. It's not easy to sew for four men in such poor light, you know that?"

Somehow I sensed there was more to it than that, but Mama kissed me and sent me back to bed and the next morning I was not even sure that I hadn't dreamed it all. Until a month later — when it happened.

That evening seemed no different from others before it. My father was shouting, shouting — and Mama was saying nothing for fear it would drive him further. But tonight her silence only seemed to anger him more. His mouth contorted with rage, he lashed at her with violent words that mounted to a final explosion while Mama stood there motionless, her eyes widening with shock, her face drained of color. Then slowly her hand touched her pale cheek. It was a gesture of infinite suffering.

I shall never forget the heavy silence in the room. No one moved. Then my father staggered to the door, slammed it behind him, and never came home again. I think Mama knew he was gone forever, and she never talked of him afterwards, but in that one naked moment she could not conceal her anguish. All the drinking and the anger and the cruelty had not erased the memory of what had once been good. Now Mama was aching with the pain of love that was lost.

Eight years old and I was growing up so swiftly. None of it I really completely understood, mind you, but from the moment one is born one begins to feel. And I was feeling something instinctively — that love can wound and love can heal. That it is some mysterious force which is bigger than hate or envy or ambition or greed. Do you know why it is so big? Because without love you are empty and poor — and with it you are rich.

All my life I have been ready for love.

7

I have found it often. It has not always lasted, for there is no guarantee that love is permanent. Yet once it has gone, the heart's unconscious search must go on and on. For as Henry Thoreau put it better than I:

There is no remedy for love but to love more.

. . . *Deux*

IT WAS 1902 and Paris was alive with color and vitality and a special kind of charm. The Eiffel Tower, nearing completion in the year I was born, soared almost a thousand feet in the air, the tallest structure in the world. It looked down on elegant ladies and gentlemen on outings in their splendid open carriages, or carefree crowds cheering the bicycle racers in the Bois de Boulogne, or little excursion boats chugging up and down the Seine with eager sightseers lining the rails. Everyone in his way was feeling the pulse of this enchanting city. So, too, was I.

High, high in the gallery of the big Eldorado music hall I sat. The stage was so very far away from the cheapest seats in the house — but at fourteen, one's eyes are bright and clear and strong. Besides, I was staring enthralled at a vision, and what my eyes missed my imagination supplied. An exciting, dynamic woman was singing and dancing. A beautiful woman with chestnut hair — not small — no, rather tall. In her late twenties at the time, she had a way of moving which was the pinnacle of grace. But she was more than loveliness alone — she was Paris, the symbol of gaiety and good humor and courage and heart.

I worshiped her from afar, never closer than this eagle's nest of a seat for which I had painfully hoarded my centimes. Like so many others in the audiences who flocked to see her, I had been captivated by Mistinguett.

Her real name was Jeanne Bourgeois, but no one thought of her as anyone but Mistinguett. And she was to become the queen of the French music hall, a kind of beloved theatre in my country in those days when the twentieth century was new. Made up of many different acts — song numbers, comedy skits, dance teams, jugglers, acrobats, pantomimists — the music hall was today's television variety show and film musical and theatre extravaganza rolled into one. It was the great popular entertainment of the day.

There have been greater comediennes, greater singers, greater dancers — but all in a single package, there has been only one Mistinguett. Complete shows were built around her, she would carry an entire revue on her lovely shoulders, the spirit of the whole evening. Truly, there is no one like her now — and if another great personality like hers should come along, she would be a star exploding across the sky.

At fourteen a storm is raging within a boy, a potpourri of curiosity and innocence and torment and mysterious longings. Suddenly love has become not just an idea or a theory but a hunger. Sex is at the core, of course, the demand of a young body coming to life. But the heart, too, is asking to be heard, often calling for the unattainable.

It was thus with me. And though I realized that even the

chance to say "*Bonjour*" to the great Mistinguett was beyond me, I knew I would scrape until I had saved enough to come here again — and dream.

I dreamed of becoming a great entertainer. Not so great, you understand, as Mistinguett — that was too much to hope for — but still important enough to know my idol as a real friend and bow when we met in public. It was a wild dream, for though I had entered the world of the theatre with a little crude act of my own, my stage was the cheap café or the dingy music hall of the side streets. Mistinguett was a star. My biggest salary to date was three francs — sixty cents a day.

Yet only two short years ago, I would tell myself, I had sung for my first time before an audience and been paid with a single cup of coffee. I had come a long way, no?

And I was lucky, this much I knew for sure. If not, I would have been a workman like my brother Paul (Charles had married and gone away no one knew where). Metal engraving held little interest for me and starting as an apprentice had even less appeal, so Paul's employer had fired me after a few weeks. From there I'd gone to a carpenter's shop. I lasted fourteen days this time. They'd caught me spending half my working hours in the rest room practicing songs. The electrician let me go because I ran errands like a tortoise; the doll painter ordered me out of his shop when I absently painted eyes where mouths should be because I was thinking of music, music, always music.

Yes, I was lucky, for I had crushed my thumb laboring in a tack factory and in the weeks I couldn't work at the machines I had found my first professional job as a singer. Rouge on my nose and cheeks, costumed to fit the mold of a typical music hall buffoon, I put across my funny songs by switching hat or jacket to portray a comically exaggerated peasant or a silly, lighthearted clown. What the words didn't say I filled in with the broad gestures of pantomime. I had become truly an entertainer, a part of the vibrant, joyous life which stirred my blood and quickened my senses and made me feel completely alive. Barely into my teens, and I was on my way to a rainbow!

There were so many new and unexpected colors in my rainbow, most of them to be found in the Boulevard de Strasbourg. Here flourished the inexperienced singer, the third-rate dancer, the not-quite-funny comedian. They worked in a host of cafés and bars along this street which half slumbered during the day and came vividly to life when the gas lamps were lit and night swept over the city. It was then that the street swarmed with denizens of a world I'd never seen. Women, singly or in pairs, with brightly painted cheeks and lips, wearing feathered hats and worn fur scarves, leaned provocatively against corner buildings to murmur invitations to passers-by. Discreetly at a distance men in striped shirts and perfumed, pomaded hair watched and calculated and joked with each other about their earnings for the evening. Men who lived off women? I was puzzled at first. When I understood, it sickened me a little and frightened me.

I was looking for work in the cafés along their street one day when someone blocked my path. I looked up into the face of a tall, heavy man. I had seen him before, but I wasn't sure where. He had a hearty grin, a bluff manner.

"Didn't I see you sing last week, kid? In a place just around the corner?" He gestured in the right direction and I nodded, pleased. It was flattering to be recognized. "You were pretty good, kid."

"Thank you, sir."

He was looking at my clothes. They were clean but that was all. Since my father had walked out, the Chevalier family had barely eked out a living. Mama had worked endlessly at making lace (the only bit of money she knew how to earn) until she had almost lost her sight from the strain, and the years had not treated us well. Paul had been our sole support till I began to add a few francs with my songs.

"You working now, kid?"

I hesitated. Then a kind of pride which happily has never deserted me took over, and I lied. I said I was waiting for a contract — the job was to begin next week.

He looked at me narrowly. "You sure you don't need any money?"

I did need money. New clothes would have given me an injection of confidence when I had so little. But again I shook my head, and doing so, in one horrified instant I remembered where I'd seen this man. He was one of the pimps. His woman was the little brunette with the dull eyes who waited outside the bar where I'd sung last week. I had never spoken to any of these men, and I felt my face flushing with fear and at the same time shame. My eyes must have given me away, for abruptly he saddened.

"So much the better, kid," he said quietly and motioned me on.

I scurried away. It was only when I was out of his sight that I slowed my pace. I felt a nagging regret. The man had done me no harm — in fact, he had tried to be my friend. His profession was repulsive and ugly, but there was surely more to him than that. It was a lesson I've carried with me always: In the worst of us, there may be good — in the best of us, there is often a little something bad. And the divine lamp which illumines it all is tolerance.

How fast the revelations began to come, once I had found my first "important" job! This historic (not for my employer perhaps, but for me) event took place on the Boulevard de Strasbourg in a café frequented by young girls who drank there with lovers forty years their senior, old girls who bought the favors of sleek, darkly handsome youths, and all the other varying shades of the demimonde.

The owner of La Ville Japonaise was hardly Japanese. She

was a faded blonde with a shrewd, hard gaze from eyes that had seen too much for too long a time. Yet something about me obviously amused her the day I wandered in to stammer a request for an audition. It was not my big head atop a little body, for these parts of me had started to catch up with each other by now. But I was still small and frightened and surely awkward enough to be an unexpected visitor to such a place. Whatever it was, it won me the chance to sing that night at eight. If I was good, maybe there would be a place on the bill. If not? Well, there was always the tack factory.

The dressing room was crowded with men and women. But as I put on my make-up, my eyes saw nothing in the mirror but a pretty, well-built dancer sitting half undressed as she pulled on her stockings. Each movement of her body revealed more to me than I had ever seen before. My throat was dry and swallowing did no good. I barely heard the stagehand's warning to be ready in ten minutes. If she had not completed her dressing, I would probably have remained rooted to the spot. But she left to join the other dancers, and I made my way to the stage pursued by the vision of those feminine secrets I had witnessed. I sang in a trance. No one, I recall, was stirred to wild applause. Yet I was hired for a trial week, and the tack factory was behind me forever.

That night at home my happy sleep was strangely disturbed. I dreamed over and over again of the dancer in her petticoat exposing her full breasts as she leaned to tug at her hose. Morning found me torn between fear and anticipation of the unknown. And there was no one to talk with at home. Innocent, simple Mama (whom Paul and I had inexplicably nicknamed "La Louque," though the name meant nothing) would only be shocked at what had happened. A world where dancers undressed before the eyes of mere boys would be unforgivable. I could not even take Paul into my confidence. His was a purity and naïveté that offered no understanding.

14

So I was on a road without a guide, but there was no thought in me of turning back. The way ahead was exciting and danger-ous and alluring. On such a route a boy could become a man — and quickly.

There are complications in this transition, however, for the greatest obstacle to learning about life is life itself. With no rules available, one must travel the path by instinct alone, and sometimes this leads to disaster. My first such contretemps came after my fourth matinee at La Ville Japonaise. On each of the previous afternoons as I finished my songs I had received warm applause from a young woman — attractive in a rather common way — sitting at a rear table beside a man old enough to be her grandfather. By the way he fondled her and kissed her openly it was apparent their relationship was far from that.

This day I smiled shyly as I passed, and I felt a hand restrain-ing me. Her fingers pressed my arm. "You sang very well today," she said in a low, insinuating voice. "I want you to join us for a drink."

I had never been invited to sit with a patron before, and it pleased me. But in our mixed dressing room backstage, I had seen men and women talk with this girl's soft look and velvet voice and known that it was often only a preamble to more. I darted a glance at her lover. His smile was kind. He seemed not at all concerned by the girl's approach, and I realized that I had been mistaken. Her warmth toward me had been pure friend-ship — and that was all.

A few days later she sat alone at the same table and stopped me again as I passed.

"My friend's away on a trip and I'm lonely," she said and made a mock sad face. "Would it be awful of me if I joined you for dinner?" I must have shown my dismay, for I could ill afford to dine in a restaurant even by myself. She winked at me charm-ingly. "I know you're not rich, so you're my guest."

The thought of saving a few centimes which I could give to

La Louque was appealing. So was her plea that I would be doing her a favor and her friend as well by giving her company on this lonesome evening. When I met her outside and she took my arm familiarly to walk along the street, I was not only pleased at this invitation, I felt a surge of masculine pride as well. Promenading beside a pretty young woman like a man of the world, I could feel the eyes of envious bystanders upon me. It never occurred to me at the time that my being a head shorter than the lady could have evoked the stares. Caught up in the moment, I had conveniently forgotten the disparity in age and size between the two of us.

In a bar where she insisted we stop for a glass of wine, she casually stroked my hand across the table, and mysteriously I felt the same sensation I had known that day with the dancer in the dressing room at the café. I had no ready explanation for this odd emotion, but suddenly its pleasure was more important than its reason. All through dinner the glow remained, and walking back to the theatre for my next performance, I basked in what had been a delightful adventure.

I didn't realize that my adventure had just begun.

The street was dimly lit and dotted with dark doorways. Into one of these the girl pulled me. "You're a cute one," she whispered. "I just have to kiss you."

Which she did, on each cheek as a sister to a brother. But in the next doorway she held me passionately and kissed me on the mouth in a fashion I had never encountered before. It was disagreeable, almost stifling, and I wanted to wipe my mouth harshly to erase it. But ten doorways and many kisses later I had changed my mind. Now I was returning kiss for kiss. My heart was hammering, and the lights of La Ville Japonaise ahead were spinning wildly. Hoarsely I agreed that we should meet again on her first free day.

Once inside, my performance was less than sparkling. My

16

mind was far away in the unknown world of which I'd caught a new glimpse tonight. This had been no furtive glance as before at a half-nude dancer. No, this was life. I hardly dared imagine where it would lead. At that moment I didn't care.

But that night, lying awake in the darkness, conscience caught up with me. Drawn on the one hand by a possible imminent initiation into the fascinating mysteries of sex, I was repelled by the feeling that I had done wrong. I knew this girl was loved by another man, yet I had promised to betray him. How could I face him tomorrow without revealing the truth in my eyes?

Tomorrow took care of itself. The old man was waiting alone at his table as I finished my matinee. He summoned me with a gesture. There was a threat in the way he motioned me to sit down, and I tensed waiting for his attack. It never came. Instead he began to tell me of all the wonderful things he had done for the girl, how much he loved her, how jealous he was. He was pleading with me now. He knew that we had dined together, but this troubled him less than what might have happened afterward. He was tormented constantly with the fear that she would betray him, and last night was no exception. He must know the truth. If he had been humiliated by this girl to whom he had given everything, he deserved at least to know it. I must have pity and tell him all.

I hesitated.

"I won't say a word to her, you understand?" He was on the verge of tears. "But you're an honest young man, I can see it in your face. I have to know the truth!"

It was more than I could stand. This old man was so hurt, so long-suffering that he must be told. To learn exactly what had happened would relieve his mind.

I spared no details. And as I spoke, his lips tightened till his face was drawn with the strain of it. Of course, I pointed out, no more would happen where I was concerned, he could depend on that. Abruptly he cut off my protestations. With a cold good-by he rose and left the café, leaving me taken aback for an instant. He hadn't seemed relieved at all, I was thinking. But this I dismissed with the pleasure of my own relief. I had acted like a man — sincere and frank — and I was proud of my forthrightness.

My satisfaction lasted less than twenty-four hours. After my performance the next afternoon, an unexpected figure was waiting for me outside the café. It was the girl, not soft and pretty and appealing as she had been two nights ago, but strident and ugly, her whole body contorted with fury.

"You dirty little brat!" she snarled, and I stared at her transfixed. What had happened? Had the old man told her after all? "I'll shut your mouth for you!"

Her hand raised menacingly, she moved closer, and I backed away.

"My friend kicked me out, you know that?" she screamed. "You and your dirty lies, I'm going to fix you for it!"

People were beginning to stare and I could feel the shame welling up in me. I had only done what I thought was right, and it had all come out wrong.

"You dirty little brat!"

As she advanced on me, I turned suddenly and began to run. I could hear her on my heels as I fled wildly, shrieking insults after me as passers-by looked on with astonishment and curiosity. The sound of her voice pursued me even after I had eluded her. It stayed with me the rest of the day and into my nightmares. It alternated the whole night long with the old man's piteous plea, "I have to know the truth!"

The next afternoon at La Ville Japonaise I went through my songs mechanically, still stunned. Then I almost missed a note as I saw them — the old man and the girl. Seated together at their usual table, they were holding hands and kissing as if nothing had occurred. And when I had to pass them to leave, holding my breath with fear, I heard them chuckle and whisper as I walked by, "The dirty little brat!"

My brain was in a whirl. I had so much to learn of love. Would every lesson, I wondered, be so bewildering? And to change from a boy to a man — would it remain so complex and difficult? Would it ever, ever happen?

The months slipped by, a blur of engagements at small cafés and theatres around Paris and some as far away as Le Havre, a hundred and thirty miles to the west, where I first saw the ocean. I remember staring wide-eyed at the green breakers crashing against the shore. Their thunder was wild, their beauty so breath-taking I would hardly be able to describe this adventure to La Louque and Paul when I was home again.

But soon there was to be only Mama to share the wonders of this life I was making for myself as an entertainer. Paul announced solemnly one day that he was getting married. Like my father and Charles before him, he was walking out, and all at once the whole responsibility for La Louque was in my hands. There was no more time to be spent in growing up. It had happened. I was the man of the house, therefore I was now a man, as simple as that.

But not quite.

It was February. The memory of the dancer in the dressing room of La Ville Japonaise had long ago been supplanted by others equally disturbing. It was time to do something about it.

The wind shrieked through the narrow, winding streets of Montmartre, and scraps of paper whirled forlornly in the air. I was climbing toward Place Pigalle and the apartment of a young woman who sang in the café where I was working. She had a rich, lusty voice and a personality to match. Many evenings I had listened as she colorfully recounted her experiences with patrons in search of pleasure after the café had closed. Perhaps this girl would be my professor in unveiling the forbidding mystery of sex. But would she be willing?

How surprised she would have been had she known my motive in visiting her apartment! I had told her I wanted to see it, perhaps to find a similar place myself. It was not very admirable of me to lie — but I was desperate.

And it worked. Somehow I found the courage to tell her that I was a man in every way but one, and though she laughed at first — disbelievingly — I protested so fervently and frantically that I convinced her it was so. She smiled gently and I blushed. But it was all right. I had found my professor. At last it was all right.

I think I floated down that hill from Montmartre, my feet completely off the ground. What a leap to freedom I had made! And now there was nothing in the whole unknown enormous world ahead that couldn't be mine if I wanted it. I grinned at everyone I passed and even the sour ones had to force a smile in the face of such extraordinary joy.

Sailing around a corner, I was almost upon the Eldorado before I recognized it. Workmen on ladders were lowering a sign from the marquee of the music hall. I stopped short. It had been months since I'd mounted to the gallery to gaze down reverently upon the fabulous Mistinguett. Now they were removing her name, and my heart was sinking with it.

Then as suddenly it bounded up again. Two men emerged from the stage entrance bearing a gigantic banner. It held only one name: MISTINGUETT.

I understood now. This was the new announcement. Mistinguett was bigger than the entire show, and the proof was there in her name alone to lure the public. I felt a kind of possessive pride as if I were sharing her triumph, and my face must have shown it.

"What are you so pleased about, kid?" One man was regarding me amusedly from his post on the ladder. "Mistinguett a friend of yours?"

"It's possible," I said and walked away with a swaggering confidence I didn't feel. But then suddenly I did feel it. I had told the truth, after all, for it was indeed possible, even probable. Today was only the beginning of a gleaming future where anything was possible. I had only to try — and everything would come my way.

Happily I whistled all the way home.

. . . Trois

THE TUNE I was whistling now was slightly off key. The slow summer season had come. My work, which had gone so well, had begun to fall off, and the little cafés and bars that used to summon me to sing and do my minor sort of comedy had become disappointingly silent. There had been months of steady jobs when I'd come home at mealtimes to chatter with La Louque and hum my new songs for her opinion. I can still see her seated at the kitchen table nodding her approval. We were closer than ever since Paul left, and she could read my moods so well. I was happy then, and she was happy with me. But now it was different. Jobs had become infrequent, and I was worried.

Still, her faith in me never weakened. When I sat disconsolate, maybe even brooding, she would look at me with her gentle blue eyes and reach across the table to touch my arm. "It will be all right, Maurice, just you see." There was a quiet and a sweetness about Mama and the beauty of simplicity. Born in the Flemish part of Belgium, she had a high, serene forehead and a fine-boned face. Her smile when it came was like a light. I adored her, and even years later when I was half a world away Mama was close to me. And I respected her judgment, too, for though she read little and could write less, she had an instinct. I remember so many times when I would bring people home and Mama would cook for them, then sit listening in her reserved way to the lively conversation around her. Afterwards she'd say, "Maurice, don't count too much on that one," or "I don't think this one is what you think he is." And you know something? Many times I disagreed with her and then, in some cases as long as ten years later, I would discover she'd been right all along. Yes, I adored her.

It was La Louque who insisted I go to the Eldorado that night after the performance to meet my friend, a comedian who had recently started in the show there. He'd asked me to come by but I was dispirited. There could be no job for me in a big music hall, so why bother going?

My manner was far from cheerful when I met him backstage. Surrounded by singers and dancers who were working regularly, I could only be reminded that I was not.

"What's this all about?" I said glumly.

"You'll find out." He motioned me to follow him along a maze of corridors. Then he stopped before a closed door. The name printed there stunned me.

"It's a very funny joke," I said bitterly and turned to go.

He seized my arm and turned me back. "You said you wanted to meet her, Maurice. I've arranged it."

It was too much to believe — that only a thin door separated me from Mistinguett and she was expecting me inside. In fact, I did not believe it. But reality caught up with me when my friend dared to knock, identifying himself, and the warm, throaty voice I'd only heard from far beyond the footlights called, "Come in."

She was sitting at her dressing table, her stage make-up gone, and the sight of her beautiful, expressive face unsettled me completely. I stood there awkwardly, not knowing what to say, and then a flood of words poured out. Compliments — deeply meant, intensely sincere, but painfully maladroit.

She had risen by this time to leave, and she stopped me with a kind smile. "How old are you, little Chevalier?"

"Fifteen, Madame Mistinguett," I managed to reply.

"Well, you listen to me." She smiled radiantly. "You've got a cute face, little Chevalier. You'll go places, you know that?"

She moved past me to the door. A man in evening clothes who was waiting there took her arm intimately, she glanced back once and was gone. I didn't move. So long as I stayed in this lavish dressing room, surrounded by her clothes and the scent of her perfume and the feel of her presence, this moment would last.

My friend jolted me back to earth. "Well?"

"Thank you," I remember saying slowly, "thank you."

I must have left the theatre in a kind of trance, much as a sleepwalker would have done, but can you blame me? I had taken a step along the road to a dream. It was almost more than I could comprehend.

But I soon discovered that dreams are no substitutes for calories. Without work there was no money, and the specter of poverty moved in to share life with La Louque and me. Baked potatoes and herb tea, it was all we could afford to eat, and the sidewalks of Paris became good friends with my feet as the holes in my shoes grew larger by the day. Unable to have them repaired, I folded newspapers and stuffed them inside and went on looking for work. But as the days lengthened into weeks and we were existing only on an occasional Sunday job in some dingy café, I began to reproach myself for having aspired to being an entertainer. If I had stayed on at the tack factory or been more attentive to metal engraving or any other job, at least now I would be able to support La Louque and myself.

One Sunday I worked for three francs and what I could garner by passing the hat. Not exactly a hat, but a collection plate that each entertainer held out to the customers at the end of his act. I'd never done this before, and I was ashamed as only the young and proud can be. Whenever I sang, I would move from the stage and tender my plate around, shrinking from the task. Apparently my distaste for what I considered begging showed through. Each time I returned backstage my plate was empty.

That next week La Louque and I ate even less than usual. The situation was indeed becoming critical. Should I throw away the profession I loved and seek another job, anything? I would sit by the window as the waning Paris day drew its curtain of amber, then pale green and finally bluish black, and I would ask myself that question over and over again. The answer was always the same: Your profession does not love you, little Chevalier, your singing, your clowning on stage, your "cute face." You were a fool to think you could climb even a tiny mountain. The ground, that's for you, my boy, with your ordinary background and your pitiful four years of schooling to help you make your way.

I borrowed newspapers from the neighbors to pore over the ads, and opportunity was surely waiting. "Three francs per day," it said and my pulse raced, "for those with splendid handwriting." In order to judge the applicant's ability to address letters stylishly, the company requested a sample letter. Feverishly I set to work, one trial letter after another, and finally I chose the outstanding example and put my signature on it with a burst of confidence. This would be perfect, for I could work at odd hours. There would still be time to look for singing jobs, and one of these days my luck was bound to turn.

Vainly I watched for the postman and the letter of acceptance praising my penmanship. Day after day, but it never came — until one morning the postman winked sagely as I met him in the street.

"You see," he said and wagged a finger at me, "patience is bitter but the fruit is sweet. Jean Jacques Rousseau."

I had never heard of Rousseau, but I nodded happily and took the envelope. Then I stopped short. It was not in answer to my application at all. This letter was from a music hall — the Parisiana. Stunned, I read its brief message. Would I come in tomorrow at two o'clock?

Would I?

I was pacing up and down outside the theatre for half an hour before the time. So much depended on this interview. If I sat down, I must be careful not to cross my legs. The holes in my shoes would proclaim how I needed this job, whatever it was. Sometimes managers shrank from hiring needy entertainers because it was embarrassing to them. This one would have no such problem with me. I was desperate, but only two people in the whole world would ever know it — La Louque and myself.

"I ran across your name on an old program somewhere," the manager said when I sat with both feet planted firmly on the floor. "Are you working this fall?"

I lifted my eyebrows in a way that could mean yes or no or perhaps. "What did you have in mind?" My voice sounded thin and faraway to me, and I prayed silently that my ears had heard me crazy.

"There's a singing spot for you in this year's revue — the opening chorus. A couple of other bit parts, maybe an understudy. Are you interested?"

Interested? I was seething with eagerness. "For ten francs a

26

day," I heard my strange voice saying, and I knew if he offered me five I would seize it.

"We'll give you nine."

I signed the contract, shook hands and was outside in the brilliant glare of the August sun before the whole significance of it hit me. Not only was I working again, in a job that would surely last six whole months, not only would we be able to eat and buy some more clothes and laugh, but there would be no more unimportant cafés and sawdust-floored bars. From now on it would only be the big music halls where important critics came to sit in somber, distinguished judgment and ladies and gentlemen of fashionable society to offer their well-bred applause — where stars could be born overnight.

This was the charmed circle of the real music hall theatre into which I had just been invited — and I had the paper in my pocket to prove it.

I had climbed the mountain after all.

There were agonizing moments before the Parisiana revue opened that fall. Rehearsals went on every day for a month, and I was trying — from my place in the back row of the chorus — to give everything I knew to my performance. It was not easy, for I was forced to stand on tiptoe the whole time in order to be as tall as possible. (I'd overheard the author complaining I was too short for the others in the line.) The combination of trying too hard and being off balance at the same time was almost fatal. The author, overseeing a rehearsal, jumped to his feet.

"Hold it!" he shouted. Then slowly he moved toward me. "Chevalier, I've yet to see anyone as clumsy as you on the stage — you'd be better off as a chimney sweep!"

I stood there in the monstrous silence, feeling every eye in the place on me, and I felt a dizzying flush of shame mount from my shoes to the top of my head. I was going to be fired, I knew it, but the greater anguish at that instant was my humiliation in front of friends.

The man barked a command at me. Do it again — and better.

Automatically I went through the number again, vainly attempting to think of my performance, but my mind was a jumble of dreadful memories: this past summer of misery, my shame at passing the plate, newspapers stuffed in my shoes, the pain La Louque would feel if I returned home out of work. An eternity passed before the author eyed me, then nodded with grudging approval.

"You see what happens when you keep your mind on what you're doing?" He turned away, and I held my breath to force my heart back down from my throat.

Somehow I survived the rehearsals, and it was October and opening night. Long before curtain time I was standing outside the theatre, wide-eyed at my first view of the glitter of an important first night. A long queue led up to the box office for unreserved seats. Carriages drew up to disgorge the smartly dressed early arrivals who would fill the select orchestra section, and I breathlessly watched the latest model 1904 automobiles approach the curb with elegant clatter. I had already seen and memorized the names of these fleet chariots which could move at a phenomenal twenty miles an hour: Dietrich, Mars, Panhard Levassor.

It was a scene out of a fairy tale. I could hardly tear myself away to run for the dressing room inside.

Moments before the curtain was to rise, I put an eye to a peephole and surveyed the glamorous audience. I recognized a man in the front row, bearded, distinguished. It was Leopold, the king of Belgium. From seat to seat my fascinated glance took in the famous personages, and I glowed with the knowledge that only the width of a stage separated me from this dazzling, unbelievable world. Sixteen years old, four years away from a tack factory — could all of this be mine?

And then I saw her.

Mistinguett sat beside the man who had called for her that

night in her dressing room at the Eldorado. I recognized him, and I felt a violent stab of jealousy. She turned to smile at him, and suddenly they were laughing together and I knew with a momentary sadness that it was not really mine, none of it, not yet. But one day? Well, if I had come this far, who could say?

My six months at the Parisiana ran swiftly by. Before they ended, La Louque and I, determined never to go through another lean summer, had amassed five hundred francs, a fortune of a hundred dollars, in the savings bank by carefully setting aside half of what I earned. Economy was still the order of the day. But one new expenditure had to be faced, a wardrobe for me. Compromise was out of the question, nor could La Louque's dexterity with the needle help out, for startlingly I had begun to grow. Not a quiet, gentle, easygoing way of growing up — oh, no. I had leaped up, almost overnight. Suddenly I was tall and lanky and much too long for my clothes.

The logical market place for bargain attire was Temple Square, a sprawling network of stalls open only till noon each day, where one could find by scrambling through merchandise on jammed racks and shelves anything from an officer's uniform to a judge's robe or from frivolous lace underwear to secondhand shirts. Everything was possible at Temple Square, and La Louque and I set out on an expedition.

The new suit I unearthed was remarkable. I was entranced by its extreme cut — ultrawide shoulders and nipped-in waist like a zoot suit — and I was undeterred by the fact that it had obviously been tailored for a big strapping man. I argued heatedly with the salesgirl and brought the price down from fifteen francs to twelve. Now the rest was up to Mama and her talent for alterations.

"Perhaps we should try something a little smaller, Maurice," she suggested timidly.

My mind was made up. I had to have this fashionable outfit. Valiantly La Louque did what she could, and I jauntily entered the theatre that night. True, I felt a little lost in the immensity of fabric, but I felt this was outweighed by the sportiness and style of its cut.

When I crossed the stage, most of the cast was chatting in little groups, and I waited for the compliments which were sure to come when they noticed me.

"Chevalier?"

I turned eagerly. It was one of the leading men in the company, a fellow with a metallic voice like the sound of a rasping file. He was looking me over with an amused eye.

"Is that your grandfather's suit you're wearing?"

He began to laugh and I could hear sniggers from the others. Again I flushed with that combination of anger and shame at being publicly humiliated. Mockery and sarcasm are cruel weapons. They can inflict great pain. When someone has struck me so, I've felt almost helpless to retaliate. I have forgiven and forgotten much graver wrongs than were done to me in the theatre that night, yet, do you know, I was never able to become that man's friend in the years which followed?

"If you don't like my clothes," I said and felt my face burn with mortification, "you've only to get me new ones from your tailor. You can surely afford it."

Then I drew back the enormous shoulders of my comic suit and made the most dignified exit I could manage. But the memory of the incident was with me till the Parisiana season had ended.

Once more I was out of a job, but I had come to realize that the chorus of a revue was not the steppingstone I needed to stardom. My talent, if I had anything to offer at all, lay in some kind of individual rapport with the audience, a feeling that I was singing to each one of them alone. I had my own funny way of selling a song to those people across the footlights. It was a sort of intimacy and friendship and exchange all rolled into one. What's more, I realized with regret, I had never really belonged in this group of experienced, worldly entertainers. Looked down on as a green kid, I'd never dared join in the jokes and discussions backstage. What had I been at the Parisiana but a kind of extra servant on the domestic staff of an imposing household, simply hired to help out for an interval? No, though this engagement had helped me financially at a crucial time, I would have to go elsewhere to entertain as myself — me alone — to find the niche I felt might someday be mine.

Elsewhere was many places. And somewhere along the way the manager of the most important music hall outside of Paris heard of me. His name was François Esposito, known in the profession simply as Franck, and he directed the great Alcazar music hall in Marseilles.

Franck was in Paris arranging his engagements for the winter season when he sent for me at his hotel. I expected to meet a middle-aged, graying impresario. The man who answered my knock was perhaps seven years older than I, rather good-looking, with an unexpected smile. We took an instant liking to each other, and I signed for a three-month tour of Marseilles, Nice, Bordeaux and other lesser towns in southern France. It was a great step forward. A reputation in the provinces would open hitherto closed doors in Paris. I could scarcely wait to get started.

From the moment my train arrived in Marseilles, however, my confidence began to go downhill. The hurly-burly of the station suddenly brought me the flavor of this bustling port where ships dropped anchor from around the globe. A babel of tongues bombarded my ears — was it English, Greek, German I was hearing, or what? And the faces — dark and swarthy, blond and fair-skinned, Oriental — they came from a foreign, unfamiliar world. They would be part of the fiery and unpredictable audiences for which Marseilles was notorious.

I'd been told about these audiences. If they liked you, they would applaud the house down. If they didn't, it would be healthy to get offstage quickly. One might even be shot at from the balcony, so the rumors in Paris had it. For in Marseilles — wild, unruly, wide open — anything was possible.

I found myself trudging across town to the Alcazar, a suitcase in each hand, with enthusiasm that waned by the minute. Passing a sign advertising the new show and finding my name in the middle in large letters, I tried to smile courageously. It was a sickly smile by the time I reached Franck at the theatre.

"Hello, kid," he greeted me. "Get ready to rehearse your songs."

I moved out on stage past a group of acrobats arranging their props and leaned across the footlights to explain to the orchestra leader the little tricks I used. He nodded, raised his baton for the down beat, and I was singing. Well, to call it singing would be an exaggeration. Truthfully, it was a kind of croak, a thin, scratchy voice that startled the musicians, halted a stagehand in the middle of arranging a set, brought Franck's eyebrows together in a taut, troubled frown.

The conductor felt sorry for me. "Shall we try it in a lower key?"

"No, no," I said with an assurance I did not feel. "I'm just tired from the trip. I'll be perfectly all right by tonight."

I finished rehearsing in the same nerve-torn voice, and when I left the theatre everyone looked my way with a pitying glance. No question about it, I could hear them saying silently, tonight's audience is going to murder this kid.

Early that evening at my theatrical boardinghouse I couldn't swallow even a bite of food. No one could encourage me. I was in for a rough time, and I knew it.

That night the Alcazar was jammed to the top balcony. It was a noisy audience, not bothering to subdue its conversation during the first few numbers, but nothing rowdy happened until an old-timer of the music halls named Bertho came out to sing in his high-pitched voice. Tonight, struck with the stage fright

32

that can sometimes catch up with even the most jaded veteran, he began to bleat the melody in tones like a goat.

A few boos started in the balcony.

Then Bertho began to do cartwheels to the rhythm of the music. Suddenly a man in the orchestra stood up. To the astonished Bertho he sarcastically shouted "Bravo" — then turned to face the audience and repeated the call. The audience broke into laughter while the angered Bertho tried to silence them with a new burst of cartwheels. "Bravo, what a dancer!" his heckler yelled and the whole house howled hysterically.

Poor Bertho could take no more. Blind with rage he ran from the stage, only to crash head on into a wall beyond the wings. It was a pitiful sight. And for me, terrifying. A woman singer was on next, and I was to follow. What would this savage audience do to me?

There was not too much time to dwell on the possibilities. The woman, too, was shouted down and rushed off in tears, and suddenly the orchestra was playing my introduction. I glanced in anguish at Franck. No consolation there in his desolate face. With the enthusiasm of a gladiator going to confront the lions, I moved reluctantly to the stage, where pandemonium from the last number still echoed up through the theatre. People were doubled up in their seats, helpless with laughter. The orchestra had reached my cue, but some instinct told me simply to stand there and wait.

The musicians repeated the opening. In my clown's outfit, painted and dressed grotesquely to add humor to my songs, I waited still. The sight of an entertainer who was simply not going to entertain must have puzzled the audience. The hysterical laughter began to break off into giggles and finally became a heavy, almost threatening silence.

I began to sing. The voice which emerged was very like my efforts of this morning, and my first song evoked not a sound from the theatre. I was beginning to wonder if boos were not a better reaction than the mute stone wall I was encountering, for at least they would show that the audience was alive. I tried a comedy monologue. Not a laugh disturbed the quiet. I could see Franck standing hopelessly in the wings.

Then, almost as if I had met their challenge and weathered it to their satisfaction, this strange audience began to respond. My third song brought sporadic laughs, and I took heart. By the time I had finished it, I was being applauded and I knew we were going to be friends. Donning a toy cap of the Foreign Legion, I marched around the stage with a tiny rifle, blowing into the barrel as if it were a trumpet. I sang a rather silly song with this pantomime. They loved it. The whole theatre was laughing with me now, and as I passed Franck still at his post in the wings, he shouted joyously, "It's all right, kid, you're in!" And each time I made a turn of the stage with new verses Franck would grin and repeat, "You're in, kid, you're in!"

Now applause was rocking the theatre where ten short minutes before it had been jeers. Franck came to my dressing room moments later, and I was still shaking from the ordeal I had been through. He clapped me on the shoulder affectionately. "You've won over the provinces, Maurice, you realize that? They like you, they like you!"

I had had my first taste of the violently fickle moods of an audience. How narrow the brink between triumph and disaster! It would be a never-ending battle, I knew that, for each time I walked on stage — no matter where or when — the issue would be in doubt until those nameless faces across the lights decided yes or no. It was terrifying. But stimulating and challenging and, for me, full of the excitement of life itself.

. . . Quatre

I WAS SITTING in the star's dressing room at the Eldorado. It was half an hour before the evening show was to begin, and on the dressing table were jars of make-up, cold cream, towels, cheek rouge, all the accoutrements a performer needs to prepare his face against the merciless glare of the stage lights. The name on the door of this room was mine. The face confronting me in the mirror was mine. Yes, I was the star in this theatre where only five years ago I had barely been able to buy a seat in the gallery.

In the mirror I glanced at the clothes rack, remembering how I had stood beside it when Mistinguett's clothes instead of mine were hanging there. She had gone from the Eldorado soon afterwards to bigger, more important engagements, and though we had passed each other recently once or twice she hadn't recognized me. I weighed my reflection in the mirror. Even if Mistinguett had cared one way or the other, I was thinking, how could she have known me? I had changed. This face was not the one she had seen in this dressing room that night we were introduced.

True, the eyes were the same and the nose and the mouth. But the worshipful young man in his teens was now almost twenty. Time and experience had changed the look of him. They had taught him, also, that to love from afar is often impractical and fruitless. I had never forgotten Mistinguett. I had simply taken my romantic adventures with women from less remote worlds. And though now I had been hired to replace the leading man of the Eldorado while he toured the provinces, I had still not arrived at Mistinguett's level.

My own level, however, was enough to make me pinch myself in disbelief. Marseilles had been a kind of turning point. From that moment on every move had been upward. Franck had signed me for another season, the music halls I played on tour gave me an extra welcome on the strength of my performance at the Alcazar, and just as I had prayed, the doors did open in Paris. It was like throwing a rock in a lake. The ripples spread out and out in a widening circle, and suddenly everything was coming all right.

People even began to talk of the "Chevalier style," a kind of comic dancing that I developed to use with my skits. Next I added tap dancing. There was always something new to be learned.

Then my pursuit of new fields took an unexpected turn.

It began one evening in a café which was a hangout for entertainers. Not great stars — just those performers on the way up and the ones who were on their way back down. One of the latter whom I'd seen staring oddly at me in this place on other occasions, a man with a surly mouth and a short, heavy neck, decided this time to air his grievances.

He staggered a little as he moved to my table.

"Well, star of the century," he said loudly and leaned on the table. "Bighearted of you to mix with us poor no-talented ones!"

Taken aback, I tried nonetheless to be as amicable as possible. "Look, my friend, this is stupid. You've had a little too much."

It was all he wanted. In a voice that silenced the entire room, he launched into a series of deliberate insults. When I said nothing in reply, this seemed to infuriate him even more. "Let's go outside and settle this," he snarled at me. "I'll fix you good, you dirty little braggart!"

My head was going around in circles. I'd never spoken a word before tonight to this man, yet he'd chosen to lash out at me in front of a roomful of people I knew. Should I let him get away with it? I could feel every eye in the place on me. I was even aware how fast the story would get around in our circle, and the thought wasn't pleasant. Yet should I walk out of here and fight when I'd done nothing to provoke it?

I ended up by muttering that I didn't fight in streets, that he must be out of his mind. It was a poor excuse. Actually, I was scared and wouldn't admit it. The room, deprived of a fight, turned back to its conversation, but not without a few mocking glances my way.

The manageress, a young, capable woman, approached as my enemy moved off disgruntled. "You did the right thing, Maurice," she said loudly and eyed the room. "They're all jealous of you, you can't fight them all."

She was trying to help, but it did nothing to allay the shame that was building up in me. I knew I'd been a coward, and sick inside I walked out to suffer alone. I got no sleep that night. I was too busy calling myself names.

The next morning I began my boxing lessons.

Every day I worked out in a gym with a professional boxer. One month of this and even my teacher was surprised with what I'd picked up. I was no champion, but I could take a punch and deliver one in return. And all this time I had been dreaming of revenge. I had spent hours scientifically planning the kind of fight I would follow. It would start with a few cautious lefts to feel him out, then I would let him have it with a solid right. After I had given him a bloody nose, I would blacken his eye and then a one-two with a left and right to the jaw would put him out cold. Each time I went over the routine I would find myself smiling a cold pitiless smile. Yes, vengeance would be sweet indeed!

I stood outside the café one night to be sure my antagonist was within and the place was filled. When the moment arrived, I took a deep breath and moved straight to the table where the man was playing cards. He turned as I touched him on the shoulder, and I felt the room suddenly become quiet.

"You insulted me a month ago, remember?" I was grim and determined. I was also a little green in the face with the tension of this moment I'd waited for so long.

"Yes, what about it?"

My throat was dry, and I was finding it difficult to speak. "You wanted to go outside and settle it, right?"

"Well, what about it?" I couldn't read his reaction, but it didn't matter. I had already chosen my course.

"I don't think a bum like you can hurt me," I said slowly. "Let's straighten this out right now."

The manageress's voice was the only sound in the place. "Bravo, Maurice!"

I heard her with my eyes fixed on the man at the table. He hesitated. Then he shrugged and backed down. "Look, I was a little drunk. I've got nothing against you. Sit down. Have a glass of wine."

38

It was my turn to pause — dramatically, to be sure that the entire room would hear me regain my self-respect. "I don't drink with a coward," I said.

With as much calm as I could muster I turned and walked the length of the room to the cashier's desk to invite the manageress to join me in a drink. What an anticlimax!

I didn't know why the man had avoided a fight. Perhaps it was because word had reached him that I'd been rehearsing daily for this moment. Or perhaps only because the surest way to deal with a bully is to call his bluff. But my revenge had been less delicious than I'd anticipated, I had to admit that to myself. The only real satisfaction I had gained from my month in a gymnasium was the knowledge that I was now able to defend myself with my fists.

Yes, I had grown up since that night at the Alcazar, I told my face in the dressing room mirror as I began to put on my make-up. No wonder Mistinguett had glanced at me in the street without recognition. But I had not forgotten her, not her gamin smile or her eyes that were always alight with the infinite joy of being alive. Perhaps one evening she would be in the audience at the Eldorado and seeing me on stage would suddenly remember. Then she might come backstage to see me, and in this very room we would have a reunion. It was a tender thought. I liked it.

My reverie was interrupted by a knock at the door. It was a note that was to thrust all other thoughts from my mind.

It said simply: "Please come to see me tomorrow in my office. Important." It was signed by the director of the Folies Bergère, the richest, most luxurious and renowned music hall in Paris. This magnificent theatre which was the mecca for international society in search of amusement always used spectacular sets on its stage, noisy and brassy enough to command the attention of the world's most famous and often most bored men and women. My act had none of the glitter and dazzle the Folies

Bergère normally employed. What then could they want of me? I found out the next day. To them, it seemed, I was not a typical singer. With my songs they would get comedy and dancing, even a boxing skit in which I fought an imaginary bout with myself and sent the audience into gales of laughter. They had seen me perform at the Eldorado and they liked what they saw. Women sipping champagne in décolleté gowns and gleaming jewels, men dressed in evening clothes smoking rich Havana cigars — the typical audience at the Folies Bergère — would like me, too, they said.

It was not too difficult to convince me. I signed for the next three winter seasons, the best contract I'd ever had. That night La Louque and I laughed and talked for hours. We made plans for a new apartment, new furniture, even a piano to lend a touch of quality. The flame of the gas lamp threw a dancing light across her hair, completely white now. Her eyes were sparkling. It was a big moment, one of those times when the horizon is altogether bright. There were so many things that this job with the Folies Bergère could bring. Acclaim, reputation, security, achievement.

The one thing I never dreamed it would bring me was Mistinguett. There seemed to be no connection between the two.

But there was.

My FIRST winter at the Folies Bergère had ended. The warm months which followed I had played at an elegant theatre on the Champs Elysées and filled the remaining weeks of summer with a brief tour of the big provincial cities. Now the sun was still bright in the cloudless blue sky above Paris, but the air was fresh and new and full of the rich promise of autumn.

Paris — like New York and London and the other great cities of the world — is born again in autumn. People walk with light, eager steps of anticipation. The shop windows which have seemed almost to slumber in the sluggish heat of summer suddenly burst into blossom. Not the soft pastel bloom of spring, but the vigorous, winy taste and color of the harvest. Autumn is a strong time of year. I've always loved it.

And this autumn seemed the best of all. Another season at the Folies Bergère would soon be upon me. I was anxious to see it started, to move out on stage and face a new audience in a new show. I awoke each morning with the delighted knowledge that I was twenty-four hours nearer.

One day over breakfast my newspaper jolted me more alive than ever. I could hardly believe what I was reading.

"P. L. Flers, producer of the Folies Bergère, announces the signing of Mistinguett to star in his forthcoming season at the music hall."

La Louque was regarding me quizzically. "Is something wrong, Maurice?"

I shook my head. Mistinguett had been on my mind, in my blood for days, stronger than she had ever been before. I had recently seen her dancing in a show with an urbane, good-looking man named Max Dearly. It was an extraordinary dance which she created, a sinuous, provocative, dramatic routine which has since been copied throughout the world as the "apache dance." She had never looked lovelier or more desirable. How I envied Dearly his chance to hold this long-limbed and supple body in his arms! And now, suddenly, Mistinguett and I were to play in the same show. Indeed, nothing was wrong. Everything was unbelievably, impossibly right.

I could hardly wait for rehearsals to begin. Time began to weigh heavily. There were too many hours in every day.

One Thursday matinee I sat in a box at the Alhambra, less interested in the attraction on its stage than in passing the dragging time. Staring down at the audience as the theatre began to fill, I saw a hundred eager glances look upward to the next box. I turned curiously, and my heart missed a beat. I should have known it would be Mistinguett. She was with another woman, and I should have known, too, that Mistinguett would choose the chair nearest me, separated from my chair by only a gleaming metal railing. It had to be that way, that we should be close enough to touch, for when destiny is bringing two people together, it is inexorable.

Mistinguett turned idly in my direction. I was openly looking at her, and our eyes met. I smiled. She began obviously to search her memory for a clue to my identity, but my words could not wait. They tumbled out. We had met before, I said eagerly, a long time ago — and now I, too, was to perform in the upcoming Folies Bergère spectacle. We might even be dancing together.

She looked at me very, very gently. Then suddenly she smiled. "I'm sure we're going to do some very nice things together, Monsieur Chevalier."

Such simple, ordinary words, yet they set off a tumult within me. I had a million things to say, but the show began at that moment and my inner torment raged unheard. I had to content myself with stolen glances throughout the performance at the most ravishing creature in Paris. When the curtain fell, she gave me her hand. I touched it with my lips and our eyes met again. There was something warm and wonderful in her glance. And now the days until rehearsal would be longer than ever. Not until then would I know if that warmth had been anything more than kindness.

Not that I entertained more than a miserable little hope, mind you, for Mistinguett was on the top rung of the Paris ladder and I had barely begun to ascend it. I knew she was pursued by celebrated men in every profession — clever, wealthy, authoritative, handsome men — and moreover, she was reportedly in love with a well-known actor. In the champagne and caviar set Mistinguett frequented I would surely be a clod with two left feet. Still I knew that a beggar could look at a queen and if I were lucky, I might even hold her in my arms and dance a number with her. I would happily settle for that.

The entire troupe gathered on stage the day rehearsals began. We stood facing the empty orchestra pit now covered with a wooden platform on which were seated the producer, the author, the director, officials of the theatre — and Mistinguett. Normally I would have regarded such a formidable array with reasonable calm. I had been a performer for almost ten years, and this waiting around for the assignment of roles in a show was routine in our profession. Not this time. Too much hung on the producer's choice.

When they announced Mistinguett's main scene, I held my breath.

"Chevalier, step forward."

I moved to the platform. Perhaps it was my imagination, but I fancied I saw a slight smile in Mistinguett's eyes. As for me, when I was told to sit beside her while the producer explained the main comic scene of the show, I was so filled with happiness that I was grinning.

First, there was to be some comedy dialogue between the two of us, nine-tenths of it for Mistinguett, the remainder for me. This was to develop into an argument, and as she lost her temper, she was to storm back and forth across the stage slapping my face each time she passed. What was I to do during all this? Nothing. Not a word of dialogue, just stand there and take it until we reconciled in a rapturous dance. Moving obliviously in each other's arms, we were to knock over chairs, tables, even a buffet, then fall over a sofa onto a rug, still embracing, and roll ourselves up in it completely. Finally, the rug would unroll, and clasping each other as tightly as ever, we would dance upstage and disappear through the window.

It was not a delicate, sensitive number, but it was perfect music hall fare. I had no illusions as to why I'd been chosen for it. Dancing experience, youth, and an ability to take punishment that had been developed through boxing — these were the reasons. But it didn't matter. The important thing was that I was to dance with Mistinguett, and every day from eleven till noon the stage was ours to rehearse alone.

There was not a chance that I would be late the next day. I had waked with the first light of dawn, and I was smiling when I opened my eyes. I lay there reviewing the miraculous events which had culminated in this meeting at eleven o'clock. Everything was so completely all right that I felt as if I had to find some flaw in the pattern. What if Mistinguett for some unexpected, untoward reason didn't like me? With great stars there was always the danger of a mercurial temperament that was warm one instant and chilling the next. My smile faded.

I was waiting on the empty stage, already dressed in my dancing clothes, ten minutes before Mistinguett was due at the theatre. I felt strangely apprehensive. I had hoped so long for this great moment and finally when it was almost ready to arrive, some of the sureness of it had evaporated. Now, instead of the savor of anticipation, I was suffering the fear of a possible disappointment.

I heard her heels clicking in the corridor and suddenly she was near. "Am I late, Monsieur Chevalier?" she said noting my rehearsal garb.

"No, no, I was early, Madame Mistinguett."

"I'll change quickly." She turned to leave, then stopped and turned back again, her eyes twinkling. "Madame Mistinguett, Monsieur Chevalier!" She threw up her hands in mock despair. "Rolled up in a rug, it'll never do. How about Maurice and Mist? Do you mind?"

Before I could reply she had disappeared. When she returned, she was wearing a dance costume that hid none of her lovely lines. She was beautiful.

My hands were trembling when I held her in my arms, and I was terrified she would notice. But there was nothing I could do. I had been waiting for this too long to react like a stone. Probably she sensed it. But there was a tenderness and a gentle-

44

ness in her that would have understood and told her to say nothing. Somehow the morning went by, and the rest of the day while the theatre buzzed with preparations for the forthcoming production I thought only of tomorrow and my second meeting alone with Mist.

She was gay and charming and enchanting in the rehearsals which followed. I learned so much about her during those happy hours we spent alone on stage. Her childhood background was much the same as mine, and time after time she would burst into laughter at some typical joke of the streets that she never had occasion to hear in the witty, brittle circle she moved among when our days together were over. For her these happy, carefree mornings when we ran through the routine of our tempestuous dance and then halted to catch our breath and laugh over some shared amusement were marvelous moments of freedom.

For me they were more than that. For me they were the zenith of each day, and when our brief hour was ended I could only wait for the one which would come tomorrow. The time between them seemed long and empty and desolate. I ached to tell Mist that I loved her. I didn't dare. I had promised myself almost at the beginning that I wouldn't try and court her, for if I'd been rebuffed, then even these sweet hours would be lost.

But they were coming to an end. Opening night would be upon us soon, and the thought of this all being over sent me into a panic of anguish. I held Mist tighter than ever as we danced, praying that some of the intensity within me would flow into her and let her know how I felt. One day we whirled through the window at the number's conclusion, and I was still holding her close. She made a movement to disengage herself, and suddenly I couldn't let her go.

"Mist, I — " I broke off, unsure what to say.

She was looking at me strangely. The spell couldn't have lasted more than two or three seconds. The rest of the cast was arriving; we could hear them noisily crossing backstage where we stood. I

45

released her, and she turned away without a word. Nothing had been spoken, yet so much had been said.

The next morning neither of us mentioned what had happened the day before. Almost businesslike in our manner, we began to rehearse the number which was now so well coordinated. The argument, the slaps, the raucous dance, and then the rug. Mist was wrapped in my arms as we began to roll ourselves up into the rug.

And suddenly my lips were pressed against hers, there in the dark and confining world of that carpet. Passionately, demandingly. Mist answered with an intensity as hungry as my own. We clung to each other as the rug unrolled itself again, still kissing, still caught in the fire that had finally sprung to life between us.

There was no turning back now, we both knew it. That entire afternoon we moved through scenes with the rest of the cast, and each time our eyes met they carried the same message — that once this day was over we had to be alone and completely together. This endless rehearsal which was to last far into the night could only postpone the moment when we would find in each other's arms the ultimate meaning of that kiss.

It was almost midnight when we left the theatre. A fiacre was waiting to take Mist home, the driver perched on his ledge above the cab, his horse a shadowy, patient figure in the darkened street. I entered with Mist, and the clip-clop of rubber-shod hoofs against the paving blocks became a muffled symphony through the still night. It was a sound that was soon unheard. For Mist and I were lost in the overwhelming discovery of each other — and love.

... *Cinq*

M IST was waiting in the theatre the next morning. I saw her standing across the stage near the footlights, seemingly deep in thought. Even in repose there was a vibrant excitement about her, and I felt my heart surge with joy. She turned as I stepped from the gloom of the wings. Without a word we moved into each other's arms. It was a tender, rapturous kiss.

"I love you, Mist," I said finally.

Her extraordinary eyes fixed me with their dark, luminous brilliance. She said nothing, but I knew that she loved me, and I was deeply happy.

I knew, too, that the days ahead would not be so simple for us. I wanted to shout my love for Mist to the whole

47

world, but I couldn't, for there was still someone else in her life — the actor whose name had been linked with hers for so long, the man who'd been waiting outside her dressing room that night when Mist and I had first been introduced. This was Mistinguett's public love, the one she dined with in fashionable restaurants, who escorted her to the lavish parties of Parisian society, who loved her perhaps as much as I. Could I ask her to choose between us? Could I in the first full flush of my young love demand that she destroy a relationship which had obviously brought her happiness in the past? Or should I wait and prove to Mist that my love was enough, that I could make her happier than she had ever been before?

Last night, after we had said good-by, I had lain awake for hours and argued with myself. Mist wanted no one to know of our love, at least not for a while. We would meet in secret at a little *bistro* on the Boulevard de Strasbourg, the Café William Tell. There were private rooms where we could be discreetly alone. Clandestine kisses in the afternoon, then, were to be mine. But her evenings were to be spent with the other man in those elegant places where stars like Mist gathered to be seen and adulated. It was an unhappy arrangement, for I wanted to share Mist with no one, and the thought of it gnawed at me. Still, I could find comfort that at least in the daytime she would be mine and every night till the last curtain call. Besides, I told myself, I desired her so much I would have paid an even greater price.

OPENING night at the Folies Bergère was always an opulent and scintillating and splendid occasion. Backstage, confusion reigned as stagehands made last-minute adjustments in scenery, half-nude chorus girls milled around to take places for the first spectacular number, the ballet master reiterated instructions for the thousandth time. Mist and I had rehearsed our complicated scene up to the last minute, for the movements of a precision dance must be honed to a fine edge.

I stuck my head in her dressing room door. "The most beautiful woman in Paris," I said to her reflection.

Mist made a face at me in the mirror, but I knew she was pleased. All women love compliments, but I had seen already how Mistinguett actually needed them. They were a kind of food for her soul, these extravagant things. Mine were not flattery or blandishments, however. To me Mist was indeed the loveliest woman in Paris. It made her happy to hear it, but also it made me happy to say it.

She turned to look at me, and her eyes made a tour of my face as if she were seeing me for the first time.

"Cio?" It was a pet name she had given me, a diminutive for Mauricio, and the way Mist said it, it was a caress. "You'll be very good tonight, Cio."

"And you, Mist."

"So young and handsome. They'll love you, you know that?"

I was a little embarrassed. I didn't feel particularly handsome, and I hated to be reminded that I was young.

"Now kiss me and go away so I can finish my make-up."

It was almost a cavalier dismissal, and for an instant I felt a tiny resentment. Mist had been a great star for years, surrounded by courtiers and sycophants whom she simply took for granted. But I knew I was not among them, so I pushed it aside. By the time we were on stage together I had forgotten it completely.

Our scene had captured the audience. They were laughing helplessly as she buffeted me around the stage, and spontaneous applause broke out as we unrolled from the rug and began our dance toward the window exit. At the window we were to fall full length to the floor to conclude the number. We had rehearsed it with split-second timing, but we didn't know that in tonight's chaos backstage the position of the scenery had been

49

accidentally shifted. My head struck violently against an unexpected protruding edge of the set and my forehead crashed into Mist's face.

We rose to take our bows and horrified I saw blood pouring from an ugly gaping wound where Mist's lip had been split. Stunned by the force of the blow, she couldn't raise her head to acknowledge her applause. It surely saved our scene, for if she had lifted her face to smile, the entire audience would have been shocked to silence. Mist's mouth, her chin and her throat were covered with blood.

Once off stage, she was quickly carried to her dressing room and moments later a doctor was cleaning the wound and assuring us that she would be all right. But I was still inconsolable when he left and we were alone in the room.

I sat beside Mist on the chaise and took her hand. "Mist, it was all my fault," I said miserably.

She managed a trace of a smile that made her wince with the pain of it. "It was not your fault, Cio, it was nobody's fault," she said gently.

"What tough luck to have drawn me for a dancing partner."

"Don't ever say that again, you hear?" Her fingers clung to mine desperately. "The day they chose you was the luckiest day of my life."

A knock sounded at the door, and our producer's voice called out. Quickly Mist withdrew her hand and whispered, "Good night, Cio. Tomorrow at the café."

"You shouldn't go home by yourself, Mist. I'll get a cab."

"No, there's no need."

Of course there was no need, I suddenly realized. The other man would be there, and it was with him she would go to her lavish apartment in the Boulevard des Capucines whose interior I had never seen but whose balcony, overlooking the trees on the grand avenue, I knew so well. I was still the hungry boy with his

50

nose pressed against the shop window, the outsider looking in. Not even the producer of the show could be told there was anything between us. The thought stabbed me. I nodded and rose to go.

Mist's voice was coolly professional as I opened the door. "Thank you for your concern, Maurice. Good night."

P. L. Flers was exuberant in the doorway. "A smash hit, Maurice. A great success." I moved past him, only half hearing the good news, for a thousand emotions were running through my brain. Here was I sharing the stage with the queen of the music halls, probably the most successful young performer in Paris, yet I was weighted with a sadness I could not dispel. I tried to point out to myself that Mistinguett had to be casual with me in front of others because she wasn't free. I pleased her, she said she loved me, but she had promised me nothing. If I were jealous — and certainly it must be that — there was nothing I had the right to do.

It was a special kind of torture. And it went with me that next afternoon to the Café William Tell. The place was almost deserted, its white-clothed tables bright, lonely circles hemmed in by the dark, somber paneling of the walls. The single waiter glanced up and recognizing me gestured to a door in the back. It was the room where Mist and I had our rendezvous.

His name was Picot. Swarthy with black hair and sorrowful eyes, the skin of his face drooping in folds from his cheeks, he had the look of a massive spaniel. He was smiling now and it was a comic sight, for Picot's appearance was so mournful that pleasure seemed out of place.

"The papers are full of your performance last night, m'sieur."

"I know, yes."

"They say you and the beautiful lady are like a pair from a romantic fairy tale. It's a nice thing to say, eh?"

"Yes, very nice."

I had resigned myself to this chatter of Picot which I was learning to endure, but he broke off abruptly. "The beautiful lady is here," he said softly and moved out as Mist entered, heavily veiled as always to go unrecognized at these meetings. So the waiter knew who she was? I told Mist.

"If he's not discreet," she said softly.

I could picture Picot talking and then others and others and finally the truth would be out, and Mist and I would not be able to hide our love any longer. It was a tempting, wonderful vista, but I knew it must not happen that way.

"He won't talk, Mist, I'll see to it." I held her closely in my arms and vowed that nothing would hurt this woman I loved. Not my jealousy — not anything.

THERE are times — most often when one is young and full of hope and verve and dreams — that life seems to be offering the best of everything. Problems? Tomorrow? What are they when all your days are made of pure cream, no milk at all? It's a floating time, when today is all that counts and inside you are light and buoyant and eager for each vivid moment as it comes. The months that followed were that way for me, and they passed in a kind of blur of ecstasy.

There was joy to be found in the simple act of waking to another morning, of tasting the sharp winter air in the few steps from my house to the Café William Tell, there to sip an *apéritif* and half listen to Picot until the telephone in the rear would ring and I would know that it was Mist. I was uncomfortable on the telephone, we had none at home, and I used it as little as possible. But this daily call was not the same, for at the other end of the line, curled up in bed with her warm voice still soft from sleep, was Mist.

"Well, Cio?" she would say, and the sound of her would start my pulse to race. "Shall we meet this afternoon?"

52

She knew what my answer would be. It was the peak of each day when she was free to join me at the café, and on those days when something interfered, I could hardly wait for evening when I would be with her at the theatre. Either way I would hang up aglow with anticipation. Because I was hopelessly, helplessly in love.

So much in love, I suppose, so lost in the contentment of this perfect time, that I forgot — for the only moment in my life — that above all else my work must always be uppermost in my heart and my mind. My work had sustained me through the good and bad years; I had lived with it, breathed with its tempo, dreamed it. Not that I gave less than everything I possessed to the audience each night in my scene with Mist. It was just that I bathed in the delight of the present with little thought for the future. I forgot that my career must go on long after this season had faded.

My plans for the coming summer were the same as last — a two-months turn with my solo act of songs, sketches and dances at the imposing music hall on the Champs Elysées, then a tour of the provinces until the Folies Bergère opened its season again in the fall. I was pleased with my act from last summer, I could see no reason to improve it, to look for something new and exciting to add. My days were too filled with love and hunger for Mist to remember that no performer can stay on top if his work does not constantly show change and growth.

But another entertainer, in a competitive theatre across the street, had not forgotten. Audiences flocked to see him that summer, to laugh as he sang his songs while moving through the crowd. Daringly he would kiss a woman's hand, still singing, grasp a man's cigar and puff it between notes, open a lady's handbag and admire himself in the mirror he unearthed inside. No one had ever done this business before. The novelty was overwhelming. Slipping over from my theatre one night to catch this

53

startling new act, I was suddenly aware that my own, to me, seemed a little stale. I was not jealous of my competition. His act had too little subtlety for me, I had outgrown this kind of low comedy. Yet, watching his success, I knew that I must inject something novel and unexpected into my routine or people would tire of me. But what? For the first time I was worried.

I had just cause for concern. The proof came at the end of my second month. A letter informed me that I was being released from my next year's summer contract. I looked at it in stunned silence. Fired. From the pinnacle to the bottom, I was thinking bitterly. It was not until later that I was to realize the lesson to be drawn from this experience. Don't get carried too high with your own importance, for that way you can't fall very far.

But at that moment I had fallen a million miles. Mist must have felt it that day in the café when we were meeting for the last time before I left for the provinces. I had never talked about my work with her, though I knew if I had a problem she would have told me what she thought, surely even tried to help. Still, I could not share this with her. It was my trial. I had tumbled myself into this crevasse, I must now try and pull myself out. Eight weeks in the provinces and we would see.

Mist and I kissed good-by. At the door she turned, her eyes grave. "Is it all right, Cio? You're sure?"

"I'm sure." I could say nothing more.

Mist hesitated an instant, then smiled a little sadly and left me alone. I watched her go, aching with the thought that fifty-six precious days would pass before I would see her again. It only added to the weight of what lay ahead.

It was a grievous weight. I had time to try and analyze it in the long train ride to the south. This discouragement I was feeling, this inability to create some sparkling innovation for my act — did it mean that my talent had run its course? Or was it simply my morale which had crumbled and with it my inventiveness and imagination? Or worse, was it simply a law which said that what goes up must come back down again?

I found no answers in the cities I played. My name, bright from last season's success with Mist, lured large crowds to the theatres. They seemed satisfied enough. But I was not. I couldn't seem to reach my audience, and I began to try too hard. My voice would start to tighten up after three or four songs. Being the star of the bill did nothing to lift my performance. Instead, it made the task seem heavier for me. The days began to be endless. Paris and Mist and the happy times were so far away now.

I left the theatre one night unhappier than ever. It was not too far to my hotel, so I walked through the humid summer night, not hurrying, for the prospect of an evening alone with the tension which had been building these past few weeks was uninviting. The tour was half over, and I'd arrived at no answers.

My door was ajar, a light was on inside. I hesitated, then threw open the door abruptly, unsure what I would find. Mist looked up at me from the chair in which she had curled herself. I stood in the doorway too surprised to speak.

"Aren't you going to even say hello?" She rose tremulously and stood there waiting for me. I moved toward her, dazed, still without a word, and took her in my arms. Her lips were real, the feel of her body was real, this was no dream.

"I didn't know you were coming," I managed finally to say.

"Nor did I," Mist said softly. "Until this morning and your letter. And suddenly I was on the train and here I am."

"My letter?"

"You were so unhappy, it was in your eyes the day you left. And this last letter, it was in every line."

"I was miserable," I said puzzled. "But I didn't write about it."

"You didn't have to, Cio." She smiled at me, a warm, tender smile. "I knew it."

It was almost too much to believe, that one heart could read another without a word being spoken. But it was true. Understanding is one of the great miracles of love. It does not always happen, but when it does, it is one of the rare moments. Mist's understanding had brought her here tonight, and the depressing weeks behind me could be forgotten. She would go on with me, I thought gaily, and I would be on velvet for the rest of the tour.

"But, Cio, it's impossible," she was saying. "I have to get back to Paris."

"Why? You're not working. Why?"

She was at the window looking out into the night. Her fingers crushed a fold of the long red drapes, and she did not turn to face me. I needed no further answer. The other man. An extended absence would call for explanations, and obviously Mist wasn't ready to offer the true reason. She loved me, I was sure of that, for she would not have been here otherwise. Then why not let the world know it? I clenched my jaw to hold back the torrent of words within me.

Mist was looking at me now. It was so easy to read my thoughts. "I loved him, Cio," she said softly, as if there were pain in this for her, "and I still have an affection for him, because we had something beautiful between us once. I don't want to finish it on an ugly note."

I said nothing.

"It will work itself out in time, believe me, it will." She crossed to my side and looked up at me imploringly. "Don't let it spoil what we have, Cio. Please."

Of course I could not. I loved her too much. But holding her close I wondered if I would always have to settle for this fraction. How long could I let it go on this way?

I FOUND my answer in Paris.

A special delivery letter was waiting for me one evening at the theatre. One glance at the signature and a knot tightened in my stomach. It was from the actor who still shared a part of Mistinguett's life, a message from the man who had cost me so much torment. He had some serious questions to ask me. Could we meet immediately?

I read the note again with a mixture of apprehension and relief. Those "serious questions" could mean only one thing: He had found out about Mist and me. Surely this was the showdown I had been secretly praying for. Quickly I scrawled a reply. I would meet him after tonight's show in a café on the Champs Elysées. I dispatched my reply by messenger and tried to concentrate on the performance ahead of me. Standing in the wings waiting for our entrance, Mist looked at me oddly as if she sensed something was wrong. I made no attempt to explain. In a few hours there might be an enormous amount to tell her, but I must say nothing until I had come to grips with my rival.

I was early at the café. Sitting at a table with a brandy before me, I felt as if every nerve in my body were screaming to break loose. So much depended on this encounter. Then I saw him coming toward me, a big man, elegantly yet sportily dressed. I had only seen this man on the stage. Now facing him across a table I was surprised at his size and his good looks. But there was no repose about him. His eyes burned with obvious anguish, and when he spoke his voice was taut with strain.

"Mistinguett has told me you two are good friends, but that's all," he said tightly. "Today I received a letter, anonymous, an accuser without a name. I didn't believe the words, I tore it up and threw it away. But I couldn't forget what it said."

"What did it say?"

"That you and she were much more than friends." He was fighting for control now, his gaze fixed on me intently. "She's my whole life, I've loved her for years and I still do, more than ever."

Perhaps at that moment I could have ended it. I had only to do as I had assumed I would, tell him that Mist and I were lovers, that his day was done. But I could not bring myself to say it. Having known the same jealous torment myself, I felt a curious sympathy for what this man was going through. The truth must come from Mist. We were both her captives, and she alone could cut the bonds.

"Those who won't sign letters are liars or cowards," I said in a flat, hard tone. "What Mistinguett told you about us is true."

I could hardly have been convincing in my lie, but he wanted so badly to hear me say it that he took no notice. Instead his face shone with relief, and he extended his hand. I shook it with no enthusiasm. I had done what I felt impelled to do, what I knew was right, but there was no pleasure in me because of it. Mist was still not mine alone, and she would never be until one side of this impossible triangle was torn away. In my heart I knew it could not continue this way. One of the two men in her life would have to go; it was inevitable. I could only pray that I would not be the one.

The season at the Folies Bergère was soon to end when a knock sounded at my dressing room door just before the Sunday matinee performance. Months had passed since I had seen the man who stepped inside. Now his face was not flooded with relief, it was livid with anger. Without a word he tossed a letter onto my make-up table.

It took only one glance to recognize it. I had written this letter to Mist during one of our absences. A love letter.

"You're going to tell me you're good friends and that's all?" The words were bitter and sarcastic and challenging. This time there could be no evasive denials, I knew it, yet still I racked my brain for some way to explain the incriminating letter. I even thought of saying that it was I who was in love with Mist, that I had been moved to write her so, but that our relations were nonetheless entirely platonic.

"Why don't you admit the truth? Are you afraid to?"

I was not afraid. But this scene was unpleasant, and I searched my mind for some way to end it without the fight for which this man was obviously spoiling.

"You're yellow, Chevalier." Contemptuously he spat out his accusation. I felt the color drain from my face, and I jumped to my feet. There was no way out any more.

"I've got a show to do now," I said and held my anger in check. "I'll meet you outside the stage entrance at midnight and we'll see how yellow I am. All right?"

He nodded grimly. "I'm going to knock your block off!"

I stopped him at the door with my voice. "Good luck," I said. Calmly I turned back to put on my make-up, but it was an exterior calm only. I was seething inside, not only at the stupidity of this man's blind rage but at my own in letting myself be provoked into a brawl. I had no fear for the outcome, though he was at least thirty pounds heavier than I, for I had kept up my boxing. For years now I had worked out in gyms at every chance. My concern was for Mist. My dressing room door had been open during this entire encounter, and I was sure that word had already started the rounds among the cast about the big event in the street at midnight. The whole affair would be known, and Mist would be caught in the middle.

In her dressing room her face was enigmatic as I told her the details.

"It was inevitable," she said finally.

Was that all she had to say? She was accepting this with no apparent concern for either me or the other man. Yet the consequences were bound to be enormous. I could not understand this seeming lack of emotion, and I turned abruptly and walked out. I had too much on my back now without having to add reproaches to Mist.

By the end of the matinee word-of-mouth advertising for the impending battle between the two lovers of Mistinguett had spread to every corner of the city's theatrical world.

A pretty youngster who was one day to become the great star Yvonne Printemps stopped me to bubble: "You're really going to fight in the street? That should be exciting!"

My mind, you can understand, was not on my performance in the theatre that evening. Confident of my prowess as a boxer at first, I had begun to dwell on the possibility of being overpowered by my opponent. Admittedly his advantage in size could be telling. He might even beat me, and that would surely mean the loss of Mist. I could hear the hypocritical condolences of my fellow performers. It was almost too much to bear, and I forced myself to think of the other side. If I won, Mist would surely be mine, and there would be no further need of loving each other in secrecy. Yes, the stakes were high.

It was a minute before midnight. I had forced myself to dress slowly, to take off my make-up as if this were any other evening, but I was vibrating thunderously inside. I opened the door of my dressing room to find the corridors darkened and strangely empty where normally there would be a hive of activity. As I stepped from the stage entrance into the narrow street, dark but for a yellow circle of light from the gas jet above the door, I discovered where everyone had gone. From all the doorways in the street faces were peering at me. In the dim shadows I recognized many of them. Dancers, comics, musicians, they were waiting for the big show to begin. A private quarrel had been turned into a circus.

From somewhere in the still night I heard the chimes of a clock. I stood there waiting, counting, until the sound of footsteps on the cobblestones turned me. A tall, solid figure was moving into the light. As he walked, he slapped his right fist hard against his open left hand. I stepped out to confront him, tensed to fight but at the same time a little sickened at being involved in this public spectacle.

"This is stupid," I said in a low voice. "And what good will it do? If Mist prefers one of us, do you think a fight's going to change her feelings?" He made no answer. "Why not let her choose for herself?"

"I'm going to knock your block off," he said tightly and drew back his fist.

I saw the blow coming and thought quickly. The street sloped downward at this point, putting him above me with a double advantage, so I backed away to the point where the pavement leveled off. My opponent mistook this maneuver for fear. Ready to attack he moved quickly after me. Standing now on flat ground I was waiting for him, and I saw my opening. He crashed directly into a hard left and then a right, and suddenly he began to crumple. Once again I caught him with a short right to the chin, and with a groan he fell against me. I was sure he was feigning, and I tried to disengage myself but he hung on desperately to my shoulders.

"Enough." He could barely utter the word, and as I pushed his half-inert form away from me, I saw his face. This man was genuinely in trouble. Unable to defend himself, he was a perfect target now, but there was no need to go on. It was over. I watched the man being led away by a friend, and I felt devoid of feeling inside.

Not a sound came from the hidden spectators. Slowly I walked past them, then glanced up at a figure in a window overlooking the street. It was Mist. She had been a silent witness, but now her face, taut with anguish, was proof that her unfeelingness of this afternoon had been a pose. It was at that moment I realized a great truth about Mistinguett — that she was a woman who would not admit the unpleasant or the ugly in her life, for by this unwillingness to recognize them, she hoped not to have to face them. It was a weakness. But it was also a gentleness, and I understood so well the pain she had been going through for all this time. Disappearing into the darkness, I could only wonder what the outcome of this idiotic, needless fight would be.

She telephoned me the next morning at the Café William Tell, still undone from the events of last night, but trying not to show it by being doubly insouciant. We made no rendezvous for that day. I felt instinctively that Mist must have a chance to adjust to this new turn in her life, for it was almost certain that the other man would never try to see her again. I knew that he was a proud man, and his pride would not allow him to be humbled by crawling to her for succor.

The story was all over Paris. The newspapers that afternoon carried vivid accounts, with no names mentioned, of the fight. They joked of the two important performers who jousted for the star's favors while she watched from a box seat. They commented archly that representatives of the legitimate theatre and the music hall theatre had fought off stage, and the music hall had come out on top.

At the Folies Bergère tension crackled that night. Everyone waited in vain for another incident. In low, discreet voices the cast exchanged views and conjectures. But Mist behaved as if nothing out of the ordinary had occurred. The show went on as usual.

I held my breath and waited.

Three days afterward Mist invited me for the first time to lunch at her luxurious apartment. I remember walking down the broad, elegant Boulevard des Capucines with my heart pounding inside me, thinking that Mist had been right after all, that it had worked itself out in time, that there was no more need for secrecy, that I was a lucky man, almost too lucky.

It was an opulent apartment, magnificently furnished, exactly as I had imagined it during the poignant months I had only gazed up at it from the street. It was like the home of a princess, and I stood there in the middle of the vast living room caught up in the spell of its magic. A picture of Mistinguett caught my eye, and I crossed to look at it. It had been taken a few years before, and I had never seen it. Her face — warm, expressive, vital — was almost too lovely to be real.

"Well, Cio?"

I turned. She stood in the doorway, as beautiful as the picture. I moved across the room without a word and held her close to me. Mist was mine alone now. And love was all over the place.

. . . Six

Finally I was openly a part of Mist's world, and moving among her chic coterie with this most adorable woman in Paris on my arm, I must have worn a perpetual face of happiness and wonderment. As if to carol the news, Mist wanted me with her in every swank restaurant or club or gala party her set frequented, and often there were all three in the same frenetic evening.

Being with Mist was all that counted to me. As for the life she led, this pursuit of after-dark entertainment, I was a part of it without ever really belonging. Mist loved tinsel and glitter, and I found them shallow and unrewarding. Though I had finally become used to wearing the dinner clothes she urged me to buy when we had first fallen in love, I still felt ill at ease and uncomfortable surrounded by her stylish, urbane friends. They seemed so brittle to me and lacking in warmth. They were a kind of people I never understood, and I still don't. Even today I prefer quiet evenings among a few friends or intelligently curious strangers from whom there is something worth while to learn, and I dislike those gatherings where people come to be seen rather than to see, where conversation is really nothing but chatter, where you're looked at oddly if you are interested in exchanging ideas, yet welcomed if you want to swap gossip.

But it was Mist's game, and I was playing it with energy because I loved her and it made her happy.

Indeed, there was only one shadow over our complete pleasure together. I was twenty-three and two years of compulsory military service were waiting. Caught up in my first glow of success at the Folies Bergère, I had asked for and been granted a postponement, but the time was coming when the army would wait no longer. Europe had passed through crisis after crisis politically, and though no one believed that a war would actually ever arrive, it was everyone's fate to be conscripted, and I was quite ready. I might not be called up, however, until I was twenty-five, so Mist and I chose not to face it before the instant it happened.

We chose not to face it by simply ignoring it. We laughed and loved and lived, and all serious things we dismissed. Not once did we speak of marriage, for it honestly never occurred to us. Somehow, no one in Paris ever conceived of it, for she was so much a part of the scene just as she was. These were the plush, florid, gaslight and hansom cab days before the first war, an era in the theatre unknown before or since, when great stars like Mist reigned as queens in a separate world of their own. Seldom did they marry into the milieu of lords and ladies or immensely wealthy men of business with whom they consorted, for this would probably have spelled the end of the careers they adored. Nor did they marry among themselves, for how could one be the darling of society and a husband at the same time? No, matrimony meant ties; and life was too full and rich and tumultuous to be leashed.

Mist and I shared many things, but none more tender than our love for La Louque. They liked each other from the start. Although she had grown up in the city and was universally acclaimed as the truly typical Parisienne, Mist had been born, as had my mother, in Belgium. But it was more than this that brought them together. Mist was unable to feel close with her own mother, an eccentric woman of whom she saw little, and in La Louque she found the simple, sweet mother she had always wanted. And Mama, in a way, had found a daughter. My relationship with Mist might not have been exactly to the standards of La Louque's world, but she knew somewhere inside that my love for Mist gave me happiness and for Mama this made everything all right.

So there were months of constant joy. But there was bound to be a day of accounting. It came as the season was ending at the Folies Bergère. My work hadn't been attracting much attention there, for the public's eye was mainly on an American who was one day to become a legendary figure in his country — W. C. Fields. I had nursed a halfhearted hope that I would be offered a new contract for the following year, though I still had not evolved any startling additions to my act. It was a futile hope. The day I learned I was out of a job, I realized that I had been confusing my personal and professional lives. In the former, all was well. As for the latter, all couldn't be worse. Lucky in one love, I'd been unlucky in the other.

But the army, which was preparing to break off my career abruptly at any time, inadvertently aided me for the moment. It had summoned many of the young music hall entertainers already, and there was a shortage of talent. The producers of a revue called *Noon to Two*, in which a beautiful dancer from the Opéra Comique was to make her debut as an actress, offered me

66

the star male part. It was like a life raft to a drowning sailor. Eagerly I accepted.

Mist was leaving the Folies Bergère also. She had chosen to star on her own again. I had not been displeased when she told me, for our being in the show together had kept us apart so little that I had once or twice wondered at the wisdom of this. Love, like any emotion, can suffer the fatigue of overexposure. It cannot sustain itself without a kind of recharging, and the tiniest absence can bring two people back together with a freshness and a newness and the wonder of rediscovery.

Now I had an important job myself. I hurried to tell Mist the good news.

"This dancer, Regina Badet, she's lovely," I enthused.

"And young?"

I thought there was an edge to Mist's voice, and I looked at her curiously. "I suppose she's young. Why?"

She turned away. "Nothing, nothing at all."

"Well, there must be something," I said half laughing. "Otherwise, why ask it?"

"It was a question, nothing more than that," she said sharply. "Now let's forget it."

In an instant she had tossed off her irritation and was smiling in her familiar impish way again. But I hadn't forgotten it. It was so clear to me that Mist was sensitive about the thirteen years' difference in our ages, that she was almost afraid to face what must happen to us all — the relentless passage of time. If she had only known that to me, and to everyone who knew her then, she was ageless. She was simply Mistinguett — the essence, the ultimate of woman.

How can a performer explain success? What is the elusive difference between audience apathy and applause? I wondered this many times after the opening of *Noon to Two*. At the Folies Bergère I had reached a peak, then gone steadily downhill. Now, in a hit revue, I had been catapulted back into public fancy. I reflected with a wry smile that I had been rediscovered by the very people who had so casually lost me in the years before. But it was wonderful to be up again, and I worked doubly hard against the rapidly approaching deadline the army had set for me, determined to make such a solid impression that no one would forget me in my two years away.

The firm notice of my call-up came in the autumn of 1913.

"When do you have to go?" Mist asked in a strained voice. I had walked in with the letter in my hand, and she had known before I said a word.

"The first of December."

"So soon?"

I forced a laugh. "Did you think after all this time they'd give me a year's warning?"

"I don't think it's so funny, Maurice," she said and turned away unhappily.

I turned her to face me. "Mist, darling, what would you have me do? Cry?"

"You could try and put it off, couldn't you?" I shook my head patiently, and she tore herself loose from my grasp. "So you're just to walk out of my life and that's all there is to it!"

"Mist, listen to me. This is training, not a war. There'll be weekend passes, furloughs, and every hour of them I'll spend with you." I had never seen her so upset before, and I groped for some way to evoke that gamin smile which lighted her face. "Look, I've got a week before the new revue starts. How would you like to go to London?"

The idea startled her, for neither of us had ever been to England before. "Would it be fun?" she asked hesitantly.

"With the two of us together, how could it be otherwise?"

"We don't speak a word of English."

"We'll pantomime." With elaborate gestures I illustrated how we would order tea and scones, visit the theatre, bet at the races, and suddenly Mist was laughing. At least for the moment the cloud of imminent separation had been blown away.

It was a carefree, vivid holiday whose adventure began on the boat from Calais to Dover, continued during the ride through the English countryside, so different from our own country just a few hours away, and reached its height when we saw London for the first time. From Victoria Station to the Savoy we were two enthralled tourists peering from the windows of our horse-drawn cab at the teeming streets of the great city, nodding in agreement as we passed each music hall marquee. We were going to cram our seven days with as many shows as possible.

It was a staggering schedule. Two o'clock matinee at the Coliseum, a performance at the Holborn Empire at six, then two hours later to the Palace for the evening show and finally a night club such as the Café de Paris from midnight till two in the morning. Anything that touched on our profession fascinated us — dancers, singers, comedians, acrobats, revues, operettas — and we moved hungrily from one spectacle to the next.

The English vaudeville performers excited me. Theirs was a kind of freshness and youth and vitality which hadn't been seen in the French music halls. And an elegance as well. In one production number, a marriage ceremony danced in ragtime, the bridegroom was outfitted completely in white, from flannel suit to shoes, bowler hat and gloves. This was quite a contrast to the costuming I employed for my brand of dancing. Mine had humor. This had style and dash. Perhaps it was the new approach I had been seeking to make my own act different. I determined I'd try it when I returned to Paris.

It was the last morning. Mist was still asleep when I left the hotel, for she never joined me on these walks through the narrow, sunless streets when I absorbed the feel of London and its people and its history. I knew this held no attraction for her, and I understood. I walked slowly, aimlessly. Once I was sure I was lost, but from a distance I recognized the stately dome of St.

Paul's cathedral and used it as a guide to retrace my steps to the Savoy.

I had begun to pack in my room when I heard a low, muffled groan. It seemed so near that I was startled, and I glanced around for the source. Then it came again, this time a sharper cry, and now I knew. The sound had come from Mist's room. Quickly I thrust open her door and moved to her side. She was lying in bed, her arm pressed against her middle, her body contorted with pain.

"Mist, what is it? What's the matter?" She gasped for answer, and I sat down beside her. "Mist, are you sick?"

The spasm of pain had passed, and the taut lines of her face relaxed. She shook her head. "I'm all right, Cio," she said in a low, weak voice. "It's gone now."

"What's gone?"

"Nothing. I'm fine."

I reached for the phone. "I'll call a doctor."

"No." She stopped me with her hand. "There's no need for a doctor. Really, Cio, whatever it was, it's passed, and I'm all right now."

I wanted to believe her. I could feel the pounding of my heart slowing down, and I wanted her to be well so much that it flooded over me. "What kind of pain was it?"

"Just a pain, that's all." She struggled to sit up, managing a wan smile. "You look so miserable, Cio, and there's no need for it. Haven't you ever had a stomach-ache in your life?" She patted my hand. "I've had worse on opening nights, so that's the end of it, you hear?"

I nodded. But I couldn't push down the thought that this was no ordinary stomach-ache. Mist, who always had the look of eternal youth, had seemed drawn and haggard for a moment. The strain was going now, but something was wrong. I felt it and I was frightened.

We talked little on the way back to Paris. Mist was silent,

withdrawn, and I was not only disturbed by that scene in her room but burdened with the depression that so often comes when a gay holiday has ended and the cares you've left behind must be faced again. It was not my new revue which troubled me nor even two years of military service but a sudden full realization that only a little more than sixty days away was my impending separation from Mist. I had reassured her with the confident promise of many weekends together and frequent furloughs, but I had really been whistling in the dark. Who could say how far I would be sent from Paris? What good were weekends if they must be entirely spent in traveling from camp and back again? And what did I really know of furloughs? Perhaps I'd have to wait months before the first one was granted.

When I left her at her apartment, Mist clung to me as if she were afraid to see me go. "There's so little time, Cio," she said in a pitiful little voice. "It's all rushing by so fast."

And it was. The weeks began to disappear. In the new revue I persuaded my dancing partner to do a scene with both of us dressed fashionably in white. I was a little worried about audience reaction when they saw me transformed from red-nosed comic to stylish dancer, but I needn't have been. When they recovered from their surprise, they seemed to like the change. It gave me a confidence I'd never had before in presenting myself as I really was, not always embellished as a type of clown. After my military service, I told myself, I wouldn't drop my comedy routines, but I would include at least one elegant scene for contrast. Somehow the simple act of making plans for the future helped to ease the pain of the present.

It could do nothing, however, to soften the anguish of the past which rose up to haunt me one evening after the show. At the stage door a number of people clustered, and I was making my way through the mass.

"Hello, Maurice," a low voice murmured as I passed. I nodded politely and started to move on when some dim, almost forgotten memory turned me around to face the man who had spoken. Seventeen years had gone by, yet I recognized him at once. It was my father. He stood there silently, a short, thickset man, smaller than I had remembered. I was a head taller than he now, and he looked up at me with infinite sadness in his eyes. I felt strangely moved at the sight of him, and for an instant a faint recollection of a long-ago family picnic darted across my mind. My father had bought me a red kite. We had flown it together in a park along the river.

"Let's get away from this," I said and led him through the crowd along the stage alley to the deserted street outside. In the flickering light of a street lamp I stopped, and the face which had once seemed so evil in the first shock of his disappearance now appeared softened and kindly enough. "Why did you come to see me?" I asked quietly.

"I saw in the papers you were going into the army." He stumbled a little over the words. "I had to see you before you went, to talk to you a little." I said nothing, and with an embarrassed smile he went on. "I've seen you from the gallery, a lot of times. You know, it's funny, but you make others laugh and I cry."

"Do you need money?"

He shook his head proudly. "No, I get along. I just came to look at you, that's all." He hesitated. "I was hoping you didn't hate me too much."

Hate? Suddenly the bitter memory of all that La Louque had suffered because of this man swept over me. Her hunger and misery and pain at being forsaken by the one she had loved. I remembered his silence over the years, and it seemed to me that he had shown up now because of my success. I stiffened at the thought.

"Listen, I don't want to see you any more, Papa. We don't talk about you at home, and you mustn't show up here ever again. It's too late, we've forgotten you." A shadow crossed his face, but I ignored it. "If you need anything, write me at the theatre, but don't come around. And I'm not even going to say that I've seen you. I think it's best that way. Good-by, Papa."

At first he didn't seem to understand. Then slowly he nodded as if on the verge of tears. "Yes, yes." Drawing himself up, he extended his hand. I took it, and we stood there for an instant before he turned and moved away. I watched his silhouette fade into the night, and I waited there motionless long after he had disappeared, shaken by what I had done, yet feeling there was no other way.

I never saw my father again. He never wrote, never tried to see me, never asked for a sou. And I never told anyone of our meeting that night, not even Mist. But I found myself thinking often of him, and more and more with compassion. He had been humble, even noble in a way and dignified. Is there a time limit to rancor, I would ask myself? Is it possible really to forget a great wrong? I had no answer, but later I tried to find him, hoping at least to talk to him further than those few perfunctory phrases. It was useless. There was no trace of him in Paris. Perhaps he had changed his name or even lived in another city. Whatever, this time he had vanished forever.

MIST stood moodily at the window of her apartment. The night outside was cold, and the glass was steamy within. She cleared a corner of it with her fingertips and stared intently into the darkness.

"What time does your train leave in the morning, Cio?"

"Seven o'clock."

She turned to face me, her hands clasping and unclasping nervously. "I know people, important people with influence. With all the army posts in France, why must you be sent so far away?"

I had been assigned to an infantry regiment stationed more than two hundred and fifty miles east of Paris in the city of

Belfort, famed for its heroic resistance during a three-months siege in the Franco-Prussian War. Just as I had feared, it would be impossible to visit Mist on weekends, and we both knew that an early leave was doubtful. Tonight I had come here directly from my final appearance at the theatre, and the room was heavy with the weight of good-by.

"I'll pull strings," Mist was saying feverishly. "Why can't you be trained near Paris? Must you go so far away just to learn how to march up and down?"

I held her close to me, and she was trembling in my arms. Mist and I were saying everything but what we really felt inside. We had talked about train schedules and the distance of Belfort and a possible transfer, but neither of us had been able to voice our deepest worry — that somehow this long, enforced separation might hurt our love. I was tortured with the thought, now that the day of departure was upon me, that Mist would find someone else while I was away, and I felt she was afraid of the same thing. Yet we were silent, and we parted that night without revealing this fear. Only at the door did Mist even hint at the truth.

"So much can happen in two years," she said, and her eyes glistened with unshed tears.

"What a Christmas we'll celebrate in 1915!" I tried to grin, but my heart wasn't in it. Then I kissed her and ran down the stairs without looking back.

The grin was even harder to summon by the time the train reached Belfort. The sky was dark with smoke that poured from factory stacks, the ground mottled with patches of dirty snow. The town itself wore a somber, grave face. Germany was only forty miles away, and the soldiers who swarmed these streets seemed grim and purposeful. Paris, the theatre, the life I loved were suddenly frighteningly remote.

At the barracks, the clerk of Company 10 watched me sign in and stared unblinkingly at my signature. The company com-

74

mander who called me in appeared to be more friendly. He'd seen my act in Paris and he recalled it smilingly. But the small talk ended quickly, the smile faded, and he warned me that military life at Belfort was tough and disciplined, that I'd have to adapt myself to it like everyone else.

I was a little taken aback. I hadn't expected to be any different from anyone else here, and I started to tell him so. He rode over my protests and dismissed me. When I found my bed at the barracks, the other men stared at me with curiosity that I read for hostility.

"An actor?" I could almost hear them saying it to themselves. "We'll take that out of him soon."

Donning a uniform and getting a short haircut made me feel less conspicuous, but my first afternoon in town diminished that comfort. Being a simple private, I was supposed to salute practically every other soldier in the streets. A corporal stopped me roughly.

"No salute, huh, soldier?" he snarled and pointed to his stripes.

I saluted. "It's my first day," I said haltingly. "I'm sorry."

He looked at me dubiously. His was a peasant accent, and my Parisian one inspired only suspicion.

"All right," he said finally. "Just watch out next time."

The adjutant at assembly the following morning was less forgiving. Lined up for the manual of arms, about which I knew nothing, he took in my obvious confusion and the laughs of the soldiers surrounding me and issued orders for special instructions for me. Later, he summoned me to his office.

"I hear you were a hit in Paris, Chevalier," he said carelessly. "Did you make much money at it?"

In spite of my ineptness at drill, I was thinking, he's proud to have me in his company. I answered simply, "Four thousand francs a month, sir."

He stiffened, and I realized I'd put my foot in it once more. I had told him the truth, but that sum was perhaps eight times the amount he earned, and this could hardly increase his warmth for me. He looked me up and down with a sarcastic smile. "You like to sing, Chevalier, so do it all you want. While you clean the latrines!"

"My darling Mist," I wrote that night in the dim barracks light. "Christmas, 1915. If it could only be tomorrow!"

. . . Sept

B UT IT was not all bad.
Somehow, the citizen became a soldier and he profited
by it. Training marches, maneuvers, gunnery practice in the
fresh, sharp open air were far more healthful than rounds
of Paris parties. Falling exhausted on my bunk after a bout
with the severe temperatures of a Belfort winter's day, I
slept through peaceful, dreamless nights as I had never
slept before. I was aglow with vigor.

And there was more to life than the army. I had found
a buddy, a young pianist who'd played at the Paris Con-
servatory. Every free evening we met at the most important
café in town, and in a room reserved for soldiers I sang to
his accompaniment. Our friends liked us. It wasn't long

77

before word got around to the townspeople, and whenever a benefit concert was organized, we were asked to entertain.

So the time was full. But there were moments to stop and think, and whenever this happened, I could see and hear and feel only Mist. Those furloughs I had so optimistically counted on, where were they? I ached to hold her in my arms, to love her, to be warmed by the tenderness of her. And though her letters described the same longings, I couldn't help being tortured with thoughts of Mist in Paris, wooed on every side with the cajolery of numerous admirers. I was not jealous at such times. I was simply miserable.

I trained by day and performed by night with doubled determination then to induce some kind of forgetfulness. It was better not to dwell on the life and the love I had left behind, but to think of what I would do when these two interminable years were finished. Why not plan a new kind of act? When my dancing number in the elegant white costume had gone over so well, I'd decided always to include one similar scene, but why not consider doing all of my routines in fashionable garb? That way I could be a new and different kind of music hall performer, a worldly one in a full-dress suit and top hat, no longer a simple clown but a young leading man whose background in comedy would give him an extra something unseen heretofore on the French stage. A comedy leading man — a rare bird indeed!

I decided to try my idea at the café downtown, and it worked. The formal clothes seemed to dismay no one. In fact, comic songs done in such fashionable attire did give them a whole new freshness. The crowd was pleased. Not half so much as I, for this was a step forward professionally — and miraculously I had taken it in the army.

Stepping out of the café into the dark night, I gazed up at a sky polka-dotted with stars, and I wanted to chortle with delight at this evening's accomplishment. But at the barracks the corporal who was in charge of quarters was awaiting me with an official envelope, and my heart sank. I was almost afraid to open it. Things had been too perfect tonight, and this was surely a reprimand of some sort to rob me of all joy.

I read the order with trembling unbelief. A week's furlough, commencing at dawn. I read it again to be sure. Yes, it was all there. I raced up the stairs to the second floor and began to pack. There was a morning train to Paris. I would be on it — and at the end of the line would be Mist. At that moment everything else was forgotten — career, army, future — for waiting for me only a few hours away was love.

IT WAS the last night of my leave. I had come to see Mist perform at the very theatre where I had sung my final evening before the army. How strange it was now, how much smaller I felt, for I was an outsider and I knew it. And though I was not in uniform, my haircut marked me as a soldier, and it seemed to me that no one could fail to recognize the private second class beneath the civilian clothes. Mist's affection had helped soothe the discomfort, her understanding had softened the unhappiness of being a fish out of water, but the applause of this audience, calling for one encore after another from Mist, made me vividly aware how much I missed the life I had known. It hurt that I would be leaving it again tomorrow, not to return for heaven knew how long.

Mist was taking her final bow. She had stepped out beyond the closed curtain, and for an instant I thought I saw her stumble. Then she seemed to recover herself and stood there, her head bowed for a moment before she lifted it to smile her gratitude. Was it my imagination, or did I see a strained tightness in that smile? I found myself rising and pushing my way through the departing throng without understanding why. Some instinct told me I should hurry.

But in her dressing room she denied there was anything wrong.

79

She laughed too brightly and announced we were going to a party and dance till dawn. Her eyes looked feverish.

"I'd rather take you home, Mist," I said, concerned.

"On your last night, Cio?" She drew a vivid scar of lip rouge across her mouth as if make-up could conceal the truth of a face drained of color. "I won't hear of it. Now, get a carriage and I'll meet you at the stage door."

Leaving the room I glanced back. With trembling fingers she was arranging her hair, and she refused to meet my glance in the mirror. Troubled, I found a carriage and stood in the doorway talking with the manager of the theatre. Too many minutes passed, and I was on the verge of seeking Mist out when she appeared. It seemed to me that she was walking unsteadily, and I reached out a hand to her. She took a final step forward and crumpled into my arms.

Her body was a dead weight, her eyes rolled back until only the whites were showing. Then slowly they closed and I picked her up in my arms and started out of the door.

The manager was at my heels, his voice quivering with fright. "Why not take her back to the dressing room? What are you doing?"

"There's a clinic a few blocks away."

"Clinic? What's the matter with her?"

"That's what I'm going to find out," I said. "Help me lift her into the carriage."

Inside the carriage we chafed her wrists and unclasped the necklace at her throat. In a moment her eyelids fluttered and she was conscious again, but we wouldn't let her talk. I stroked her hand and fear was a tight knot inside of me.

The chief of the hospital was summoned, and I waited tensely outside the room where Mist was being examined. The memory of that day in London assailed me over and over again, and I was sure that this was somehow involved with it. In a way I blamed myself for having listened to her then, for having believed her when she said nothing was wrong. She had probably been ill for months, and being Mist with her great courage and joy of living she had ignored what was happening. And now?

"Internal organs," the doctor was saying gravely. "Something should have been done a long time ago."

"Something?"

"Operation, I'm afraid."

"When?" My throat was dry and the word seemed to stick there.

"We'll keep her under observation for a few days. Probably the end of the week, I'd say."

"Is it serious?"

The doctor looked at me almost pityingly, reading my panic for a form of stupidity. "Of course it's serious," he said and walked away.

I stared at the door which separated me from Mist and I was heartsick. There would be no way of extending my leave. I must be on that train to Belfort tomorrow, and in all the days ahead I would be torn with the knowledge that I was powerless to help the woman I loved.

And the days were agony. Mechanically I moved through each twenty-four hours, my body in Belfort but my mind in a clinic on a small street in Paris. Who could know but that at the very moment I was drilling with my company or firing my rifle on the wooded range outside of town Mist was fighting for her life on an operating table? I had a wild notion of deserting, of fleeing to her side, and I drove it away. There was nothing to do but wait till word came from Paris.

Then at last it was over, and Mist had come through the ordeal. It would be a long recuperation in the hospital, more weeks of rest afterwards at home. I had to see her.

"You had a furlough less than a month ago, Chevalier," the adjutant said sourly.

"Yes, sir, but this is an emergency."

"It's always an emergency." He had never forgiven me for that first day's revelation of my earnings, but months had gone by and at least he had the satisfaction of knowing that now I was far inferior in station to him. Apparently it slightly softened his heart. He signed orders for a three-day pass and tossed the paper across his desk. I was grateful, even for three brief days.

Mist's room was at the end of a long corridor, and I knocked softly before I moved inside. She had not known I was coming, and she lay there with her head turned toward the window, as if she ached to be free in the world outside. How forlorn she looked and wistful, until our eyes met and she smiled in startled joy, suddenly my Mist again. Gently I kissed her. All was right once more.

"Cio," she said later, and her hand tightened around mine, "there's so much about war in the papers."

"It makes good headlines, that's all."

"But it could happen," she said anxiously.

"And it won't," I replied. "Now, all you're to worry about is walking out of this place and getting well."

"You look thin, Cio."

A frown creased her forehead, and I pressed it away with my fingertips. "Thin, Mist — and happy and very much in love."

IT WAS April, but Belfort had not yet thrown off winter. The mountains surrounding it were a barrier to spring. Not so Melun, only twenty-five miles from Paris, where miraculously I had just been transferred. Here nature had sprung to life again and around the little town the first green shoots were burgeoning on tall poplars and the fields were painted with wild flowers.

82

These were pleasant agreeable weeks, made doubly so because Mist, finally dismissed from the clinic, took a small house at a village called Bois-le-Roi, only a few minutes away from our barracks. Each night I was free from five to nine. I could be with her every day, and in the flush of this joy of an ideal summer ahead I could almost forget that there were still eighteen months to go before I would be out of uniform.

June 29, 1914, was a Monday.

Mist met me at the door, newspaper in hand. She had been reading a dispatch from Vienna concerning the assassination in the Balkan town of Sarajevo of Archduke Francis Ferdinand of Austria and his wife. It seemed remote and unreal to me, this political unrest so far away, and certainly Mist understood none of its implications. But the story was alarming. It spoke of repercussions that could echo throughout Europe.

"What does it mean, Cio?" she said anxiously.

I didn't know. "Surely it's exaggerated, Mist. Nothing will come of it."

"There could be a war, you could be killed."

"There could be an earthquake, we could all be killed tomorrow," I laughed.

"It's no joke," Mist flared, and I realized how tense she had become. Quickly I brought the subject around to La Louque, whom Mist had invited here for a visit, and soon this momentary upset was forgotten.

But it had not been buried. War rumors were thicker now. Paris at the end of July had been declared out of bounds to keep all outfits ready for instant mobilization. I managed a weekend pass, however, on the promise that I would report back immediately in an emergency. The gravity of the times had reached us all now, and I was hungry to spend at least one weekend there with Mist.

It was destined not to be completed. We awoke the next day

to a Paris charged with emotion. Germany had declared war on France. Thousands of people thronged the streets, some laughing and singing patriotic songs, others crying, still others staring in stunned silence. Crowds milled around posters hastily affixed to walls, placards proclaiming in bold black print the ominous words: GENERAL MOBILIZATION.

I stood there, my arm around Mist, and read the orders which applied to me. 31st Infantry. It would leave for the front in four days. For an instant I stood there hardly believing what I saw. Then I took Mist by the arm. I must rejoin my battalion at once.

"Cio, wait a minute," Mist said with a note of urgency. At that moment we were whirled into a milling group moving down the avenue, caught up in a mass of violent demonstrators shouting for a quick march on the enemy. Mist was twisted from my grasp, and I fought my way through them to seize her arm and finally pulled us free.

"Did they hurt you, darling?" I shouted above the clamor.

She shook her head, and I saw she was near tears. I drew her into the safety of a doorway.

"They've gone now, Mist, it's all right."

She looked up at me with eyes that seemed bruised with pain. "I knew it would come," she said, haltingly, "and I wanted to stop it but I didn't dare."

"The war, Mist?" I said puzzled.

"Your going away." Her gaze was fastened on me. "Why couldn't you simply stay at Melun? Or Paris even?"

"When my outfit moves out? What are you talking about?"

"Those friends I have, Cio," she said hastily. "You wouldn't let me talk to them, but it's not too late, and if ——"

"I have to shave every day, Mist," I interrupted tautly. "That means looking at myself in the mirror."

There was nothing more to be said. We walked away in silence, and I was thinking that I was no hero, that I had little taste for what obviously lay ahead. But I had come this far, and in this moment there was no question of a detour.

THE Germans had moved into Belgium. Denied free access to France through Belgian territory, they had marched in nonetheless, and now England by this act had been brought into the war as well. In Melun, our outfit was in battle dress, laden like mules, preparing to move out toward the approaching front. It had all happened so fast that my head was spinning. Battlefield? I didn't even know what it would look like. I only knew that I was a soldier, and I hoped I'd fight as well as I could.

But marching through the streets of town lined with shouting, flower-throwing men and women and children, I felt as if I were being drawn into a bottomless chasm. At the railroad station I saw Mist and La Louque in the mob, not cheering as the others were, but standing rigidly with drawn faces. I mustered a smile I didn't feel, hoping in their brief glance they wouldn't read what I was trying to hide, my misery at leaving behind everything in the world that mattered to me. Then in an instant I had passed them. Only fate now knew what lay ahead.

Apparently our officers were as much in the dark as we. Passing through the packed cars they shook their heads in answer to all questions, and that night we left the train to camp outside a village, convinced the morning would find us in combat. I lay awake staring into the blackness. Tomorrow. Our months of playing at war had ended. This game was real, and the stakes were life and death.

In my platoon, we had teamed up in pairs, and when the war reached us each man was to fight alongside his partner. I had drawn a little fellow with a pinched face, narrow eyes and almost bald head whose nickname in the outfit was "the Mole." How resourceful he was! Whenever we halted, the Mole would disappear to forage for supplies, always to return with plenty to eat and drink. Moreover, in these expeditions he managed each time to find a nearby barn with straw-filled corners to serve us as beds and a private dining room.

"How do you do it?" I would ask in admiration.

"I'm the Mole," he would reply with a wink. "I dig."

It was the 21st of August.

All night long we had listened to the distant thunder of artillery. The gunfire grew steadily nearer as we ground off mile after mile in a grueling, fatiguing march. Word spread from man to man that something was about to happen.

It came late that afternoon in the tiny village of Cons-la-Granville. Instead of the usual command to halt and make camp for the night, we were ordered to fix bayonets. The enemy had occupied the nearby village of Cutry, and we were to surprise him this very night and wrest his position away in hand-to-hand encounter. This was to be no attack accomplished with rifle fire where the enemy was only a distant, impersonal target. We must stealthily approach, and then rip human bodies apart with harsh, violent thrusts of the lethal blades protruding from our weapons. War had suddenly become a very personal thing. I had had nightmares about bayonet attacks. The bad dream was on the verge of coming true, and I felt nausea mount in me at the prospect.

It was dark now. Sporadic gunfire broke the otherwise silent night. Quietly the order to attack filtered through, and we took a deep breath, so sharp it coursed within us like a gulp of straight whiskey and burned deep inside. Bayonets at the ready we began to move out toward Cutry. On my left I could hear a man praying as he advanced, and the Mole was swearing beside me in a low, strained voice. We continued steadily forward, stumbling over rocks and abrupt slopes in the hilly ground, tensed for the fight which must come at any moment.

But each moment came and passed with no sound from Cutry

dead ahead. We halted while scouts went beyond to reconnoiter. The wait for their return seemed interminable, but finally their shadowy figures emerged from the darkness to report that the town was deserted, that the Germans had withdrawn. A laugh leaped up from the blackness. "Do we have to go all the way to Berlin to see them?" somebody shouted.

"When they heard the 31st was on the way, they took off like rabbits!" another voice added with the bravado of relief.

It all seemed too good to be true — our first victory, even though without combat. We were drained with fatigue and spent emotion, but it called for a celebration. As the outfit bedded down, the irrepressible Mole slipped away to search for food and drink. Half an hour later he was back, loaded with provisions abandoned by peasants who had fled their homes at the approach of the enemy. There was a bottle of wine for each of us, and God, how good it tasted! We slept like babies that night.

We woke at dawn fired with the hope that the Germans had met with reverses and decided to retreat. A patrol would have to find this out, and the Mole and I, with four others, were sent to scout the enemy. We advanced almost confidently, then stopped short at the sight of a uniformed figure seated upright on an embankment. Our first view of the enemy. We inched forward. Sightless eyes were staring at us. This dead soldier was barely more than a kid, and his rigid hands still clutched his gun. We could feel our hopes waning. The enemy was near, and we could sense it in the air. The Mole hissed a warning and pointed above the bank to a wooded slope beyond. The sun was rising now, and metal gleamed from the base of a dozen trees. As quickly as possible we slipped back to Cutry to report.

We hardly made it to the center of town before a burst of artillery fire slashed across the square. I saw a handful of men fall, and the Mole and I leaped for the protection of a low wall beside a church where our platoon had been placed to face a possible attack. Now above the town we could see a gray-green line forming and moving down beneath the cover of an artillery barrage.

The enemy bombardment was sharp and accurate. Somehow the church remained standing, but walls of houses were crashing to the ground and the air was filled with the dust of falling debris. We were firing mechanically at the approaching wave of Germans, but each instant there were fewer of us to try and stop them. The man on my left toppled over. I glanced at him. There was a bullet hole in his forehead, and a thin trickle of blood inched down his face. Reload. Fire. Reload. Fire. It was automatic, and all the time a part of me was adding up the days and years which had combined to put me here. Ménilmontant, the tack factory, La Louque. And Mist. Was it all to end behind a wall with a bullet in my head?

From somewhere in a dream a voice came to me. "Don't worry, Maurice, your Mole's right here beside you!" I patted his shoulder without looking at him.

The Germans were closer now. The uniforms had faces. There was no chance of stopping this gray tide of men, but we were trying. Then the Mole called out that we'd been ordered to fall back, and I strapped on my pack and started crawling toward the church. Bullets were whining continuously above our heads; it was impossible to straighten up.

The ground beneath me heaved with a giant explosion, and a white-hot pain seared my back. I fell flat, gasping for breath as two medical orderlies ran toward me. My eyes seemed to be focusing oddly, for their faces grew longer and narrower as they leaned over me. Their voices, too, were strange and bizarre and faraway. Where was I hit? I tried to turn my head. One of them pulled my pack off.

"Right through his knapsack," I heard him say, and the other one asked, "Can you move? If we don't get out of here soon, we never will."

Crawling on their bellies, they helped me drag myself along the ground to a shallow ditch that offered little cover. Each movement was agony, the pain twisting from my back through my whole body, and from the edge of consciousness, I heard enemy fire on three sides as they began to encircle us. Dimly I could make out the falling forms of our men as they tried to double back to new positions, and then I was being carried by the two orderlies down a road raked with bullets until finally the slope of a hill meant shelter and safety for the flight backwards to Cons-la-Granville.

Vaguely, as through a mask of gauze, I recognized the one big house in the village. A large flag of the Red Cross was draped near its door. I was being lifted up the stairs, then slowly lowered to a bed. I felt my shirt being torn away and hands that bandaged the excruciating wound in my back. It was the last thing I remembered before I fell into a deep sleep. It lasted for ten hours. Shells fell, bullets smashed windows and spent themselves in the walls of this room with its twenty wounded men, but I heard nothing.

My sleep was dreamless until from its dark depths a shadowed form approached, and as I recognized the supple, graceful figure I fought to come awake. It was Mist. Her arms were outstretched, and she was crying, the only time I had ever seen her in tears. Her lips were moving, she was trying to tell me something, but the voice was not hers. It was loud and harsh and guttural, and I struggled to understand.

"*Achtung!*" the voice seemed to say. "*Durchsuchen Sie das Zimmer!*"

This was not Mist speaking, and I moved toward her to protest, to break through this barrier, but as I strained to reach her she disappeared and my eyes were open in the half-darkness of twilight. I was struggling to sit up in bed. Hobnailed boots echoed in the corridor outside. In the distance two rifleshots sounded.

"*Achtung!*" Now I saw the owner of the voice, an officer in a gray-green uniform. He was brandishing a revolver and gesturing toward the men in the beds. "*Durchsuchen Sie die Gefangenen nach Waffen!*"

It was suddenly clear. Mist had been a dream. This was the reality. We were being examined by the Germans to see if we were wounded and disarmed.

We were prisoners of war.

. . . Huit

THE EYES of the young lieutenant in the bed to the right were fastened blankly on me, and in growing horror I saw the bandage that circled half his body growing bloodier by the minute. The German doctor muttered something to the orderly who stood beside him with more bandage, then pushed a hypodermic needle into the lieutenant's forearm. The eyes did not even blink. To my left I heard the man who had screamed through the night. Now he was too far gone for that. He simply groaned with every painful breath, and I tensed at each agonized sound.

"*Drehen Sie ihn um,*" the doctor was saying when he reached my side, and the orderly pulled against me to turn me over on my stomach. I felt the cloth being stripped away from the wound in my back and gasped with pain as the doctor began to probe.

"We leave the shrapnel inside, soldier," he said in heavily-accented French. "That way we avoid an operation, and if you are quiet, it will heal. We hope." He was closing the bandage again. "You are lucky, you know that?"

It was true. My knapsack had saved my life, for it had slowed the force of the metal fragments which had struck me. As it was, I had been badly wounded in the back of the right lung, but I was not going to die. In a few days the man to my left would be dead, and dozens of my friends had fallen in the churchyard at Cutry never to rise again. Even the Mole might be lying there, his bantam figure twisted in death. The thought stabbed through me. Somehow I knew I would never see my little friend again.

But fortune had picked me to smile on. With our allies we were bound to win the war in a couple of months, and I would be alive to return to Paris. La Louque would welcome me with her gentle old smile, and Mist's lips would be passionately pressed against mine again. I need only hoard my strength as I convalesced in this château. It was only a question of time until all of this nightmare would be over.

It was a thin thread of hope, but I held to it doggedly through the interminable days that followed, even when those of the wounded who could walk were suddenly ordered to leave this makeshift hospital and assemble beside the cemetery wall in Cutry. Shakily I moved out to face whatever lay ahead, trying hard not to believe the stories that had circulated among us about the fate of other prisoners.

Inside the cemetery dozens of headstones had been shattered by the enemy's shells. Others had tumbled grotesquely to the ground. Leaves were falling forlornly to add to the desolation. "When they shoot us, we won't be far from the grave," somebody muttered despairingly as we took our places in front of the wall.

But we were not to be killed, at least not then, we told our-selves, for other groups of wounded men were herded into the road to join us in some kind of march. There were hundreds of us, and for the first time it began to be clear that our defeat at Cutry had not been an isolated setback. Obviously the war was going badly for us in many quarters, and my thread of hope snapped. There would be no return home in a few weeks. What then was to be our destiny?

The little railroad station furnished the beginning of an answer. On a siding stood half a dozen cattle cars. We were shoved inside. The sliding doors were bolted closed, and our world became the sweaty, narrow confines of a wooden box for two days and nights, broken only by the endless shunting of our car to different engines as we traversed one station after another across the German countryside. At times the train would stop and curious men and women would peer with hate-filled eyes through the bars of our car to see the human animals trapped inside. There was seldom a flicker of pity in their gaze.

Once I caught sight of a girl moving along a station platform, and I felt as if my heart had abruptly stopped. Her hair was long and reddish brown, falling away from her as she walked with easy grace. It was Mist! Here, somewhere in northern Germany, Mist had gone by within twenty feet of this moving prison cell, not even guessing that I was near. Then she turned in my direction, and suddenly I was looking at the face of a stranger. This girl was not at all like Mist, and desolation welled up inside me. Every turn of this train's wheels was taking me farther away from Paris. I might never even see Mist again.

The morning of the third day we learned our destination. We were outside the city of Magdeburg, only a few hours west of Berlin. The door of our car was unbolted and thrown back and some of the stench within was washed away in the welcome morning air.

"*Raus! Raus! Schnell!*" The harsh voice rasped along the

barrel of an ugly rifle. The soldier behind it gestured us out. One by one we moved to the edge of the car. Those who were slow to leap were shoved out with the gun against the back of their knees. I jumped to the ground and felt a tearing pain in my back, which had not completely healed. But the pain was forgotten in the joy of standing on earth again, of delight in freedom from our dungeon.

It was a short-lived happiness. Ahead of us, stretching as far as we could see was row on row of grim, drab huts behind barbed-wire barriers, and everywhere inside this prison compound was a sea of mud, churned up by trucks carrying supplies to laborers hurriedly building still more barracks. This was the prison camp of Alten Grabow. We were among the early arrivals. Soon thousands of prisoners — French, English, Belgian, Russian — were to swell Alten Grabow to one of the largest camps in Germany.

Alten Grabow — my new home for how long? Wearily I fell into a bunk with only a thin layer of straw to cover its boards.

Above me a voice was saying, "It'll be over by New Year's, you wait and see."

The new year was less than three months away. I wondered.

A young soldier was staring down at me. A lock of lank, blond hair had fallen over one eye, and he pushed it aside to see better. "Aren't you Chevalier?" he said oddly. I nodded. "I read in the Paris papers you were killed."

"Almost," I laughed without humor. "Not quite."

He had walked away before I realized what this meant. A false report in the newspapers. Mist and La Louque believed that I was dead. Somehow I must get word to them. But the sentry posted at the entrance to our enclosure only stared coldly as I tried to explain, then brusquely ordered me back inside the barracks in the sign language of a gun.

Days were to pass before the prisoners were allowed to write. Only post cards were permitted for easier censorship. My hand

94

trembled as I wrote that I was alive, that I'd been wounded but I was healthy and strong and everything would be all right soon. I had already discovered there were captured French doctors in our compound and they would be caring for their wounded countrymen. It was just a matter of time. That was the consolation for all of us. If you could survive the food, the dragging hours of boredom, the insidious tearing away at already-raw nerves, the petty arguments born of tension, the aching hunger for just the sight of a pretty girl, the growing hopelessness, the thoughts of home, then time would do the rest.

Suddenly among a host of strange faces, familiar ones appeared. Those who came from Paris naturally looked for other Parisians, and one gray, miserable day in the yard as we walked in our perpetual, hemmed-in circles, I saw a young stage designer I had known casually for years. But in the confines of a prison an ordinary acquaintance instantly becomes a friend, and Joe Bridge and I stood there in the cold drizzle talking obliviously for the full exercise period. I learned there were other men we both knew in other barracks. Some astute maneuvering would be necessary, but we must manage to wind up all in the same hut, and then we must plan entertainment for the camp. Joe would write revues, I would sing and dance, the others would do their acts. We were planning so excitedly we missed the warning signal to reassemble. A few loud angry shouts from our German overseers separated us in a hurry. We had just time to arrange a meeting for the next day — same hour, same place.

That afternoon, an envelope was thrust at me, its address almost obscured by the censor's stamp. But no blatant seals could blot out for me the handwriting of my beloved. For me, the way Mist wrote was as familiar as how she spoke or laughed or sighed.

"My darling Cio, you are alive! It's my last thought when I go to sleep, my first when I awake, and every minute of the time between — wherever I am or whatever I do — I say a thank-you to God because you are alive!"

Her voice rose up at me from the page, intimate and caressing. I had only to live through this and come back one day, and she would be waiting for me. She loved me, she would be faithful to me, she would take care of Mama, and soon we would be together.

I still remember how I felt that day, the warmth that glowed within me at the knowledge that I was Mist's man, that no one could change it. There was no marriage tie to keep her true to me, there was only the fidelity of love, but it was an unbreakable bond. From this moment on there would be the thought of Mist waiting — warm, tender, desirable — to make the future weeks move swiftly by.

But New Year's Day came and went. News filtered in that both sides had dug in for the winter. At last we faced the truth — that our captivity might last for years. The weeks abruptly slowed down. The shows Joe Bridge and I staged, weekly letters from Mist and La Louque with twenty francs enclosed to buy cigarettes and similar luxuries at the canteen the prisoners had organized, the packages from home — they could offer everything but hope.

I was given a job. Several of the French doctors who had seen me perform in Paris gave me perfunctory lessons and the post of pharmacist for the camp infirmary. Joe Bridge had already been made chief enlisted man in the hospital, living there in a room of his own, and we were now neighbors again. I was not a particularly inspired pharmacist, but each day, after assisting the doctors by giving injections and taking temperatures, I would take my satchel of medicines and make the rounds of the camp, going to any enclosure I desired.

It was in the English compound that I met Sergeant Ronald Kennedy. Friendly, smiling, soft-spoken, he was the ideal teacher for a man who had determined to learn the English language. I had no idea that I would use it to work in England or America, for I honestly didn't think I had the talent to measure up to their music hall performers. But I recalled the trip Mist and I had made to London and how lost we were with only French, and I could picture her look of disbelief and admiration when I returned from prison speaking another tongue, conversing easily with the English and American girls who came to work in our Paris theatres. Also it would give me an objective to help the endless days seem shorter. I hadn't counted, however, on the problems.

"It's an impossible language," I exploded one day to Kennedy. "Why doesn't 'daughter' rhyme with 'laughter'? Or 'waked' with 'naked'? And how can 'bow' rhyme with 'how' and at the same time with 'grow'?"

Kennedy grinned. "Why do you Frenchies have masculine and feminine words? And adjectives that have to agree in gender and number with the nouns they modify? We don't."

I had to admit he had a point. Just as English was difficult for me, so my language was a trial for him. I shook my head determinedly. I would learn to pronounce this unpredictable English tongue, I told myself, even if it took me fifty years! And you know something? That was forty-five years ago, and I'm still working at it!

It was now the autumn of 1915 with another grim winter looming ahead. We had been at Alten Grabow for fourteen months. In my old barracks the boy with the lank blond hair was haranguing a circle of thin tense men.

"This war could go on for twenty years, you realize that? You want to grow old in this rat trap?" An uncomfortable silence was his reply, and he jumped to his feet. "I guess you do," he said tightly and walked away.

A week later he was dead, shot trying to escape over the barbed wire on a dark moonless night.

I thought a great deal about it afterwards. Sitting in my tiny cubicle of a room at the infirmary, I remembered the failure of other escape attempts. And if anyone had made it over the barrier, how could he hope to escape with nearly all of Germany to traverse? Yet the desperate gamble might be worth it. In my hands was a letter from Mist, worn from many readings. She had been on a long tour with a revue, and now she had returned to Paris and the fever of a new season. Life. This was the lure which had tempted that boy to try the impossible. Outside that wire were living, breathing people. Inside were weary, dispirited robots — corpses going through the motions of being alive.

The door of my room burst open. Joe Bridge stood there, his face ashen.

"They just brought in six guys, Maurice. We're needed up front."

"Six? What's the matter with them?"

"Typhoid. It looks like an epidemic."

It was. From that night on helpless men, their bodies racked with fever, began to fill every one of our fifty beds. And the moment a man died, another victim took his place. There were four of us laboring in this room of death, ignoring the hours in a blur of work, sleeping only when exhaustion drove us to it, and by some miracle not one of us or the doctors came down with the dread disease. Perhaps we were too busy to become sick.

We saved the lives of many as the typhoid raged through the entire camp, but dozens of others died. We stood by their bedsides and watched hopelessly as the fever mounted, mounted. I found myself playing the role of comforter over and over again, mouthing confidence I didn't feel. There was a boy of eighteen who came from a small town in the provinces I had played when I was near his age. His eyes were glazed, his forehead glistening with sweat. His breathing was heavy and strained. He would be dead soon.

"It's a nice town," I was saying. "Who's there waiting for you? Your mother?" His answer was a groan that meant nothing. "And a girl maybe?"

98

I waited for some reaction, some sign that this fever-ridden boy heard me and understood. There was none.

"Well, just think about it for a moment. You'll be seeing them, I promise you. A long time before I ever make it out of here." When I got no response, I went on tensely. "I'll be in this place till the war's over, but you, once you're well enough to travel, they'll have to send you home, you realize that? Home!"

Did I read a flicker of emotion in his eyes? I leaned over his bed to see him better in the fading light. There was a trace of a smile on his lips, and I sat back feeling as if I had moved the world. I had reached him. And he believed me. In the little time he had left, he might be happier because of the lie I had told.

In all the years that have passed I have never been prouder of a performance or similar ones I gave in those tragic weeks. But that night when I passed the bed of that boy, I felt only despair. Already another man had been moved there. He, too, was dying. Suddenly the hopelessness of everything at Alten Grabow seemed almost too much to bear. I wanted to run till my lungs burst with the effort, but in a prison one runs nowhere.

And long after the epidemic had ended, despair remained my companion. Another summer had passed, and autumn of 1916 only served to remind me that more than two years had gone by with still no hope of escape or release. Mist, La Louque, Paris. They were only words now, so remote they seemed unreal.

BULLETIN

Red Cross exchange of doctors and medical corpsmen between belligerents. All orderlies bearing proof of assignment to the Medical Corps prior to their capture will be returned to their country of origin immediately.

Joe Bridge and I read the notice for the hundredth time. We were not genuine medical corpsmen; we'd been pressed into service after our arrival at camp. The other two orderlies in our infirmary had proof of their status, a stamp on their army identification cards certifying their assignment to the Medical Corps. Our only hope for repatriation was forging such a stamp on our own cards. But how?

We both thought of the man at the same moment. In Barracks Three was a thin, round-shouldered dour soldier who had been an engraver before the war. If anyone could copy the official stamp, it was he.

"If they find out it's a fake," Joe was saying, "we'll be the last ones to walk out of here after the war's over."

"Unless they just decide to shoot us," I replied grimly.

The gamble was worth it. We didn't even hesitate. And there were others in the French enclosure who were willing to take the risk. Dozens of them. Quickly the plan was set in operation. From an ordinary potato a "rubber stamp" was skillfully carved. Inked and pressed onto identification cards it made a passable imitation of the legitimate stamp, and for hours that night men stealthily made their way to Barracks Three.

But this was only the beginning. The German lieutenant glared suspiciously at the mass of cards, then announced that no action would be taken for fifteen days.

"Why the delay?" Joe asked nervously when we stood outside alone.

I didn't know. I only knew that the time of waiting would be an eternity, and I was right, for there were surely forty-eight hours in every one of those days. Then suddenly on the night of the fourteenth day a rumor spread through camp that an assembly was to be called the next day of all men who had claimed to be medical corpsmen, that we were to be interrogated by the German doctor-general. I was thrown into a panic. How idiotic to have hoped for clearance on the basis of an identification card alone! What better way to separate the genuine from the false than to question us on our medical knowledge?

On such a basis I knew I would fail. But I sat up most of the night cramming facts into my weary brain. The position of the liver, location of the vital arteries, a thousand complicated details. Finally I fell asleep over my book.

Joe and I read our names on the list the next morning. Report at ten o'clock. It was a bright, sharp October day. I stood outside the infirmary in a line that formed from the right. I was number fifteen. I remember that my hands were shaking violently, and I was unable to stop them. And in one horrified instant I knew that I had forgotten everything I had memorized the night before.

Through an interpreter, the German general was questioning the first man, one of the infirmary's two legitimate orderlies. He answered with professional sureness, and the general, a tall old man, very, very military and distinguished, nodded curtly to indicate approval and moved to the next man in line. The question concerned methods of treatment for kidney injury. If I stood in the shoes of that fellow, I was thinking, I would be finished, for I had no inkling of the answer. The man hesitated, stumbled over his reply and was roughly ordered out of line. From the corner of my eye I saw his face, gray with misery. Soon I would wear that face.

Each minute was a lifetime. The general was interrogating the fourteenth man. Only two had been passed so far. Frantically I tried to summon up the pages I had pored over last night. It was useless; my mind was a blank; I was doomed. I caught the glance of the French doctor who was introducing each man. He was one of the officers who had selected me as camp pharmacist and I felt he was my friend, but I knew he was helpless to intercede. All he could do to aid any of us was to reveal nothing of our desperate bluff for freedom.

The man beside me was rejected.

"This is medical corpsman Chevalier, General," the doctor was saying. "He's the star of our shows here in camp, and a good pharmacist, too." He paused. The general was finding my name on the list the interpreter held.

"Maurice Chevalier," he read slowly.

"Perhaps you saw him on the stage in Paris before the war," the doctor said.

The German was looking me over, eyebrows raised in a quizzical way. I held my breath and waited, braced for whatever was coming. But he remained silent, his expression unchanged. What was this man thinking? Was he delving into his mind for a particularly tricky question to trip me up? Or maybe that wouldn't be necessary, I thought almost hysterically. Maybe my fear of being exposed wasn't hidden at all. He could be reading it right now in my face and realizing that any question he chose would eliminate me. His unblinking scrutiny seemed to go on forever. I was certain I was lost.

Suddenly the general gestured to his interpreter and muttered something aside before he turned back to me. The query seemed to be poised on his lips, then abruptly he changed his mind and moved on to the next man. I looked in anguish at the interpreter.

"You pass, Chevalier," he said and joined the general. I stood there transfixed, unable to believe what I had heard. I had been approved, I was on the list of those who would be leaving Alten Grabow, but why? Had this general seen me on the stage three or four or five years ago? It was possible, for the Germans adored Paris, and before the outbreak of war they had thronged along our beautiful tree-lined boulevards. But could this explain his failing to ask me a single question?

I would never know, for I never saw the general again. Perhaps it had been pity for the panic that must have been in my eyes or a whim or the convincing air of my friendly French doctor. Whatever the cause, only thirteen out of all those who tried it succeeded in their masquerade as medical corpsmen. Joe Bridge was among them, and we were given orders to be ready to leave the following morning.

I awoke with the first light of dawn and stood at the window of my room to stare at the grim outlines of barbed wire and wooden watchtowers. This prison had been my world for twenty-six months. I had inured myself to believe that a day of release would never come. Now it was almost here, and the heavy weight of doubt dragged at me. We were not beyond the gate of Alten Grabow yet.

Joe knocked at my door and when he entered his face was drained of color. "I just talked with the guard out there," he stammered. "They're taking us in a truck to some town down the road and dumping us there."

I felt panic race through my body. "What for?"

"Another camp maybe. They wouldn't tell me." He turned back at the door, his shoulders suddenly sagging. "They wouldn't do that to us, would they?"

I had no answer for Joe. So near and yet so far, I was thinking, so near and yet so far.

THE TOWN was Merseburg, a short journey south of Alten Grabow. Our guards herded us into another barracks and stolidly refused to reveal what was happening. We were restricted to this drab building, but it was a different kind of prison, for there were no fences of wire to be seen. Only a soldier at the door stood between us and liberty. Oddly, instead of comforting us, this absence of forbidding walls was doubly unsettling because it was unfamiliar. At least in Alten Grabow we had grown accustomed to our fate. Now, with only the unknown waiting for us out there, we were meeting a new kind of fear.

We waited for days. Finally we were ordered to march to the railroad station, and the explanation appeared simple enough: Merseburg was an assembly point for medical personnel from all camps involved in this exchange, and we were to be part of an entire train of repatriates headed for Switzerland.

Ahead the Alps loomed and then a frontier was crossed and

Zurich was only miles away. Switzerland. We were no longer in the land of the enemy, and no one could seize us in this neutral country and drive us backwards into captivity. I remember crying quietly, without shame, until the train pulled into Zurich. There, friendly Swiss faces beamed as men and women and children milled around outside and Red Cross workers boarded our sealed cars to hand out chocolates and cigarettes and congratulations. We were all laughing and shouting as the full happiness of this moment swept over us. Joe pounded me on the back and I pummeled the next man and the train was moving without our realizing it. Impulsively I started to sing, and one voice after another joined in. Time ceased to exist.

Suddenly voices began to break off as if some signal had been called for quiet, and a silence settled over the length of the car. The train had ground to a stop, and slowly as if we were hypnotized we moved to the windows.

We stared at the striped pole of a barrier which was being raised to open the tracks. Another border. Hanging on the squat hut which housed the mechanism to raise and lower the barrier was a sign, its blue letters washed clean in the brilliant afternoon sunlight. It bore a single word: FRANCE.

Home. My God, we were home.

... Neuf

P ARIS.

The Gare de Lyon seethed with people as the train rumbled beneath the dirty glass roof of the station and halted beside an army band playing its noisy welcome for all of us. Our faces had been pressed against the windows to search the crowd, but the steam from the engine swirled back and obscured our vision. I looked anxiously for Mist and failing to find her turned to leave the car, but the corridor was blocked by a paunchy, middle-aged captain who stood in the doorway. His uniform, new and unwrinkled, had obviously never seen the front lines. He had a speech prepared to greet us, and there was no escape until it was delivered, along with instructions to spend this day as we pleased with our families and report in the morning to head-quarters.

At his last word I pushed from the car to elbow my way through the throng until a voice I had heard only in my dreams for so long wheeled me around. Mist stood slightly apart from the others, half in shadow. Crying and laughing at the same moment, she held out her arms to me, but as we moved toward each other the crowd shifted slightly and suddenly we were surrounded. Mist was recognized, and I could feel the curious stares upon us. It seemed to throw a blanket of restraint over us both, and our lips met almost with embarrassment.

"How are you, Mist?" I said and the words sounded inane. After all this time, was that what I had to say?

Her eyes filled with tears as she searched my face. "You've lost weight, Cio, did they treat you badly, was it terrible?"

She ran all the words together in a kind of breathless burst of sympathy I didn't want. It made me feel uncomfortable. It never occurred to me that Mist at this moment might be just as uncomfortable as I. "It was all right," I said and looked around questioningly for La Louque.

"She's waiting for you at home, so let's hurry. My car's out this way."

"Your car? Do you have a car now?"

"One of a thousand changes," Mist said and put on a smile that was too bright. "You didn't expect to find everything the same, did you?"

It was such an innocent remark, and I knew it, yet I found myself trying not to resent it and Mist's sudden gaiety as she led me to the coupé parked outside. She was chattering about the theatre and the way Paris had changed because of the war and how we would get to know our city all over again and have such wonderful good times together. And somehow, for no reason, the harder she tried to cheer me up, the more lost I became as I sat beside her and she raced through the streets I knew so well.

I was watching Mist as she talked. She hadn't changed, this much I knew, though up to now we had come together almost as strangers. Her beauty was the same, her eyes still laughed at me and dared me at the same time, her throaty voice still had the same warm catch in it. But there was a change in me, one I couldn't understand, and it frightened me. Was it that two years in prison without the nourishment of outside ideas and enthusiasm and spirit had forced me to feed upon my own resources too long? Was that why I felt empty and drained with no brilliance and sparkle and vigor inside myself?

Then we were outside my little apartment where La Louque was waiting and the door was thrown open and Mama was there. I held her frail gentle body close to me.

She was crying softly. "You've lost weight, Maurice, you must eat." It is an instinct with all mothers to want to fatten up thin sons, and I had known Mama would say something like that. For the first time that day I laughed almost easily as she hurried to the kitchen to ready the lunch she had been cooking the entire morning. It made me feel momentarily as if I were my old self again, and I turned to sweep Mist into my arms. Now we were alone, and I could kiss her passionately as I had ached to do for this lifetime I had been away.

But though Mist was soft and yielding, I began to tremble intensely when I pressed her near, for no passion welled up inside me as our bodies met. Rather there was almost an absence of feeling, as if our love were in my mind but not in my physical being. The dead void I had felt within me earlier was still there. I shall never forget the violence of my reaction, the shock of that moment, or the fear engulfing me that truly I had been consumed by those grim years in prison and would never be alive again.

Nor will I ever forget the tenderness of Mist.

"It will be all right, Cio," she said and her eyes glowed with love. "Soon it will be all right."

SLOWLY my appetite for love returned. Not so the other normal hungers — to eat, to drink, to work. The sumptuous meals I had dreamed of at Alten Grabow had no allure when set before me, and though the army doctor who examined my wound pronounced me fairly healthy, I could barely force myself to eat. I'd been given a three-months leave. At the end of that period, the decision would be made as to whether I would remain in uniform or be honorably discharged, probably the latter. In the meantime, I was urged to try and adjust to life again.

Adjust? It was a difficult word. How adjust to the fact that my strength seemed unwilling to come back, that friends whom I saw persisted in shaking my hand with obvious pity at my failure to be myself again? I spent more and more time alone with Mist, who was kind and understanding, and less and less time in the outside world of noise and traffic and the demands of other people. It was a kind of retreat from reality.

Yet at the same time a warning voice within me insisted that I stop, that I reverse direction and seek out the public rather than avoid it. The day was coming when I would have to work again, so I'd better face it now.

The place I chose for my first civilian performance in three years was a music hall in Montparnasse. I had been popular in this neighborhood before I went into uniform, and it seemed a good idea to give myself all the help I could, for I knew I was rusty and this would be no barracks entertainment but a real stage in a real theatre. I had some old songs and some new ones I'd learned in prison camp, and to be on the safe side I decided to wear my familiar comedy costume instead of the dress clothes I'd experimented with so successfully in the army. I felt more confident that way.

108

But confidence soon disappeared my first night before the audience. These people didn't react as a roomful of soldiers had done. I couldn't seem quite to reach them. My jokes fell a little flat. My voice which, in those days before microphones and amplifiers, had always reached the balcony now seemed a little feeble to make it. In the middle of my performance, I had the depressing thought that I didn't really have enough strength to do this work any more.

After this engagement ended I went on tour in the provinces. The same thing, except here they had less pity than Paris for one-time stars who had seemingly lost their ability. The journey home was endless, and its despondency stayed with me through the days when my discharge orders came from the army, through another two weeks of performances which I'd obtained at a major music hall in Paris on Mist's recommendation and where I still couldn't deliver on stage the performance I wanted to give.

"You? Quitting?" Mist said almost angrily later in her apartment. "How can you even think about it?"

I was sitting wearily, my head buried in my hands. "Believe me, I don't want to, but it goes from bad to worse. Whatever the spark was, I've lost it and no matter where I look I can't get it back."

"You need time, that's all. You'll be yourself again."

"When? I've been home three months. How much longer am I supposed to wait?"

"Forever, if you have to." Mist was pleading now, deeply moved by my depression. "Don't bury a career, my darling, that hasn't died." I stood up with a humorless laugh. "Cio, I want to help. What can I do?"

"No one can help me but myself, Mist, I've always been that way. The problem is, how can I help myself if I can't find myself?"

Unhappily I left.

A bitter cold wind pushed along the boulevard and fought me as I walked, but I hardly felt it, for a thousand thoughts were tumbling through my brain at that moment. The hour of decision was near; I could not go on this way, yet deep within me I knew that there was nothing else in my life but the theatre. I was recalling the years of struggle and poverty, the little triumphs and bigger setbacks, the night I had whirled around the stage in Marseilles and Franck had shouted, "You're in!" each time I passed the wings. Well, now I was out. Shrapnel in the lung and twenty-six grinding months of captivity had apparently done what all the difficult times had never succeeded in doing. They had destroyed my avidity for life and with it my will to fight.

I do not know to this day why I stopped in that little restaurant. Perhaps I was finally conscious of the cold, for it was surely not from hunger that I entered the deserted room. I ordered lunch mechanically and stared at my food without appetite, and all the time I was still reviewing the past. One harsh fact kept intruding: I had never quit before. I could not quit now. If it required a hundred years to find myself, I still could not quit. It was as simple as that.

I remember the waiter had put a Camembert cheese on the table, assuming that I would cut a wedge of it, and a tiny wedge at that, considering how little of my lunch I had eaten. But it tasted good, and suddenly one morsel demanded another. For the first time since my return I was hungry, and I devoured the entire cheese with a silly grin on my face. And as I did so, I seemed to feel a kind of miracle happening within me, a kind of fantastic bubbling up of the life force. The grin became a laugh. The waiter approached and stared at me as if I were insane, but I only laughed harder and soon, without knowing why, he was joining me.

It was the happiest duet I've ever known. For with that laughter I knew that I was being reborn, that the bright days would come again after all.

THEY did come. The year 1917 was one of renewed hope for all of us, for the United States had come into the war, and for me it was a year of beginning anew. Mist and I were signed for a revue at the Folies Bergère where seven years before we had first danced together. This time our number was far different from that original burlesqued fight and raucous dance. Now, costumed all in white, we danced stylishly to an American hit tune, "Broken Doll." Mist, of course, was still the top star, but I was on my way up again and I felt my sureness and poise returning with every new evening on stage.

A jarring note sounded the night Mist and I opened in an operetta called *Gobette of Paris*. Heaven knows there shouldn't have been such a note, for this was my first chance to appear in a lavish production as an actor rather than simply a specialty singer and dancer. The author had especially written a love scene for me to play with Mistinguett, and I was in the clouds. When I said "I love you, Gobette" to end the scene, I was going to speak with such fervor that everyone in the audience would be moved as never before.

A prop had been rigged to add to the effect. Mist and I were to sit on a love seat, lighted only by a pair of spots mounted in the eyes of a large porcelain dog. Hidden behind my back in the cushion of the sofa was a switch controlling these lights, and as I uttered my final words I was to flick the spots off simultaneously, plunging the entire stage into darkness. It was a novel, charming idea. At least it should have been.

That opening night all went smoothly. Our love scene enthralled the audience into total silence, and a moment before my final cue from Mist, I reached surreptitiously behind me for the concealed switch, just to reassure myself that it was in place. To my horror, my fingers touched nothing but air. During my next few lines I fumbled frantically behind me in the depths of the cushion and from the audience I heard a confused murmur rising. People were obviously asking each other what was wrong, and vital seconds passed before I located the switch. It had slipped from its rehearsed position. It now resided directly beneath me, in such an embarrassing spot that as I groped in panic for it and spoke my fervent last line, "I love you, Gobette," it appeared that I was scratching my posterior for emphasis!

Hysterical laughter broke out in the theatre, lasting long beyond the blackout on stage. I rushed off heartbroken, all my hopes for dramatic success smashed. In my dressing room later I was inconsolable.

"You're too sensitive," Mist said, a little annoyed. "It's not the end of the world."

"For me it is."

"You're acting like a child, Cio."

She spoke with a trace of condescension as if she were patting me on the head, and it stung me.

"Am I?" I said tightly.

"Just because they laughed at you. So what?"

"So how would you feel if they laughed at the great Mistinguett?" I lashed out at her and then was quickly sorry. Sharp words were so rare between Mist and me that I felt unhappy at having spoken this way, but still I could not apologize or try to soften this tiny rift, because I realized it had sprung from something that had been vaguely troubling me since my return. Mist expected me to accept passively every opinion she offered, every criticism she leveled, and before the war I'd been willing, even happy, to do it.

Now I was different; the army and imprisonment had seen to that. I had gone away from Mist a youngster, content to offer the homage she expected, but I had come back a man, and I had ideas and opinions of my own. I still loved her passionately, I still admired her professionally as the greatest light in the

112

French music hall theatre, but in the realm of emotion and intellect I was certainly Mist's equal and I had to be treated accordingly.

She walked out of my dressing room without a word. I made no effort to stop her. I only hoped this wouldn't happen again.

I WAS about to meet my first king, Alphonso XIII of Spain, but this was no typical command performance where a large number of show people are summoned to entertain before royalty. That sort of affair is a kind of public spectacle as one performer after another steps up to be formally presented, says four or five words and steps back again. In this case, however, Mist and I had been invited with only a few others to entertain Alphonso and his queen, in Paris on a visit, at a very private party at the Ritz. Our introduction to the King would be much more than a cursory presentation. There would be personal conversation with His Majesty, and I was nervous at the prospect.

In later years I would perform at similar intimate gatherings for other rulers — Leopold III of Belgium, England's Edward VIII who gave up his crown for love, his brother George VI and the present young monarch, Queen Elizabeth, but Alphonso's soiree was my first, and I wasn't at all sure how to act. Mist was completely at ease. Social protocol never disturbed her as it did me, and I envied her grace and ability to forget the rough, earthy background of her childhood. Even now, when I'd found a new success in a marvelous revue with Mist at the Casino de Paris, the glamorous, elevated world beyond the theatre was not my element.

Just before Mist and I were to go on I whispered to Sacha Guitry, the famed actor and writer who was to play a sketch with Yvonne Printemps, that I could use some guidance in comportment before the King.

His voice was grave. "Never address royalty as 'you,' Maurice. It's always in the third person." I nodded seriously. "I humbly thank Your Majesty," he recited. "Your Majesty honors me very much."

He went on to warn me that no one would applaud until their Gracious Majesties gave the signal, that even then Alphonso and his lady would only look politely amused and clap with the tips of their fingers. The others would have to be even less demonstrative, lest their fingertips drown out the feeble sounds of the royal applause. To a performer whose heart quickened at clamorous acclaim from his audience, this was hardly reassuring.

I danced as well as I could in this refrigerated atmosphere, and afterwards, waiting to be presented, I repeated my "third person" lessons under my breath, aware that this headwaiter's language fitted me not at all. Sacha and Yvonne were first. They did well. I went forward with Mist, who was natural and self-possessed. What about me? My knees were shaking, my throat dry, and I wanted nothing more than to sit down.

"You danced very well, Monsieur Chevalier," Alphonso said.

"Your—" The words stuck and I cleared my throat. I felt foolish and reluctant. "Your Majesty is too kind."

"Your dance seemed to be so easy, yet I'm sure it's difficult and tiring."

"Your—" Again the frog in my throat. I was concentrating so hard on the third person that I couldn't seem to get past "Your Majesty." Finally I thought of a word. "Your Majesty is too indulgent," I said painfully.

The King's eyes were twinkling now, and suddenly he smiled. It was obvious that he understood my discomfiture, that he knew I was lost in this world of stiffness and formality. I broke into a smile myself, and then we began conversing spiritedly as friends—in the second person, not the third—for this sovereign's genuine warmth had dissolved the artificial barrier between us.

When I parted from the King of Spain a few moments later, I had gained a new appreciation for kindness and understanding.

In the decades that followed I was to meet Alphonso XIII again, but if our paths had not crossed again, I would never have forgotten him — not because the man was a king, but because the king was a man.

THE hope for no more tiffs with Mist proved futile, and the villain turned out to be her insatiable search for amusement when our nightly performance at the Casino was done. It was spring, 1918, and thousands of American soldiers were pouring into France. German air raids had brought a blackout to Paris after dark, but behind heavy curtains from which no glimmer of light could escape a frantic search for pleasure was taking place. Everyone was trying too hard to have a good time. To the blare of jazz bands in crowded, smoky rooms, French, English and American officers and aviators traveled on a boisterous wave, and Mist and I were with them almost every night.

Still ill at ease and lost at such get-togethers, I gathered courage from one drink after another, and I'd return home each dawn drunk and weary of alcohol. Not so Mist, who barely drank at all. Her own natural exuberance sustained her, and she was the life of every party, but for me it was a crippling pace and finally I rebelled.

At first Mist thought I was joking when I said I was going directly home.

"It's not even midnight, Cio. You're not serious."

"I'm tired, Mist. People do go to sleep at this hour, did you know that?"

She held out her lavish furs to me. "Darling, sleep is for the very young and the very old and we're neither, so let's go now, shall we?"

"I'm sorry, Mist, I've been trying to tell you for weeks that these things night after night just bore me. I'm not asking you to give them up. Apparently they mean a great deal to you. All I want is to be free of this whole mess once in a while."

Mist's eyes flashed. "Free? That's a peculiar choice of words. I expect you to be my slave, is that what you're trying to say?"

I tried to calm my temper in the face of her shrillness. "You said it, Mist, not I."

"But you meant it, didn't you?"

"Not exactly, Mist," I told her, and I knew this would be a fight if it went on. "But I'm not the lady's servant, I'm her lover, and I'm going home to sleep."

It was my turn now to walk out.

I stayed away from Mist's apartment that night and all of the next day. In my own place that I shared with La Louque I sat unhappily through most of the afternoon wondering what we would say to each other when we met at the theatre. My answer came as a shock: Mist was not speaking to me. As soon as this was established, I naturally was not speaking to her, so between us a cold, hostile silence reigned for days.

A lovers' quarrel — nothing so rare in that, you say. Perhaps not, if the two can stay apart. But in our case it was different. In this latest revue at the Casino we were playing a torrid love scene in which passionate kisses and soft glances and tender caresses were exchanged. It was a long scene and a vital one to the show, and it was very difficult to carry off, believe me.

Six days it went like that.

On the seventh the routine started out the same. I clasped Mist in my arms and our lips met in what would appear to the audience as a deep, emotional kiss, but which for this eternal week had only been a cold, impersonal embrace. My whole body ached with longing for Mist; it was torture to go on this way.

We still held each other, and suddenly in Mist's eyes the implacable hostility we had been sharing was gone. "Oh, God, Cio," she whispered. "What are we doing?"

"We're out of our minds, Mist," I whispered back. "Let's stop it now."

116

And there on the stage of the Casino before a packed audience who knew nothing of the drama that was actually happening on stage we kissed again and, though the script did not call for it, still again. There was something so sweet about that reconciliation, for love that survives the bitterness of a quarrel seems twice as strong when anger subsides and tenderness returns.

What I failed to realize was that love may seem stronger at such a time, but often the repair you've made in its structure remains as a weak point which can rupture again at a moment of strain.

For a precarious instant that moment seemed at hand with the opening of the Casino's new autumn revue. With each succeeding show I had been trying to add an extra zest to my performances on the theory that you must give the public always a little more than they expect. And I felt it had been worth while, for every audience had seemed to respond with more enthusiasm. Nothing riotous, you understand, but a slowly growing acclaim, and I was happier because of it. And still more pleased the day after the première of the autumn revue, for the papers carried glowing praise for me from several critics. They had loved Mist as always, and our numbers together, but they had also liked me very much for myself.

I wanted to share my joy with Mist, and I went to her dressing room before the show that night. The door was open, and several of her entourage were grouped around her. I liked none of these people, but they were Mist's court of admirers who always hung around to fawn and I had long since given up the hope that she would drive them away.

"The people are out there because of you," one of them was simpering. "Does Chevalier think he fills the theatre?"

"Listen to this one, Mist," another said and began to read in a derisive voice that part of the newspaper review which dealt with me. At the end of each phrase he stopped for the group to punctuate with sarcastic laughter. It was a childish mockery, and I waited with annoyance for Mist to interrupt. When she didn't, I stepped inside and the game stopped abruptly. I waited without a word until the group filed out and closed the door behind them.

"Apparently your friends don't agree with the reviews, Mist," I said. "Do you?" I tried in vain to meet her eyes in the mirror as she put on her make-up.

"They were only joking, Cio. Where's your sense of humor?"

"You didn't answer the question, Mist. Do you agree with the reviews?"

"They said you were wonderful, darling," she shrugged. "Isn't that enough for you?"

"No. I was hoping you thought so, too. That means a great deal to me, or didn't you know?"

She turned finally to face me. "It doesn't really matter what I think, Cio," she said enigmatically. "It's really the audience who makes a star, isn't that right? Of course I agree with the papers, you were fine." She returned to her mirror and said pointedly, "You'll look better in make-up, too, darling."

I nodded and left, not angry, because I had no reason to be — at least no reason that I could touch. Yet I sensed within Mist, or thought I did, a resentment, and it made me wonder if she considered me a rival. The idea was ludicrous, I told myself, for there would always be but one Mistinguett, and if I established Maurice Chevalier as a personality, it would not be as a competitor but rather as a colleague. Surely Mist loved me enough not to want me to stand still in my profession, not to want me to remain forever as her junior partner on the stage?

I dismissed my doubts, but they were still there, and the foundation of love unknowingly had weakened a little more.

The Armistice came and the lights went on again in Paris and there would never be another war and the world was aglow with joy. Now the boulevards milled with celebrating soldiers on leave, marking time till boats could take them home again. I guess in a way Mist and I were marking time as well, because we were caught up in the hysteria of the day and tomorrow was forgotten, for today was too wonderful. The Casino de Paris was jammed solidly with uniforms every night, but a tall girl with a slim, sleek body and a dazzling smile managed to catch the show. She came backstage to see me afterwards — Elsie Janis, the sweetheart of the American forces in Europe, who had sung and danced and won the heart of every doughboy.

When I spoke to her in English, she was delighted. "I'm doing a revue soon in London," she said. "How would you like to join me?"

The idea was appealing, but I remembered the English music hall performers, how good they were, and I was afraid I'd suffer by comparison.

Elsie was a direct, candid girl who spoke straight from the shoulder like a man when I told her my fears. "Why, none of them's got what you've got, at least not as much."

"What's that?"

"Personality. Charm."

Charm. This word had never been applied to me in France. People had said I was warm or amusing or full of pep — but charming? I laughed out loud, but Elsie was not joking. She pressed me for an answer. I could only reply that it was impossible for the moment, that I'd let her know if the situation changed. The offer was a great compliment and tempting, but I couldn't walk out on Mist, even for a single engagement. I owed her a great debt, but more than that, I still loved her.

I decided to say nothing about the London offer to Mist or even about Elsie Janis's visit, but I'd overlooked the underground that exists with every theatrical production — backstage gossip. Mist heard of my talk with Elsie probably hours after it happened, though she made no mention of it for several days, and then only casually.

"Is she pretty?" she said, and I nodded. "Did you like her?" I nodded again. "Well, what did you talk about?"

I could be as offhand as she, and I shrugged. "The show, London, Paris — the usual things."

I wondered at the time why I didn't reveal the whole story, and later I had to admit that I was keeping the Janis offer in my pocket just in case Mist should underestimate my worth as a performer, at which time I would quietly point out that I had a certain important value elsewhere. Another crack in the wall of love, even if I was not admitting it was there.

Mist turned away, trying to hide her annoyance at my reticence, but I knew her too well and I could see that she was piqued, although I was sure she'd forget the whole thing before the night was out. Here I was apparently wrong, for soon afterwards the same backstage tattle reached in my direction to repeat little remarks Mist had reportedly made to others in the cast that I would never have gone anywhere in the profession without her, that she had guided me and lifted me as well. I wanted not to believe these tales, so as fast as I heard them I dismissed them. After all, I could honestly tell myself that I had come a long way before that first dance with Mist at the Folies Bergère, and the plaudits I was receiving now from the public were for the work I was doing on my own.

Then one day the story which couldn't be pushed aside found me: that I was disloyal, that I was saving my big efforts on stage for the moments that made me look good by myself and holding back in those we were together. It wasn't true. Having too great a respect, almost worship, of the audience who had paid to see me, I had never been and was never to be a performer who coasted, who ever gave less than his best. And if I had stopped to weigh the rumor at that moment, I would surely have decided it was distorted and alien to the Mist I had known and loved for so long. Anger, however, seldom allows for reflection. I cabled Elsie Janis in London.

That afternoon I had my reply: "All right. Come over. Will start in four weeks in show." They were offering me five hundred dollars a week.

Mist was standing with Volterra, the manager of the theatre, when I arrived that evening, and they broke off their discussion when they saw me near. I had the feeling that I was the subject of their talk, but it mattered no longer, for I was handing in my notice. When I announced it, Mist's eyes were wide as if she had been struck, and Volterra regarded me with a look of stunned amazement. Finally he shook his head and smiled thinly.

"You're playing a losing game, Maurice," he said.

"Striking out on my own? I don't think so."

"But maybe it'll teach you a lesson." He laughed and walked away.

Mist was still staring almost fixedly at me, and in that instant we could have been complete strangers. I remember thinking it and feeling suddenly hollow inside.

"Well, that's what you've wanted, Cio," she said and left me standing there alone.

I was still alone in the early morning hour when I stood on the railway platform waiting for the boat train which would take me to London. Mist and I had said our cool good-bys the night before, yet somewhere inside me there had been the hope she would be here for a warmer farewell. Gazing around vainly for at least some member of the cast who had braved the dawn to see me off, I felt forlorn and disappointed and frightened of what lay ahead. Had I been a fool to do this just for the sake of proving I could succeed without Mist at my side?

In London that evening I still was haunted by that question and by sights and sounds of memory on every side — Victoria

Station, where Mist and I had arrived almost ten years before, the lights of Piccadilly Circus past which we had rushed from one theatre to the next, the Savoy, with a room where once I had cradled her in my arms to comfort the pain that racked her body. Remembering these times, I could suddenly no longer recall the angry words, the petty disagreements of the past months. Only the good moments, the happy hours were there with me, and in the act of regretting that I had left them behind, I knew that love, though abandoned, would not die without a fight.

Whatever befell me in this foreign land, an unfinished part of my life waited for me in Paris. Mist and I had yet to settle the fate of love.

Or love to settle the fate of us.

"From the time I was twelve I dreamed of becoming a great entertainer, a part of the vibrant, joyous life which stirred my blood and quickened my senses and made me feel completely alive."

*"The boy became a man
—and just as I had prayed,
the doors did open in Paris."*

ALLIED ARTISTS

ALLIED ARTISTS

ALLIED ARTISTS

WALERY

*"By 1908, people even began
to talk of the Chevalier style,
and suddenly everything was
all right."*

"Mistinguett was Paris — the symbol of gaiety and good humor and courage and heart. And she brought me the greatest love I would ever know."

"In my World War I uniform."

"1914. Standing third from the left, my arm around a buddy, I little realized that a few months later some of us would be dead, others prisoners of war."

"Rehearsing with the Dolly Sisters, 1925 — the first time a male star had headed the bill at the famed Casino de Paris."

"Marriage was to fail with Yvonne Vallée and me, but I would always have an immense gratitude to her for all she had done for me."

*"With Jeanette MacDonald
in* One Hour with You.*"*

*"With Baby Leroy
in* Bedtime Story.*"*

"*After the 1932 premiere of* Sign of the Cross. *Marlene Dietrich was an extraordinary comrade, a woman of great intelligence and sensitivity, amusingly and charmingly unpredictable in her moods.*"

UPI

EMKA, LTD.

"*An Apache dance from* Love Me Tonight."

"*In* The Smiling Lieutenant, *with Claudette Colbert — lovely and talented and a delicious comedienne.*"

EMKA, LTD.

(Left) "*On the set of* The Merry Widow *— with Norma Shearer, Maureen O'Sullivan, Herbert Marshall and Ernst Lubitsch.*"

"At La Bocca with Nita Raya
— and love had come back into my life again."

. . . Dix

How often in the next month I wished I had never
heard of London or the Palace Theatre or our revue,
Hullo, America, or even Elsie Janis! Charming and friendly
and encouraging, she had done all she knew to put me at
my ease as my opening appearance neared, but there were
so many problems I hadn't envisioned which tumbled
through my brain night and day.

Language. Suddenly I was to perform before a public totally unfamiliar with me or my work, and I was to do it in
a tongue where I must think and translate before each
phrase I uttered. If something went wrong and I were
forced to improvise, I would be lost.

Dancing. I was to waltz with the girls in the company,

and I had never waltzed in my life and felt clumsy in the part. Moreover, I had a tap-dancing number, and I felt that even kids in the English streets could tap-dance better than I. My own brand of eccentric humorous dance had no place in this show. Yes, the foreigner had come to a strange country, and the moment he stepped onto the stage, the natives would do everything better than he.

Finally, there was Elsie, a bundle of dynamic talent. Her work lacked the provocative style and warmth of Mistinguett, but she made up for it with precision and drive and power. I stood a good chance of being overwhelmed by her personality, and once again, I reflected, I had put myself at the mercy of a forceful, compelling woman behind the footlights, and I might well disappear in her shadow. Elsie must have sensed my feelings from the moment rehearsals began, for in these past weeks she had been an angel, constantly going over my lines with me, teaching me every intonation in English so the audience would clearly understand my accent. The same thing with my dances. When opening matinee came, however, I was still doubtful, and I finished the show ready to leave for home the next morning.

Backstage, the producer's smile was forged of cold steel. "You're under a three-months contract; you'll board that boat in ninety days, is that clear?"

Elsie's glance was gentler. "Monday matinee is the coldest day of the week, Maurice. I said you had charm in Paris, I say it again. Now, don't be so temperamental and for the evening show everything will be splendid."

Happily she was right. It went a great deal better. The critics weren't bowled over but they liked me, and I slowly became one of the foreign entertainers accepted by the English public.

But always the dilemma of love. Mist and I were writing letters that carefully ignored the tension which had erupted in my leaving. I admitted it was not terribly gay in London without saying I was almost unhappy because I didn't want it to look as if I had made a mistake. Between the lines of what she wrote I could sense that something, too, was missing from her life, yet neither of us went so far as to say we were sorry this whole thing had happened, not even when Mist suddenly decided to spend a long weekend in London and it would have been so easy to confess that we were a little miserable without each other.

Instead we played a kind of game that happens so often in love: we were casual, we made small talk, yet all the time we had so much to say to each other and couldn't. In my dressing room after seeing the show Mist was astonished that I spoke English apparently well and rapidly, but she had little to say about my performance. And though this irked me, I said nothing, for it was all part of the game of being intimate strangers.

The pretense ends, however, when the lovers have gone apart again, and so it was with me. The moment Mist had left London to return home I missed her more than ever, and I determined that we would patch things up on my return. We had our professional differences, there was no evading the truth, but why must this destroy a love that had lasted for nine years? Why couldn't Mist and I disagree as performers and still agree as lovers? Somehow it all seemed so logical when we were apart — it could surely make as much sense when we were together.

When my three months with Elsie Janis were over and I returned to Paris to open in a revue at a beautiful theatre belonging to my London producer, it seemed more logical than ever. Mist was still starring at the Casino, so we would each have our separate careers without the friction that apparently came from working together, and every day we could meet with the eagerness of new young lovers.

Mist was in my arms, her eyes soft and glowing. "Is it a good show, Cio?" she asked. "Will you run forever in it?"

"A few days less." I grinned and kissed her again.

It was many days less. Two months after our heralded opening we closed, for the revue had never caught on and was losing money every day. And I suppose what happened next was inevitable. Volterra ran into me in the street and wanted to know, now that I was free, when I was coming back to the Casino. A warning voice should have told me that I was tempting fate in going back to work with Mist when all had been so calm and happy playing apart from each other, but no whisper of alarm sounded. Instead, it was flattering to be in demand for the most lavish production in Paris, one that was guaranteed to run for a complete season.

"I'm booked for ten days out of town," I said. "Let's talk about it when I get back."

In my heart, however, I had already decided. I would accept with only one stipulation: that the co-stars in this production, an excellent comedian named Dorville who was a friend of mine and myself, be given slightly larger billing. To a performer, you understand, the size of type in which his name is printed in programs and advertisements is in a way earned recognition. Money is satisfaction for his pocketbook, billing for his pride.

Volterra listened me out unhappily upon my return. "It's the same billing you had before you left, Maurice."

"But I'm not the same man. I've been to London, I've done bigger things."

"You won't sign otherwise?" I shook my head and he sighed. "Mistinguett's the star of the show, I'll have to talk to her and straighten it out, I hope."

He seemed so lugubrious about his mission that I almost stopped him to offer reassurance. I was sure that Mist wouldn't object to something as fair as this tiny request.

I could not have been more mistaken. When I saw her that evening Mist was smiling too tightly, and I knew she was hiding annoyance.

"What's this about billing, Cio? Isn't it a little ridiculous, your pushing Volterra in a corner over the size of a name?"

"It wasn't very much to ask, Mist."

"I think it was."

It was my turn to be annoyed. "Why? I'm not asking for equal billing; it certainly doesn't affect you."

"People will feel I'm going down."

"How so? Your name will be in as big type as ever. It's just that Dorville and I will be less small." Mist turned away angrily, and I began to understand. "It's the contrast you want, isn't that right, Mist? So long as those around you look small, it guarantees you'll look big." As I said the words it saddened me, because I knew that Mistinguett should not need this kind of artificial assurance that she was a great star. She would have been a queen with only rags for a robe and paper for a crown, yet something petty inside made her jealous and fearful of what she mistakenly considered competition.

"Good night, Mist," I said and before she could turn back to face me, I walked out. Almost blindly I moved down the stairs to the street, and I began to walk without purpose, unheeding of people and cars and the myriad noises of the city. A terrible thing was happening within me, a kind of truth welling up to be recognized and confronted.

It was a truth about love, and it was harsh and painful and naked. Love is only strong and durable, the truth was pounding at me, when respect and esteem are there to share its glory. To be completely in love with someone you must like her as well as love her. You must adore her — but admire her, too, and at that instant I had no admiration for Mist.

Volterra saw me the next day. "It's all arranged," he said. "You've won."

But what had I won? It was an empty victory, for I had lost my illusions, and I knew it. There would be wonderful moments again, but fewer and every day farther between. And now I realized that we had passed the crest, and the road could lead only downhill to the end.

Mist and I never mentioned the incident of the billing. Rehearsals began, and we did but one number together, while a young American dancer, Earl Leslie, was her partner in two. My solo contribution to the show was to be a ten-minute singing performance done first in my own style and then as three other well-known French personality entertainers would do the same song. I had insisted over the objection of Volterra that this would be my specialty scene, and even up to dress rehearsal night he was worried that it would slow down the pace and rhythm of the revue as a whole despite his having cautiously placed my turn at the beginning of the second act when people would still be seating themselves after intermission.

"Imitations," he said mournfully the afternoon of the opening. "Tonight tells the tale, Maurice. If the audience doesn't like them either, out they go."

It was all I could ask for, a chance to see how much weight I could carry in a big spectacle when I stood in the spotlight on a giant stage alone for the length of a good solid number. For me it was an important gamble, and I was lucky enough to win. Even the dour Volterra was chortling after the last curtain call.

"It was the high spot of the evening, Maurice. Give them something new and original, and they'll love you every time, isn't that right, Mist?"

"Every time," Mist said and moved away.

Watching her go without another word, I felt a pang of regret. It was so clear that now I was openly to be Mist's rival, but something else was clear as well: from this day on I would have complete confidence in my ability to fly on my own wings.

Volterra had followed Mist, and I stood there in the wings savoring tonight's success almost unaware of the bustle around me. A soft, caressing voice was at my ear. "Monsieur Chevalier?" I turned to see a dark-haired girl beside me whom I had seen scores of times before during the rehearsals of our show, but she had been one of the dancers in the company and that was all. Now in the shadowy light backstage, there was a quality I hadn't noticed, a kind of deep beauty in her face and a subtle promise in the way she held her body.

"You were wonderful tonight," she said, so coyly that in someone else it might have seemed vacuous, but there was so much pure animal magnetism in Simone that the words didn't really matter or how she said them. You cared only that this was a ravishing, voluptuous creature to be looked at and enjoyed.

"Thank you." I said it caught up in this first startling awareness, and when she had gone away the nearness of her lingered. No one but Mist had stirred me so in many years. And disturbed me, too.

When I joined Mist for the celebration we'd planned after tonight's opening, Earl Leslie was waiting with her.

"I've invited my other leading man along, Cio, do you mind?" She graced Earl with her brilliant smile, and I watched him bloom in its light, but within me there was no jealousy. I think at that moment I felt relieved, and I must have sensed the way it was going to be, that more and more often the three of us would make the rounds of the night clubs Mist loved, and that each time I inevitably rebelled Earl would escort her alone.

Something else was inevitable: Simone. Mist and I kept up our public pretense that all was not over between us, for indeed it was not completely and finally done yet. Our relationship was rather like a marriage which has had its day, when husband and wife have separate bedrooms and separate hopes and thoughts and fears yet still dine together and live together and even sometimes make love together because they have shared too much to take the ultimate, permanent, irrevocable step which means farewell. But my meetings with Simone were bound to happen. She was exciting, bewitching, wanting nothing from passion but passion itself — and I was human. We met in secret. I was determined that no public knowledge of this would hurt Mist.

This was an affair of the flesh, an enormous attraction between two people whose hearts were not involved as those of Mist and mine. One night I sat moodily and stared at the lingering flames in the fireplace, and Simone, at my feet with her head resting against my knees, looked up to ask, "What are you thinking of, *chéri?*"

"Nothing." It was not the truth. I had been thinking of an evening six years before at Bois-le-Roi when Mist, convalescing at the little house near my army camp, had curled up just this way with me to share the rich, happy silence that only lovers can know.

Yes, it was almost but not quite the end with Mist and me.

1920.
MIST had left the Casino for a new production, and I had become the star there for three shows in a row. In the last one, a summer revue, I decided to do my solo specialty number for the first time dressed simply in a tuxedo. The English were wearing top hats with dinner jackets, but that seemed pretentious for a Paris stage.

"A black fedora," Volterra suggested, and I shook my head.

"It's a little sad."

"Well, name me a hat that's lighthearted," he snorted. "A derby?"

Lighthearted. There was the key to what I wanted, and I ran down the list of every man's hat I could remember. When I reached the stiff straw hat known affectionately as a "boater," I stopped. This was it. Perhaps a boater was not the standard headgear for formal clothes, but who could complain at its sunny gaiety and insouciance?

I didn't know then that I had chosen the hat which was to become my trademark around the world.

On my way home from the hatter's I slipped into the theatre where Mist was starring and took a seat at the rear of the house to hear her sing a song which had enraptured all of Paris. It was called *"Mon Homme,"* and it was to cross the sea later to become a fantastic hit in America — "My Man," introduced by the great Fanny Brice.

I shall never forget the way Mist did that song or my own stirring within at the haunting fervor of it, for I was the man she was singing of, her man indeed, even though the enchantment between us had faded and almost disappeared, Mist sang the last wailing notes, and the audience burst into applause. My own handclaps sounded hollow and desolate and sad, an elegy to what had once been love.

But there was little time to mourn days gone by, for the days still to come were offering a new and daring challenge. I was approached to play the lead in an operetta called *Dede,* and if I accepted, this meant carrying an entire show on my shoulders for the first time. To perform a ten-minute sketch or monologue in a revue was one thing, but to dominate most of the scenes in a musical play which lasted almost three hours was altogether another.

Rehearsals found me too anxious, too strong in my attack, and the director was constantly softening my approach to the part. Slowly, it began to work. To my own pleasant surprise, I was becoming an actor, there was hope for me yet, though at dress rehearsal a group of my old colleagues from the Casino dropped in and privately predicted disaster for my efforts.

Volterra saw me at his theatre that night. "I hear it's not good, Maurice," he said with a kind of mocking compassion. "You shouldn't have swapped a good thing here for that, but don't worry, there'll always be a place for you with me whenever you want to come back."

"I'll remember," I said dryly and wished I had stayed away from the Casino. With all that faced me tomorrow night, I should have spent the evening at home with La Louque and tried to rest. But I was too keyed up and tense to be alone, so I remained to face Volterra and Mist and the others who were so sure that *Dede* would be a debacle.

How wrong they were! Off to a slow start on opening night, the show picked up momentum, and I danced and spoke and sang to audience enthusiasm such as I had never known. *Dede* was an immense, extraordinary hit, and Paris was predicting a run of at least two years. The most important critics devoted columns to my emergence as an actor, and important people from everywhere knocked at my dressing room door each night, people who six months before hadn't bothered to toss a glance in my direction. It was all too unbelievable, this explosion of good fortune. With one smash success I had become a star like Mist.

"I'm so happy for you, Cio," she said soon after the opening. "You've come a long way since that scene with me in the rug, haven't you?"

The words had a little edge to them, but it didn't matter any more. I was beyond being hurt by Mist or needing her approbation, and she knew it, so the moments of tension between us actually began now to lessen. Unfortunately, tenderness had gone as well, and what we had left was habitude. We were used to each other, and somehow it seemed more comfortable to remain together than to admit the failure of a long, long rapport. Naturally it would not have continued if either of us had fallen in love with someone else, for that would have provoked a move to end it once and for all. As it was, we saw each other almost every evening when our performances on stage were done, and life drifted on in an almost aimless pattern.

The design was destined to change the night Douglas Fairbanks and Mary Pickford visited me after the show. We had met earlier and had become three great friends, and all of Paris was wild about them.

"You have to go to New York and play this in English," Doug said in his ebullient way. "You'll be a sensation."

"I think maybe I should stick to Paris," I said, remembering my London experience, and all of Doug's enthusiasm and Mary's golden smiles failed to move me.

Later they returned with reinforcements. The director of New York's famed Globe Theatre, C. B. Dillingham, was in Paris, and the arguments he offered, seconded by Doug and Mary, were too persuasive. A guarantee of fifteen hundred dollars a week against a percentage possibility of double that amount was a staggering sum of money. One's misgivings could bend under such an onslaught, and I signed an agreement to come to New York at the end of the run of *Dede*.

"It might be a year before I get there," I pointed out to Dillingham, but he didn't appear worried. He was convinced that he had a potential hit on his hands, and he could wait.

I could not. Now that I had committed myself to America, I was seized with a desire to see that incredible country, and I decided to spend the summer weeks when *Dede* would be closed in taking a look at New York. I explained my plans to Mist, secretly a little relieved at our impending separation, even perhaps hoping that distance would finally sever the ties which neither of us seemed willing to cut.

"I think I'll go with you," Mist said slowly.

Taken aback and trying not to show it, I protested that this was really a business trip for me, that I would be trying to get the feel of a new city, perhaps even to adapt my style of playing to fit New York's demands.

"Well, what better way to know the place than to have Earl along to show it to you? It's his home town after all."

"Earl?"

"Of course. He'll introduce both of us, take us to spots we'd never get to see otherwise." She stopped with a challenging glance. "What's the matter, doesn't my coming along appeal to you, Cio?"

Instantly I felt remorseful. If Mist wanted despite everything to hold on to some remnant of our past, whatever her reason I was not going to dispute it. But I agreed with misgivings, for though I could only guess at her relationship vis-à-vis Earl, which I suspected had become more and more intimate, a group of two men and one woman could in any case well become an uncomfortable arrangement.

I was right. Tension was the fourth member of our party from the moment we debarked from Le Havre. Mist, apparently annoyed by my determination to be alone to enjoy my first long ocean voyage, made little effort to hide her irritation toward me, and the oftener I withdrew, the oftener she insisted that the three of us be together. Earl, a charming and likable fellow who was obviously as captivated by Mist as I once had been, was caught in the middle of this strain with no choice. Before the other passengers we wore a politely civilized mask, but had the trip lasted too many days I'm afraid the disguise would ultimately have crumpled.

As it was, we were saved by our arrival in New York and freedom from the cramped quarters of a ship. I stood on the top deck drinking in the fairy-tale view of Manhattan, awed by the skyscraper splendor into forgetting the unpleasant days of travel. What a miraculous island! I could barely wait to explore this magic city with diamonds of sunlight bursting from the windows of its towering façade.

"Earl has plans for us," Mist said when we had settled into our hotel rooms. "Dinner in a wonderful room at the Ritz-Carlton, then one marvelous speakeasy after another!"

I shook my head. I had come here to see music halls, singers and dancers, and not night clubs. On my first night in America, I was asserting my own Declaration of Independence.

"As you will." Mist turned away.

That same evening I found myself alone in Harlem devouring a revue whose reputation had reached as far as Paris: *Shuffle Along*. Excitedly I listened to a new rhythm, an incessant, dynamic beat like nothing I'd ever heard before. A startling girl dancer contorted and writhed her sinuous body in a way that was to conquer Paris not many years later. I sought her name on the program. Josephine Baker. There were Negro comedy dancers, too, shuffling, soft-shoeing, swiveling in a jazz syncopation that was gay and free and at the same time electric and hard-hitting. Fascinated, I watched them all, feeling the vitality of it, knowing that I must master this special kind of magic for myself.

The next morning Dillingham found me a teacher of eccentric dancing. I had come here planning simply to alter my style if necessary for New York, but instead I was changing it for Europe as well. In three short weeks of intensive dance lessons in the morning and watching one revue after another in the evening I was to learn as much as years in France had taught me. I was going to wed the Parisian approach to entertainment with the American approach. It was a happy decision. I've never abandoned it since that day.

Departure time was near. The four of us — Dillingham, Mist, Earl and I — were lying on the warm sand at Atlantic City with the clamor of the boardwalk behind us. It had been a lazy summer weekend. The air was soft, a little breeze stirred off the ocean, I was feeling a deep contentment with all that had transpired in this fabulous new country. Dillingham for the dozenth time was outlining his enthusiastic plans for *Dede*.

"It'll be a smash, Maurice, a new kind of entertainment for us, and who knows, maybe we'll take it on tour when we finally close in New York." I nodded happily. This was pleasant to contemplate. "I think he'll take America by storm," he went on, turning to face Mist and Earl. "Don't you think so, Mist?"

"Yes, yes," Mist said and closed her eyes.

"The question is, how long will he run in Paris?" Dillingham said to her, and when Mist didn't reply he pursued it. "You've seen the show, what's your opinion? Another season? More?"

Mist sat up abruptly. "Why ask me, Mr. Dillingham? Your star is right next to you, ask him."

She started off down the beach and Earl scrambled to his feet to follow while Dillingham looked puzzled at me. Had he done something to make Mistinguett angry? I shrugged it off and quickly changed the subject, but later I sat in my room and watched the gray of evening climb from the horizon in the east till finally the sky was somber above, and all the time I was reviewing the years which had brought Mist and me so close together and now so far apart.

The fault lay not in either of us, I could see it so clearly now, but simply in the profession we adored. Work had joined us and then separated us, for we were competitors on the stage and love could not be the referee. Two performers, I was thinking sadly, might succeed in making a career together if the work of one complemented the other. But if each were an individual, stamped with his own unique mark, and if each were driven by some inner fire to guard his cachet as jealously as his life, then it was simply a fight for survival. Mist and I were entertainers first — and lovers second.

Perhaps, somewhere along the way, if we had realized that our métier would one day doom our love, we would have desperately tried to change the path. Now it was too late. Too late.

A knock sounded at the door. It was Dillingham. "Are you ready for dinner, Maurice?"

"I think I'll skip it. I'm not hungry."

He was eying me, concerned. "What's wrong?"

"Nothing that time won't heal," I said with a weary smile. "Even the scar will disappear finally."

THE BOAT was heading for home, and we were dancing at the Captain's gala on the next to the last night out. The number ended with Mist in my arms, and a wave of applause rose from the crowded tables around the salon. No one in the audience could have guessed that our dance had been a quiet fight, for our bodies had efficiently gone through every movement of this routine we knew so well. But great dancing is more than a series of graceful steps. Like an actor's performance, it is not just technique, it's built of emotion and drama and finesse, and all of this had been subordinated to our own personal feelings by Mist and me tonight. The days of taut restraint which had begun more than a month ago when we sailed for New York were finally taking their toll.

A few minutes later we stood alone on deck, and in the phosphorescent glow from the sea, Mist's eyes were almost too bright.

"That was quite a battle we had in there, Cio," she said tensely.

"Well, at least we were the only ones who knew it, Mist."

"What about Earl? Don't you think he realized something was going on?"

"One dancer can always tell when another one's holding back, surely. But Earl's not blind, he's seen us these last four weeks, he knows everything."

Mist said nothing for a moment. Then finally, "I'm going to leave the ship at Southampton, Cio, and go to London."

"Oh?"

"Earl will be with me, of course."

"I'm glad, Mist," I said simply. "You won't be alone that way."

"Is that all you have to say? You mean you'll go on to Le Havre without me?"

"Yes, Mist, and on to Paris."

She seemed about to say something more, then slowly turned without a word, and moved back inside the salon. As the door swung open, the music poured out and faded as it closed again, leaving the night silence broken only by the sibilance of the water as it rushed away from the slashing prow of the boat.

Standing there in the ghostly half-light, I suddenly knew that it was all over with Mist and me, that this was the final hour, and that each of us had somehow realized it in one single instant of awareness. The flame had gone out at last. We would say no more. There was no more to be said.

The next day slipped by and the night and then it was morning again and our ship had halted in the deep water off the green shore of England. The tender waited alongside to transport passengers and luggage to the Southampton dock in the distance, and I stood at the railing to look down at Mist and Earl as they boarded.

The breeze was whipping Mist's dress against the supple outlines of her body and her hair was a chestnut halo around her lovely face and I was remembering the years our lives had been woven together into a single story. Love had come to us like a gift with a thousand tendernesses to share, a living, fragile, vulnerable thing which had finally died.

But at least, I was thinking, we had allowed love to die without saying bad things to each other. We were disappearing from each other's lives without those fights in which brutal and ugly and regretful things were said. To end like that would have been to murder the memory of every happy and charming moment with which love had so abundantly blessed Mist and me. Love would go with as much grace as it had come.

At that moment she looked up and our eyes met, and then the chugging engine of the tender accelerated and the little boat turned in a half circle away from the mother ship. Mist waved and I raised my hand to answer. Slowly, slowly the distance between us grew until at last I could barely make out her figure and still I gazed at the receding vessel.

Ten years of my life were on that boat. It was impossible to see them go without a pang of dismay.

Good-by, Mist.

Good-by.

Can Wisdom be put in a silver rod,
Or Love in a golden bowl?

— Book of Thel

II

Love
in
a
Golden
Bowl

. . Un

GOOD-BY.
It's a very final word. Mist and I had never spoken it.
Still it had happened. The feeling of ending — of something
finished which cannot be again — rode inside me while the
boat train clicked its way toward Paris.

The dust of late August had coated the compartment
window and I watched the Normandy countryside slip by,
neatly marked off into hedgerowed squares, still green but
with the freshness exhausted. The fields had a melancholy
look. Maybe they knew, even while the sun still warmed
them, that soon this summer would be lost and though
others might come to bring them new life, the enchantment that belonged to this particular one would be gone

143

forever. It can be like that with a summer, I was thinking, or a love affair. Not a sadness, exactly, but a nostalgia for something beautiful which will never return. I had the feeling that nature and I were caught up in the same mood.

The train whistle made a sudden, sharp little cry as we approached a crossing. It sounded human. Like a protest. Suddenly I wanted no more of this landscape. I turned from the window restlessly.

The man seated opposite me caught my eye. He was perhaps in his middle fifties, with a sober, responsible businessman's face. "The last hour of the journey," he said. "It's always the longest."

I nodded in agreement, searching my jacket pockets for a package of cigarettes.

"You must be anxious to get back to Paris. I mean, the stage and all that excitement."

His face had lighted up when he said those words, as if for me Paris must be a special and magic place. Well, wasn't it? Until this moment I had given no thought to my homecoming. Now I began to fill my head with visions of it. Paris. My beautiful city. I had never returned to her with my professional star shining so high. In a matter of weeks I would be opening the second season of *Dede* which promised to be as great a success as the first. And until then?

Until then, I had only to let Paris carry me on that sweeping wave of joyousness I had always found as I wandered her great avenues and narrow, crooked side streets. Paris. Alive and gay and soaring, where the very air was charged with intoxication and promise. Anxious to get back? Suddenly I couldn't wait. This heavy shadow that had been hovering over my spirit would vanish in the dazzling light of Paris.

But the shadow wouldn't leave.

It followed me along the white stone quays beside the Seine where the usually carefree fishermen seemed sullen and dispirited

144

in the August heat. It stayed as I walked the paths of the Tuileries Gardens and found them lonely and deserted where a wonderful, tumbling knot of kids were wont to play and laugh and shout. Even the summer tourists who normally crowded the boulevards seemed to have outstayed their enthusiasm. They strolled along a little like mechanical dolls when the key is winding down and the dance is nearly over.

I had been back in Paris for five hours and no matter where I turned I couldn't find my city. Somewhere a baby began to cry — a soft, irritated, fretful sound in the weighted, windless air. Two leaves, brown and curled, dropped with a hollow rattle from the wearied branches of a chestnut tree to the bench where I had paused. Impatiently I brushed them to the ground. Was this the sparkle of Paris?

I heard a voice calling me and turned to see a figure hurrying my way, a well-dressed man whose rounding body strained a bit at the buttons of his coat but who moved with a light-footed, almost comic grace. It was Felix Mayol, a friend who two decades ago had been the greatest music hall star in France.

"I just came up from Toulon," he said as we shook hands. "So, Maurice, how are you?"

"Better now," I told him happily. "Of all the days you could choose to be in Paris, this is the finest. For the first time since I unpacked I'm beginning to feel at home."

"Oh?" A little puzzled frown came in his face. "Then you're staying in Paris?"

"But why not? I've just arrived."

"I read in the paper this morning that Mistinguett was in London." He shrugged to cover the natural conclusion that if I were not with Mist I would surely be joining her.

I felt the smile slipping from my face, but I said as noncommittally as I could manage, "No, I won't be able to meet her there."

I could have explained why right then. One simple sentence:

Mist and I have parted. I couldn't speak it. Because I couldn't face it? Or because I was tormented with unhappy memories? Not that either. Maybe it was to delay for a time something which would be inevitable once the news became public. A feast of gossip, for the theatre world would turn our breakup over on its tongue until it had extracted the last soupçon of flavor. It wasn't a happy prospect. Maybe, too, there was another reason. At a moment like that one has a strong hunger to look ahead, to find a new direction, and talking about what has gone can't feed it.

"Then come back with me to Toulon," Felix was saying. "Take a rest in the Mediterranean sun till Mistinguett returns."

I invented an excuse to say no. How could I explain that I still hoped to find in Paris one whiff of that special air with a promise of stimulation and new enthusiasm for the future?

Later, when I was alone again and the soft blue night came and the lights began to catch the plumes of fountain sprays, it seemed very close, just beyond the next square or hovering above the small round tables of the next café. But it was an illusion that faded as I arrived at each spot, as if I were pursuing an emotional mirage. Finally, I found myself at the top of the hill of Montmartre, weary of the whole quest, and sat down at the first empty table at a sidewalk restaurant.

By now I must have covered all of Paris. All? Well, not quite. Certain streets, certain buildings, certain cafés were too closely bound up with memories of Mist. Those I avoided. Tonight I wanted no reminders.

But they were to confront me, even here.

"M'sieur?"

I glanced up to give the waiter my order and stopped short. I was looking into a face that evoked a hundred moments from the past. The years had barely altered the sagging jowls or the doleful eyes. It was Picot, the gloomy philosopher with an understanding heart, the waiter who had looked after Mist and me in the days when a café in the Boulevard de Strasbourg had been our private paradise.

In the same instant we recognized each other. Pleased that I remembered him, he began to reminisce enthusiastically, pouring out a flood of details that had colored those afternoons with Mist. I waited, silent, hoping my lack of response would put an end to his conversation. Finally he turned away for the cognac I'd ordered.

Suddenly I no longer wanted a drink. Nor did I want any more conversation with Picot. Not tonight.

I pulled out a handful of coins. I could leave money and be gone, unnoticed, before Picot returned. But just as I started to get up, a young couple stood before me. A little shyly they told me they had seen me play *Dede* the last night before we had closed for the summer. They had been timid about coming around for my autograph after the performance. But if I wouldn't mind now? I signed the paper the girl offered me. As they turned away, Picot was back bearing the tray with my drink. Now it was too late to flee.

As he served me he noticed the lovers strolling off. The man's arm circled the girl's waist, and her head rested lightly in the hollow of his protecting shoulder. They moved like one body, in a single fluid rhythm, an image of complete and loving harmony.

Picot turned to me, amused. "Those two. So lost in each other." He chuckled softly. "They remind me of you and the beautiful lady."

I tasted my drink without answering.

"Here." He took a folded newspaper from beneath his arm and placed it on the table before me. "I thought you might like this for company."

I looked down. The paper was folded so that it framed a

picture of Mist, arriving in England. She seemed to be staring directly at me with that insouciant, slightly challenging expression I had responded to a thousand times.

He was still speaking. "So then, now that you know where old Picot is, when she returns you can bring her here in person, eh?" I nodded mechanically without looking up and he drifted away. Now there was only Mist's face on the page before me.

I could hear her husky voice, provocative and a little bit daring you: "Well, Cio?" It was a question that always came with that expression and it said, "It's your move and what are you going to do about it?"

I knew what I was *not* going to do. I was not going to spend another night in Paris feeling let down and restless. The whole day had been flat and disappointing. The city I had rushed toward with such enthusiasm this morning I suddenly wanted no more of.

Abruptly I pushed the paper aside and left the café. I found a telegraph office and pulled a blank form from the pad. Then I wrote hastily: "Mayol. Toulon. Arriving next train. Maurice."

BUT Toulon, serene and lazy, was no help at all, perhaps because one must be in need of calm to enjoy its benefits. And when you are thirty-three years old and so vitally alive that it pounds like a fever, then serenity can become a mocking thing. Instead of soothing you, it only makes you more restless.

Work, I told myself, would surely be the answer — long and demanding and stimulating hours on stage. The *Dede* company was assembling in Vichy for a brief summer tour before the show opened again in Paris, and I went there confident that this career I adored would dispel vague dissatisfaction and restore the fine, happy edge to my life.

Yet somehow it didn't, not quite. My spirit was lifted, only not high enough or for long enough. I tried to analyze what was missing. Was it Mist? No, I had honestly to answer at this point that it surely was not. Mist and I had accepted the loss of love long before that final night aboard ship.

The loss of love.

I remember thinking the words and for an instant my heart seemed to stop, for suddenly I knew why there were no longer those glowing mornings when the joyous singing of my own blood awakened me with its wonderful melody. Love was the missing ingredient, and I had not known it because it had left my life so slowly and quietly. When love dies swiftly and violently, how easily recognized is its stabbing wound of anguish! But with Mist and me love had simply faded away, so that by the end its wound had really become only a scar, with little pain left to scream out that love was gone.

But in that moment of knowledge that it was love I wanted and needed to change the face of my days, I felt a weight descending on me. In all my life I had never sought love, I had waited for it to come my way and I could never change. How long would it be before fortune smiled and brought me love again? Or would it ever?

I was standing alone on the bare stage of the theatre in Bordeaux where tomorrow night I would begin a solo engagement between the end of the *Dede* tour and Paris. I moved beyond a work lamp with its naked, harsh bulb, my footsteps echoing hollowly in the silence as I paced off the area in which I would be performing, then stopped to look out at the cavern of darkness in the auditorium.

What a lonely place, I was thinking, to be by oneself. There is a kind of ghostly sadness in the air of an empty theatre, the disappointment of an unkept promise, for those rows of seats out there need people who will laugh or cry or applaud or even

149

boo. But whatever they do, they'll be responding, and it's only then that a theatre can come alive.

Tomorrow that would happen. But many long hours stood between now and tomorrow, and ahead of me was the dismal prospect of an evening by myself in a town full of strangers. I sighed a little wearily and turned to leave.

"Monsieur Chevalier?" It was the gnome of a watchman who guarded the stage door in a sort of perpetual half-sleep. He seemed awake now, bristling with authority. "It's a lady. She wants to see you."

Who even knew I was here? "Who is she?"

"She says she knows you," he answered in a way that said he didn't believe her, "but I told her you couldn't be disturbed."

"And I said he would like being disturbed." The voice came from the shadows, gay and playful but with a tone that had the softness of a caress. "Now we'll see who is right." She came into sight, moving with slow, sensuous ease and stopped before me with a pleased smile.

"Simone!"

"It's a nice surprise, yes?"

Nice? Suddenly it seemed wonderful. "But what are you doing in Bordeaux?"

"I used to live here, remember? I came back to spend the summer." Her enormous velvet eyes were fastened on me. "I saw your picture outside and took a chance I'd find you."

"I'm grateful to chance." I was only saying words without thinking, for I was taking in the vibrant beauty of this girl with whom I had spent so many passionate hours. She glanced at the doorkeeper who was hanging on every word between us. I turned to him. "Thank you for showing the lady in."

Unwillingly he left. Simone didn't move until finally his footsteps faded away, then slowly she faced me. Her eyes were luminous now and filled with candid delight. She was beautiful and desirable; and she was in my arms so quickly, so inevitably that I can't remember which of us moved toward the other. I only recall that she said it had been a lonely summer and added in a whisper, intense and ardent: "Loneliness frightens me, chéri. I don't have to be afraid any more, do I?"

I kissed her warm and appealing mouth with the feeling that a wildly beautiful wave was breaking over me, claiming me by its sheer magnificent force, and suddenly joy seemed to be singing in my blood again.

. . . Deux

B UT IT was not really love.
Love is a nourishment for the body and the spirit and
the soul, and what I was caught up in again with Simone
was simply a magnificent blur of passion. Every hour I
could manage I spent with her, drunk on a kind of ecstasy
that was beyond reason. I was like a man who dives into a
brilliant sea and is seized in a rapture of all his senses. It
was a sexual hunger so intense and compelling that it had
become a demanding force I couldn't resist.

Yet I knew the danger of such an obsession. I knew that
it could rage like a fever through my blood until it ultimately would consume both strength and logic. Painful
experience had taught me that an excessive streak existed

in my character which was capable, if unchecked, of sweeping me over the brink of disaster. I had been shocked into learning this lesson fourteen years earlier, the first time a strong and frightening passion had claimed me.

It had been the year before Mist and I fell in love. I was making a name for myself at the Eldorado, and the girl was a young singer who had already become the darling of the night clubs. Drawn to each other by our youth and vitality, we had plunged into a carefree love affair that was soon to distort into a nightmare of jealous quarrels and tempestuous reconciliations.

She would sing from midnight until two in the morning, then insist on making the rounds of every night club in Montmartre to sample every vice of that noisy, smoky, frantic world. At first I would accompany her to these places, though I hated them, but then I rebelled, for I saw that they were destroying her and begged her to stop. But the lure of alcohol and orgies and drugs was too much, and she would angrily go on without me.

I should have been strong enough to put an end to it, but I was torn with desire for her, and despite one stormy battle after another, I would find myself waiting each dawn when she returned to her apartment. Possessed by her, I was not only draining my physical energies but seducing my ambition and my ability to think as well. It was almost a kind of madness, and it lasted long enough for people to gossip about what was happening to me and to say I was on the verge of ruining my career.

Even so it had taken an enormous punishing effort of will to break that alluring, devastating tie. Finally I had found the courage to do so. She went her way, and I — weak and spent, but, I hoped, a little wiser — went mine.

Now I was doing it again and I knew it, but I couldn't say good-by to Simone. I argued with myself that she was different, that in her entire, seductive body there was no trace of evil or vice, so where was the danger of the story ending the same way? It was a question to which I wanted no answer. I only wanted the joy of her mouth, the warmth and responsiveness and fire of her, the feeling of her in my arms.

Mist and love had gone from my life. Now there was Simone —and the delirious substitute of passion.

OUR first night back in Paris we sat in a velvet-curtained restaurant surrounded by gay, laughing people and I watched Simone across the table from me and thought of all the marvelous things ahead for us. My hand closed around the stem of my champagne glass.

"To you, *chérie*." I lifted my glass and my hand froze in mid-air. I was facing the entrance to the room and there pausing on the threshold, receiving the headwaiter's effusive welcome with that friendly but always elegant smile, was Mist.

I felt completely numb, as if I were caught up in that game of living statues where nobody is allowed to move or react. Earl Leslie was with her, following an attentive few steps behind as the headwaiter ushered them to a table. They couldn't reach it without passing the spot where I was seated, but Mist was coming toward me without a flicker of recognition and the instant of encounter was here.

In that instant the choice was made. Our eyes took in the image of each other but they didn't actually touch, for between people who have loved a simple meeting of eyes is a kind of talking, and Mist and I, each having found someone else, had nothing left to say. As she moved past me that night I didn't know that our silence would last for ten long years. I only knew I was waiting, expecting some reaction of pain or regret to stab me. None came.

Then suddenly I remembered my incomplete toast. As I raised the glass to my lips the bubbles seemed to come rushing up from the pale gold depths to meet me. I took a sip. It was like the promised kiss of gaiety and joy.

DISTURBINGLY it was a kiss that soon became a constant embrace, for Simone adored the sparkle of night life and champagne with the same open delight she brought to passion. I found myself playing, working and making love with such intensity there was little time left for sleep. If I had known the price I was paying for burning the candle so profligately, it might have sobered me into ending the affair with Simone then and there. But life seldom provides one with previews of personal disaster.

I was performing in *Dede*, whose second season was proving to be even more flourishing than I'd anticipated, for three hours each night and six hours on stage on matinee days, and my success here had brought me an offer to star in a series of four silent films. It became a backbreaking schedule. Except for matinee days I would work at the studio just outside Paris from early morning to nightfall. Then I would race back to the theatre with barely enough minutes to change before the curtain went up. I was forever tired, but somehow I managed to push it aside.

And when the curtain came down there was always Simone and her constant enthusiasm for touring the gala *boîtes* of Montmartre, floating around the city, clinging to my arm in a giggling champagne haze. It was a game she never tired of playing. So it continued that way, with exhaustion still tagging along like an ignored, uninvited guest — until one night it refused to be snubbed any longer.

Jammed into the uncomfortable few inches of space allotted each ringside table in a club we'd often closed before, we were applauding the final number of a singer who starred there. For me this simple gesture suddenly seemed to require monumental strength, as if hundred-pound weights had been attached to both my arms and only with great concentration could I lift them. Tiredness seemed to have fallen on me with the weight of an iron blanket.

Simone was draining her glass, her smile as vivacious as it had been three hours earlier when she picked me up at the theatre. She was no longer sober, but charming with it like a slightly tipsy butterfly. She tilted her head toward me appealingly with an air of mock secrecy. There was a new place, halfway across the city, that stayed open all night. She had just heard about it. Would I like to go?

"Perhaps tomorrow night," I answered wearily.

She looked into my face, surprised, unable to read what I was feeling. "All right." She paused for a moment, baffled, then went on. "But why not tonight? It's still young, *chéri*." She giggled, a pleased little sound. "And so are we."

She was right, I told myself, we were young. And if I had the strength to work as intensely as I did, surely I had the strength to play intensely, too.

And with enough champagne I managed to convince myself. By the time we were out in the sharp, biting air the iron blanket had disappeared. I was light again. I could fly without wings through this whole enchanting night until it finished in Simone's endlessly desirable embrace. And if the heavy weight came down on me again tomorrow, crashing with such force that I couldn't push it off? Well, tomorrow would be time enough to worry about that.

But though I didn't realize it, tomorrow was surely on its way.

The one richness my fatigue had been unable to wrest from me was the pleasure of my hours on stage. From the time I was a boy I had received a marvelous lift from my work before an audience. Waiting in the wings for the moment I would perform I would always have a happy, keyed-up feeling of anticipation that thrust everything else from my mind and body. Then one night I discovered that feeling was gone.

Before my first entrance I felt strangely tense and on edge as if something troubling were nagging at me. I didn't know what it was until I looked down at my fingers. I stared at them, realizing that I was counting off how many numbers I would have to sing before this night could be over. It was suddenly obvious that what had once been my wonderful joy had now become a draining, fearsome chore. Shocked by this discovery, I tried to stop myself from going on with this depressing inventory, but it was useless. Night after night my fingers would begin their unconscious counting until finally I was just too tired even to care.

So fatigue became an old pal I simply took for granted. By the time I was shooting the third of my four films in the cavernous studio at Vincennes it had become my apology and explanation for every strange reaction or angry outburst over nothing. Before one scene I berated the old wardrobe mistress for a loose button on my jacket, then sought her out after the take was done to apologize.

"I was tired," I said. "I'm sorry."

"Monsieur Maurice?" Very gently she touched my sleeve with her wrinkled hand. "Please forget it, we all have nerves."

Nerves. Was that the cause of all this? Not fatigue — but nerves? Was my entire nervous system going to pieces? The idea started a kind of panic inside me. Despite the intense heat of the set lights and the jacket I was wearing, a cold chill suddenly enveloped me. Was that kind of destruction in store for me?

It was a question that began to ring in my head like a sinister echo whenever I had a few minutes alone. It would be waiting for me in the silence of my bedroom when I awakened in the morning, and soon I found myself jumping up from sleep tensely, calling out as quickly as I could for La Louque to come in and visit.

Starting our days with a few minutes together was an important little tradition between us, one that had carried over from the bleak mornings in Ménilmontant when we had been two alone against the world. But now as she came in to greet me, carrying a tray of breakfast coffee, the frightening feeling would sweep over me that the earlier struggle was much less ominous than the current one. And this time it couldn't be shared with La Louque, for she was simple and direct and thought that problems must be tangible. If you were troubled, she wanted to know the cause. Or if you were suffering, where did it hurt? But there was no way to explain the apprehension I lived with now. I understood neither the source of the pain nor its location.

So instead I tried to hide its existence with nonchalant chatter, but the clatter of my coffee cup replaced in its saucer with a shaking hand finally gave me away. She took the tray away with a troubled frown. "Maurice, are you sick?"

"Sick?" I forced a surprised laugh. "Where'd you get an idea like that? Of course I'm not sick!"

The performance was convincing enough for La Louque. It even managed halfway to convince me. At least for a time.

But destiny has a way of exploding self-deception in your face.

One night in my dressing room, I was in the middle of removing my make-up when an old friend, a newspaperman who had come around after the performance, suddenly turned to me with an ironic smile. It was one of the rare evenings when I wouldn't be seeing Simone and I'd invited him for a few drinks after the show. Now he was asking me to join him after that on a story he had to cover.

"What is it?"

"Something that might interest you." His smile became even more ironic. "You play a character named Dede. Tonight they're going to execute a man by the same name. You want to go?"

He proposed it so suddenly, in such a matter-of-fact way,

that without even pausing I heard myself answering, "Why not? I've never seen anything like it."

Almost in the same instant that I spoke I regretted it. I wanted no part of the macabre human drama that would be climaxed on the guillotine a few hours from now, but when I started to tell him so, no words emerged. Strangely I found myself unable to back down.

A small stack of saucers, one for each drink consumed, had piled up on the veined, marble surface of the café table where we waited. Ten cognacs, I thought. Prelude to an execution. The man named Dede had committed murder, and before the sun came up in the morning sky he would be paying the supreme price. I tried to concentrate on the justice which had dictated his dying but it was useless. All I could think about was that it would happen before my eyes.

We approached the second of two police barriers and waited in the cold night air to present credentials before entering the cobblestoned area where the execution would actually take place. Then finally we were checked in, and suddenly in the eerie light, just ahead of me was the soaring outline of the guillotine. As I faced that terrifying silhouette, the staggering enormity of its purpose hit me with the impact of an acute physical blow, freezing me for a moment in my tracks.

With great effort I managed the mask of a man to whom this was an accustomed sight. My legs, threatening to give way beneath me, could buckle at any instant and expose my masquerade, but somehow I forced them to go on supporting me until I had joined a group of perhaps fifty men made up of officials and police officers and journalists.

Now the frightening machinery of death was less than four yards away. Each separate part of it seemed to rush at me: The ominous balance of the counterweight which, released, would trigger the blade, the gleaming steel cutter, honed to a fatal edge, poised at the top of the shaft; and finally, the basket which would receive the body and severed head when this ordeal came to its agonizing end.

With a sickening thud the blade fell again and again as the executioner tested it. A cold sweat began to drench me, and I turned away to glance at the faces of those around me. They all carried a look of waiting calm. One man was chatting quietly with two others, then regarded his watch with the gesture of someone who has a train to catch. Suddenly with a stab of fear, I felt as if my logic had gone out of focus. The others were here because their jobs forced them to take part in this grim spectacle. But what was I doing caught up in their midst? What had happened to my balance? I was going through this ordeal without any reason.

A wild clatter of horses and iron wheels abruptly drowned out my thoughts. A covered van arrived in the courtyard. It stopped near the spot where I stood, and immediately the back of it was opened. I watched numbly as a priest emerged, holding a raised crucifix before the face of a man whose shirt-sleeved arms were bound behind his back. The condemned and his comforter.

Then as they turned to pass before me the prisoner lifted his head and my numbness turned to horror. That tall, heavy-set frame and that face with its rough, dark good looks. Suddenly the years between were wiped out. I recognized him instantly and I thought I would cry out with the staggering shock of it!

The man I was about to watch die was the first man in my life who, for no reason except that he wanted to be my friend, had offered me assistance. The "Dede" a grotesquely twisted fate had reunited me with tonight was the pimp I'd encountered as a struggling young kid near the Boulevard de Strasbourg.

With a strength and dignity he had surely never managed before to bring to his life he began to mount the steps toward

160

his death. From that moment I could no longer see clearly. Too stunned to move I waited, in a kind of anguished, blurred trance, until a sound broke the tense silence and a violent shudder ran through my body. And I knew it was over.

But that wasn't the end of it for me. For days afterwards I was haunted by the fear I'd felt in the prison courtyard — the fear that my logic had gone out of focus. First fatigue, then nerves and now this seeming inability even to think straight. Was it all part of some sinister pattern that was taking over my life?

This new worry clung to me like a melancholy shadow until at last I grew weary of trying futilely to throw it off by myself. I desperately needed a holiday from my own depression, and I wondered if seeing a few old friends as I used to do before this whole cycle of misery began would provide that welcome change of scenery.

I decided to give a big, festive luncheon, and when the afternoon arrived it got under way so happily that for the first time in months I really felt like my old self again. It was one of those rare gatherings when everything was perfect — the food, the wines, the friends. We ate and drank and laughed and drank still more while the afternoon shadows lengthened unnoticed. Lingering over brandy glasses that were refilled again and again, exchanging stories, I couldn't remember when I had felt so relaxed or at peace. Then somehow it was suddenly six o'clock, and there was an evening performance to make.

I wasn't concerned until I'd bid my last guest good-by and closed the door behind him. But suddenly the feeling seized me that I'd had too much to drink. In the foyer mirror my face was brightly flushed, and I reeled a little as I looked. Still, I was thinking merrily, it's early. I would have a good nap and then a cold shower. It was a combination that would surely make me feel brand-new by theatre time.

Quickly I got into bed. When I lay back against the pillows I had the strange sensation that my brain was trying to float out of my head, but it didn't upset me. I was confident that all would be well after I'd napped. I dropped into a deep, dreamless sleep that lasted till my servant awakened me with the news that it was nearing eight o'clock and I must get ready to leave for the theatre.

Groggily, what had happened came back to me and with it came confidence. I'd had almost two hours of sleep. Certainly by now all the alcohol must have worn off. I started to get up but when I lifted my head I fell back shocked. Something odd and frightening was still happening inside of it. It was on fire, and the sensation that my brain was trying to escape continued, only now it had become an urgent struggle and I felt it would burst my skull open with its frantic pounding. Painfully I forced myself to sit up and the terrible conviction hit me that my blood was circulating backwards. The idea was eerie and unreasonable but I couldn't dismiss it. When I pulled myself to my feet they didn't feel the floor. I rushed for my shower, praying that the force of the icy needles would put an end to all this strangeness. But it changed nothing.

Panic began to mount in me. How in the name of all the saints was I going to be able to sing and dance and act in this terrible state?

By the time I arrived at the theatre I was convinced that all my nerve centers had been stricken. Their jangled messages were assaulting my brain one on top of another, and in the shrieking confusion I felt as if I were being pulled in seventeen different directions at the same time. I looked down at my hand. It was filled with grease paint. But each time I tried to apply it to my face, my image seemed to fade and disappear from the mirror, only to come floating back when I'd drop my hand in defeat. Stunned, I realized I couldn't even accomplish this simple task without enormous struggle and my terror for what would happen to me on stage became acute. I needed help. And I needed it fast.

The doctor I'd summoned appeared at the door of my dressing room only minutes before the curtain was to go up. With frantic haste I told him about the afternoon and what I'd been suffering since. He listened and calmly explained that the mixture of rich foods combined with so many wines and liqueurs could easily account for an upset violent enough to produce such intense reactions. He prescribed a powder mixed with water, and while I gulped it down he assured me that all would be right again.

Heading for the wings to await my first entrance I kept hollowly repeating his words. I had heard the backstage warning call and the other actors' answering voices as if they all came from some remote other world. My feet were moving but they still couldn't feel the floor beneath them and the fire in my head seemed to go on burning despite the thick cotton padding it now felt crammed with.

Then through the cotton some familiar sound must have penetrated. Apparently it was my entrance cue, for I found myself crossing the stage hearing laughter and applause as I went. But there was something disturbingly wrong about the way I was moving. My physical equilibrium had completely abandoned me. It must have been obvious to everyone in the theatre, yet I couldn't worry about it. I was too intent on reaching the actor before whom I was supposed to stop, and now on the dizzily spinning stage he seemed an almost impossible distance away.

Finally we were facing each other and his lips were moving. Though the words sounded faint I recognized them. The cue for my first speech. I answered with the expected line that both of us knew so well. But he seemed to react oddly. I saw his eyes widen in surprise and he paused for an instant before throwing me my second cue. When I responded with my second line I saw his surprise turn to alarm and I suddenly realized with horror that I'd answered both his speeches with my lines from the third act instead of the first.

I saw the startled faces of the musicians staring at me over the footlights and I could read the shocked question in their eyes: What's the matter with Chevalier?

In that suspended nightmare moment with all their eyes on me I knew I was no longer drunk, nor was I any longer in a state of wandering confusion.

I was totally and hopelessly lost.

My mind had stopped dead, refusing to work. Feverishly I tried to lash it into responding. It gave back only blank silence. Not a single word of the lines I was desperately groping for came through to me.

It couldn't go on like this. The audience, which luckily didn't usually pay too much attention to the dialogue of a lighthearted operetta, had nonetheless begun to stir restlessly, sensing by instinct that something strange was in the air. My fellow actor stepped in quickly to break the tension. Giving a false laugh to divert the audience's attention, he turned quickly and whispered my next line in my ear. I grabbed at it like a man who is falling into a black pit. He went on this way, phrase by phrase, and like a wooden robot I repeated aloud each whispered word that reached my ear.

My fingernails had pierced the flesh of my clenched palms before he had carried me to the place where my seething head began to function and I got back on the track. And finally the first act was over.

In my dressing room where the other actors had gathered around me solicitously, I was racked with a feverish trembling that refused to stop, despite their friendly assurances that nothing irreparable had happened on stage. All I could think about was the yawning pit of disaster that had opened beneath me. Thus far I had managed, by holding on for dear life, to cling to its edge. But it had taken all my strength. Now exhausted and with my nerves shredded from the strain, I had two more acts ahead of me.

For those two acts an almost irrational terror of my lines tortured me. I forced myself to repeat silently each word I would have to speak aloud to be certain it was still there. It was a killing burden to add to the fear I was battling, and despite the fact that it caused me to stumble over almost every line, I could no more stop this wild constant monitoring of my memory than I could silence the roiling noise that had built to such volume inside my head that it now sounded like an angry, boiling sea.

Then, after an eternity, the last curtain came down. But its falling brought no relief.

In that pitching, menacing night of distorted visions and unbearable torment I somehow found my way to Simone's apartment. I was in a state of almost hysterical despair when I arrived, with no clear notion of how I'd gotten there. All I knew was that I was sitting on a couch pouring out all the horrors that had closed in to claim me, when suddenly I became aware of an incredible sound.

It was Simone's laughter.

I lifted my head, baffled, halfway expecting to discover it was a new turn my auditory hallucinations had taken. But no, it was real. She was chattering away gaily about how high I must have been, and what a marvelously funny business it was, turning the lines around. She was sorry she hadn't been there to see it for herself.

I stared at her, dumfounded. I was going through an experience of living, suffering hell, and all her giddy little mind could understand was that an amusing lark had taken place.

It was too much to deal with. Already I was wrestling with the staggering fear of tomorrow's performance. What mistakes might I make? What new, ominous plans did my mind have for deserting me? As her empty jabbering continued, I found myself compulsively repeating line after line of dialogue and song lyrics to myself. I was so lost in my own anguish that I didn't notice when she stopped talking. Then finally it came to me that the voice I was hearing was my own. How long had my frantic recital been going on aloud? I glanced up again and she was standing across the room regarding me silently.

"Tell me something, *chéri?*" Her expression was solemn now and a worried frown was on her face. She hesitated, and then went on a little apprehensively. "By any chance are you going crazy?"

I stared at her for an instant, completely unable to speak. Then, like a man moving through a bad dream, I got up and walked out. I turned blindly down the narrow black street, wanting only to escape that paralyzing question. But it pursued me. The entire world seemed to be made of nothing but darkness and swirling mist and Simone's voice. No matter how fast I went it followed me, rising from the cobblestones and echoing off the damp walls, calling out insistently. Crazy? . . . crazy? . . . crazy?

. . . *Trois*

CRAZY. When does it cease being merely a word and turn into a dread actuality?

For a man trying desperately to inch his way across a high wire with the chasm of madness threatening each footstep, it's an unbearable question. I know, because in the months that followed, that thin, treacherous wire is where I lived.

And there is no lonelier place on earth, for help cannot reach you.

From the time of that nightmare performance I lived with the most devastating fear an entertainer can suffer. I was obsessed by the terrifying idea that I could no longer trust my memory, that it would betray me and make me forget my lines. No matter what I did, I couldn't escape it. Anguished, I stumbled through weeks in which sleep became almost an impossibility. And when it did come, instead of bringing rest and relief, I was pulled down into a labyrinth that led always to the same tormented dream.

In my troubled sleep I was always lying behind the low stone wall at Cutry as the Germans were advancing. I knew I'd been hit but when the soldiers who were trying to get me out asked if I could move I didn't answer. I heard one tell the other I was dead. Then together, they would crawl away. I wanted to shout to them to come back, that I was alive — but each time I tried to cry out I'd realize in horror that suddenly I'd forgotten the words I needed to save my life. Uselessly I struggled to recall them, to force some sound from my constricted throat, until suddenly I knew I was going to die here because my memory had deserted me.

Then abruptly I would come awake, exhausted and drenched with icy, panicked perspiration, my heart pounding, to find myself sitting up in bed surrounded by the gloomy shadows of my own room.

I know today what was at the core of my suffering, for since that time many psychiatrists have written about mania and hallucination and fixed ideas — infecting and tormenting the mind as germs invade and weaken the body. But I only knew then that I was being consumed by fear, and I felt I couldn't go on enduring it — and survive.

Haggard with the toll it was taking of me I began to haunt the offices of one doctor after another, searching out specialists for every kind of nerve malady. None of them could tell me what was really wrong. They could only listen while I tried to explain what I was going through and suggest treatment that might bring me relief. I gave up smoking and drinking and went on a rigid diet and waited vainly for my strained nerves to calm down as predicted.

I dragged myself back day after day to try a series of glandular injections, and when those failed, massages that didn't work either, and finally involved electrical therapy that also did no good until in a burst of despair I knew that nothing was going to help. I had searched endlessly for a cure, and for what? Through the cab window as I left the latest doctor's office I could see the first tender green of spring veiling the trees. All around me Paris was blossoming to promising new life. I closed my eyes. When you have just run out of hope, the sight of spring is a bitter mockery.

Perhaps the seeds of what had brought me to this awful crisis had always been inside of me. I knew I carried in my blood some of the calm, practical balance of La Louque, but it was mixed with another legacy — the wild emotional peaks and the plummeting descents into melancholy, the almost uncontrollable drive to push myself to the very limit of endurance — that surely came from the unstable temperament of my father. And added to the mixture were the myriad experiences that since my childhood had shaped many qualities in me but never the one I most sorely needed — confidence — deep, unshakable confidence. The combination of everything I was and everything I lacked, was that the answer?

I didn't know for sure, and I think I never actually will. But of one thing I am convinced: In one evening of too-violent battle for control, I overforced the complicated human machine and gravely injured my nervous system.

But at the time the doctors who were offering their assorted cures didn't think anything so critical was happening. And even La Louque, who had seen me arrive home that first night white as a ghost and half out of my head, wasn't alarmed. She, too, seemed to believe I would get better and finally the whole problem would be forgotten.

I couldn't share their belief. For every night the monstrous fear that my memory would fail was waiting for me the moment I stepped out on stage. I no longer dared relax, even for an instant. Instead, as I spoke each line my mind was racing feverishly beyond to grope for speeches as far away as the next act or words from a song I wouldn't be singing for another ten minutes.

Sometimes after several punishing minutes of this ordeal of concentration I would be lulled into feeling that everything was going to be all right, but the instant I tried to stop this unbelievable policing of my memory a kind of spasm would seize me and I would stumble over simple words, and sweating and trembling I would start the whole ghastly pattern again.

It was taking a constant, draining toll of me, and though my pride stubbornly refused to let me tell the other members of the company what I was suffering, it was impossible to keep them from seeing that something strange was going on. We had been playing *Dede* now for more than a year without using a prompter, when one night things suddenly got worse and in a panic I demanded he be hired again. I read the suspicious reactions in the faces around me. Hastily I explained that I was so familiar with the role that I often couldn't help thinking about other things while I was performing and might get stuck.

But the sight of the prompter back at his old spot didn't relieve my staggering anxiety. Appearances on stage were a series of calvaries and each night, getting through them a little more shattered and back to my dressing room, I would bury my throbbing head in my hands.

I had given up Simone. Because I wanted to? No. But the moment had come when finally I knew I must. So long as she stayed in my life, the temptation of her was too powerful to resist, and my nerves, stretched almost to the breaking point, could no longer support a tempestuous relationship impossible to limit. If they snapped, so would the high wire I was treading so precariously. And whatever sanity I still possessed warned me this would be the end of my ever making it back to solid healthy ground.

Although I was sick to the very bottom of my soul a kind of frantic determination was inside me to finish out the season my contract called for. I felt that if I could just hold on and keep going, somehow I might be able to work my way out of this black despair. Yet some awful conspiracy of strains seemed to be working against me. I would no sooner finish wrestling with one than another loomed up threateningly. Now it was the problem of tackling a whole new operetta.

After a matinee one afternoon I listened in stunned silence as our producer announced the closing of *Dede* and the mounting of a new show to run the remaining three months of the season. I learned that we would begin rehearsing and polishing the new production immediately, and suddenly all I could see before me was an impossibly high wall built of words and songs and dance steps and a thousand intricate details of gesture and timing. And to scale it I would have to commit every bit of it to memory. I could feel myself choking on the panic that rose in my throat.

Faintly I heard him explaining that the setting for the new play was the Kingdom of Heaven. Did I like the title, *On High?* I couldn't answer. I could only nod and pray that he would leave before the terror inside me escaped my tightly clenched teeth into an open scream.

Rehearsals, even under the best of circumstances, are a time when a hundred little crosscurrents of tension begin to build up within a company. They go on mounting into a kind of cumulative anxiety that reaches its climax on opening night. Everybody is concerned about the show, but because the star carries the largest responsibility for making it a success or failure, his worry is often largest as well. Maybe because everybody I was working with knew this, nobody seemed to notice that my distress was surely out of all proportion to the fate of any single production.

From the moment of my first entrance on opening night I knew I was in the gravest trouble of my entire career. Already shackled by fear of my memory failing, I suddenly encountered a terrifying new danger — a kind of vertigo. The floor of the stage rushed up menacingly to meet my footsteps, then as I tried to adjust my balance, it would quickly melt away leaving me teetering in empty space. Over and over it happened and my head swam so that only monumental effort kept me from falling. God, this was too much! Now my sight was betraying me too.

Despite my difficulties, *On High* proved to be a hit, and as soon as the reviews appeared, tension dissolved into exultant relief for everyone in the company. Everyone, that is, but me, for the critics were saying that apparently Chevalier was having to work much harder to achieve less. They were polite and even complimentary about certain numbers I did, but no glow of enthusiasm lighted their words. It was a subtle thing, the tone of these new notices. At least on the surface it was. But as I turned from one to the next my depression deepened. Obviously the warm and wonderful reactions were missing because I was no longer able to inspire them. I pushed the papers away, sick inside. Why should anybody be enthusiastic about a performer whose *joie de vivre* and gaiety had all but disappeared?

If I could just manage to hold on, I had told myself. But as the weeks dragged by in a repetitious agony of that first night's performance, I began to wonder. Even if I could get to the end of the interminable season it would only bring me face to face with the next impossible struggle — playing *Dede* in the United States for C. B. Dillingham. How was I going to last long enough to "enchant" America, when already I was on the verge of losing the footing I'd struggled so hard to gain in France? My professional life was in peril, yet I was helpless to protect it. And my personal life? It was empty of everything but despair. Yes, despair seemed to be the only emotion left.

Then one evening I wasn't quite so certain after all.

I had no idea how many times I had stood in this same spot backstage and watched a quiet and surprisingly earnest little figure always seated in the same corner of the wings calmly knitting a sweater while she waited for her next scene. She was a young, dark-eyed dancer, and this show was her first chance to play a real part. We had exchanged a few casual words every night because the specialty dance coming up was the one number we had together.

Perhaps the sweet, serene smile she was offering me tonight had existed in that gentle, pretty face since the first day of rehearsal. But sealed off in my own misery I had never noticed until now, nor had I seen the expression of warmth and patient understanding in her eyes when I spoke my usual tense greeting.

I had the strange sensation that somehow she was trying without words to say something to me, almost a kind of message of hope. I didn't see how that could be, yet the feeling was so strong that when she turned back to the darting needles in her slender hands I suddenly heard myself asking her if she would lunch with me the next day.

The flashing needles paused for just a split second, then she answered quietly without glancing up. "Yes. That would be very nice."

But by the next morning I was already regretting the invitation. Hadn't I exhausted the lists of the greatest doctors in Paris in my futile search for help and understanding? What idiotic quirk made me think I could find this now in a retiring, inexperienced girl named Yvonne Vallée? What had made me think I could even talk honestly with her when for months it had been an impossible thing to do with old and close friends? I had been avoiding them because the strain of making hollow conversation, pretending that everything was fine, was more than I could stand. Now I had let myself in for exactly that kind of trial with a girl I barely knew.

I had decided on a restaurant near the park of St. Cloud. When we arrived I felt certain that lunch, for me, would be an ordeal. And for Yvonne? Probably a terrible bore.

But as we sat at a quiet window table that looked out on the peaceful greenery of the park, the strain I was anticipating never arrived. Instead of trying to talk, I found myself comfortably listening as she chatted easily about the pleasant, ordinary little details of her life. She was from Bordeaux, she lived with her family, and the fact that fancy dresses from the famous designers were well beyond her means didn't depress her. She could admire the elegant trappings other women in the theatre possessed without a moment's envy. She was simple and sound and sweet.

It didn't seem necessary to make any effort with her. She accepted my silence as a natural thing and made no attempt to probe my disturbed mood. I began to wonder if her own wholesome outlook toward life was some kind of insulation, if perhaps she hadn't been aware of my problem after all, if I had only imagined that message of hope. But after lunch when we emerged into the soft early summer air and decided to walk in the park, I discovered I was wrong.

We had strolled for a time without saying much when she paused to pick a wild flower from a cluster that bordered our path. She handed it to me with a gentle, knowing smile.

"You see, there still are some beautiful things in the world, Maurice." And when I looked at her oddly, she added, "I know it's hard to believe sometimes, but I promise you, it's true."

She was gazing at me with infinite compassion and warmth, and in that moment I knew that somehow this quiet girl truly had recognized and understood the despair that was hounding me. At least now I was not completely alone.

There were other lunches after that day, meetings in little out-of-the-way places, and she listened patiently as I stumbled and hesitated and then bit by bit revealed all the desperate troubles that beset me. Many times I broke off tensely, strangling on my own agitation, and she would reach across the table and gently touch my hand as if she would give me serenity from her own deep reservoir of calm. In my entire life I had known no one quite like her. A contrast to the kind of woman I had been attracted to in the past, she offered instead of glamour a shining sweetness and loyalty which let you know without words that if you needed her she would be there.

But sadly I needed more than sympathy and understanding, so these meetings with Yvonne were not enough to rescue me from my private hell. My hours on stage were still pure terror, and every minute off stage was haunted with fear of the next performance. Slowly, inexorably I began to drift into a kind of acceptance of this dread I lived with. It was a limbo where nothing seemed important enough to care about, not even survival, for what did life mean but more of the same torture?

One morning I awakened to the familiar pattern of dappled sunlight on my bedroom ceiling and knew that I had reached the nadir. I could only close my eyes again. What could this new day possibly hold for me that was worth getting up to face? Wretchedly I searched my mind, trying to dredge up a single reason and could find none. I was locked in a prison cell of despair, and there was no key to free me.

But suddenly it came, a thin high sound in my head at first, and then the sound became words running through my brain and they made miraculous sense. Of course there was a key, the words were saying, a simple answer: If I wanted to escape, I had only to destroy myself!

My eyes flashed open. I propped myself up against the pillows. This ingenious thought had never occurred to me until this moment, yet there seemed nothing surprising about it or shocking. As a matter of fact, examining it I found myself almost smiling at the simplicity of it. Suddenly the torment and agitation lacerating me all these months were gone and relief was flowing through my body like a magic medicine. I threw back the covers. Now I did have a reason to get out of bed, I told myself with a strange kind of elation, I had plans to make.

I started to shape these plans carefully, for instinct warned me that I must move with caution, not risking my new-found hope for liberation by letting anyone even guess that it existed. I must take one wary step at a time. First there was La Louque to consider. I must be certain that she was safe and protected when I would no longer be here to look after her. Providing money for her would be a simple matter of an hour in a lawyer's office arranging a will, but protecting her against the shock of my suicide was more complicated. She must be out of Paris, I told myself, away from witnessing what would scar her gentle heart.

"But why, Maurice?" she said with a shrug. "I'm happy here with you, why must I move to the country?"

"I've already told you why!" I almost shouted and instantly regretted it. La Louque's protest was something I hadn't expected and it had thrown my delicately balanced plan into a temporary panic. "Listen, Mama," I said, struggling to sound calm and reasonable, "it's going to be a hot summer. There's no reason for you to suffer through it in Paris." Finally I convinced her, and days later, when I had seen her comfortably settled in her new home, I breathed evenly again.

Now alone, I turned to the question of final details for killing myself. The quiet of my own apartment would be the place. And a revolver the means. And until I found the moment of absolute courage in which to act, I must continue to lead what

176

looked like an ordinary course of life, neither saying nor doing anything that would arouse suspicion.

How careful I was and how sly with my pose! I was sure that no one at the theatre suspected, and one night when Yvonne caught an odd look in my face and asked what was going on, I covered up with an invented story of an adventure I'd had that afternoon. And all this time, you understand, I was consulting with myself about the date of my own death. It was a weird situation that could only serve to make me still more tense.

One morning at home the phone rang and a feminine voice said, "The doctor wants to see you half an hour earlier today, Monsieur Chevalier, is that all right?"

My routine visit with the doctor, an appointment set up the last time I'd seen him. It was useless now, for I was handling my own treatment and the cure would be certain and forever, so shouldn't I simply cancel? But no, I was thinking, this could arouse his suspicions. Worried that I was worse, perhaps he would insist on seeing me and then, probing, he might even discover my well-hidden plan to end it all.

"I'll be there," I said and hung up, already deciding how I would conduct myself in his office. This doctor must never guess what was going on in my mind.

Seated in the deep leather armchair he offered me that afternoon, I drew a deep breath and warned myself that I must hold on with every bit of my strength and control. If I remained calm, my secret plan would be completely safe.

The warning seemed to work. I could hear my voice quietly responding to every question. Then suddenly in the middle of our conversation I heard something else, the sound of deep, terrible sobbing. To my horror I realized that these racking sounds were emerging from me, and then wildly in this crisis of tears I could no longer hold back what I thought I had been guarding so well. In a gasping river of words I began to pour out every single detail of my plan for suicide, every nuance of the scheme I had worked so hard to keep locked and hidden in my mind!

The doctor was leaning over me anxiously. My confession must have been shockingly complete, for his face was pale and his expression was different from the tolerant look I had been accustomed to seeing in all the months that he had heard and taken not too seriously my complaints. Now, apparently he was shaken by their gravity.

He spoke earnestly for a long time, saying a jumble of words concerning nervous exhaustion and unrelieved strains and breakdowns and fixed ideas. It was imperative I have a complete rest, and how soon could I quit working? Was there someone close to me he could discuss arrangements with? How soon could I leave for Saujon?

"Saujon?" I asked woodenly.

It was the name of a tiny village in the southwest of France. There was a rest home there to which he was ordering me. I would be in the care of a Dr. Dubois, a specialist in nervous disorders. My reactions to everything he was saying must have been strange, because finally he took me by the shoulders as if to force my attention back into focus.

"It's important that you go as soon as possible, Maurice. Do you understand?"

I nodded numbly, trying to sort it all out. A nervous breakdown. For all this tragic, desperate time I had been living and working with a nervous system that had been slowly disintegrating to the point of collapse.

"This Yvonne Vallée," the doctor was saying. "Will you tell her to see me right away?"

"Yes." There was no one else I could turn to, for La Louque was not strong enough to cope with such a load. And of all the people I knew, there was no one with the compassion of this girl.

178

I was walking out of the office. A question, a fear, turned me back at the door. "This place you want me to go," I said. "How long will I have to stay there?"

"That depends," he answered. "Maybe several weeks, maybe a few months, maybe —" He broke off and his troubled frown deepened as if he had already said too much.

"And maybe forever?"

He shook his head. "Of course not, Maurice. These things just take time and no one knows how much." His denial seemed a little too hearty. "But you'll be well one day, don't you worry."

How hollow his reassurance rang! I left, weighted with the irony of the bitter joke fate had saved for the last. For months I had frantically sought to discover what was wrong with me. Now, finally, my illness had been recognized and all I had gained from the discovery was an unshakable feeling that it couldn't be cured.

A terrible kind of death settled in my soul and mechanically I groped and stumbled through the performances I still was obligated to play. Through it all I was aware that Yvonne rarely left my side. She had become my shepherd and my constant source of strength, and she had taken on the burden of handling everything that had to be dealt with before my departure.

A cable had to be sent to C. B. Dillingham, explaining that my health was forcing me to cancel my contract to come to the United States. Yvonne saw that it got off. La Louque must be told where her son was going and why. Yvonne went with me and thanks to her sweet calm and her air of complete faith that I'd soon be well again, my mother embraced me when we were parting, no more disturbed than if I were going off to bask in the sun to shake a nagging cold. Closing my apartment, preparing me for the journey, even personally accompanying me down to Saujon, though it would mean having to turn right around again for the lonely six-hours drive back to Paris to make her performance in the show — nothing was too much for her.

On the trip, our road narrowed to pass through the winding main street of an old village, and as we slowed down I glanced at the clean, strong lines of her profile. She caught my eye. "Hungry?" she asked lightly. "Shall we stop for lunch?"

She made it sound so nonchalant, as if we were off on some holiday jaunt through the countryside to amuse ourselves, instead of en route to a hopeless destination, but I knew it was a tremendous effort for Yvonne, keeping up this cheerful attitude. I knew, too, it would make it less difficult for her if I played the game. Yet I couldn't, because in that moment all I could think about was that she was transporting a hollow broken man to what would surely be a well-guarded hell which would swallow him forever. Sitting beside her, I felt a little like a corpse who weirdly is forced to drive to his own funeral before he is dead.

"I can't eat," I mumbled miserably.

What I was feeling must have been there to read in my eyes, but her warm smile never wavered, and all she said was: "Then we don't have to stop. I'm not hungry either."

She had taken this difficult moment, as she had a hundred others with me, in willing, cheerful stride. It was almost as if the backbone of that slim, graceful body were made of absolute, tireless dedication. But realizing it only made me sadder. Yvonne Vallée was quietly offering me all the love and devotion and energy of her vital young heart. And it was a terrible waste. For I was certain that in this world of breathing death where I wandered, I was completely beyond the miracle of love. It could never reach me nor could I respond to it again.

By the time we turned in at the hedge-flanked entry, the afternoon shadows had already stretched in long fingers across the curving, graveled drive that led up to what looked like a large, pleasant, rambling country hotel. It bore no resemblance to the "rest home" I had been imagining with mounting foreboding this past hour.

As Yvonne stopped the car I glanced around apprehensively. I musn't be taken in by this peaceful camouflage, I warned myself. Surely, if I looked carefully I would discover, skillfully hidden behind the trees and rustic walks and clumps of gaily colored summer flowers in extravagant bloom, the restraining fences and stolid guards and desperate, demented souls who, like me, had been condemned to this dreaded place which wore the mask of a paradise.

I found no sign of them, but that didn't seem to relieve my anxiety that they existed, and once I was ushered to my comfortably furnished room, I waited tensely, listening for what I didn't know. Yvonne had gotten me settled and now it was time for her to leave. She came to the window where I stood. Gently she reminded me of the appointment that was arranged for me in the morning, when I'd meet Dr. Dubois, and that I was to relax and get a good night's rest and there was nothing to worry about.

I nodded automatically.

Then she touched my arm lightly. "Maurice?" I turned to face her. "I'll write to you, and please, promise you'll write to me." I nodded again. For just an instant a worry came into her eyes. "You will be all right, won't you?" Then she made a little gesture with her hand, as if to wipe out the question, and went on quickly. "Of course you will."

"If you say so." My voice was thin with strain.

"I say so." Her shining conviction had returned. "Everything will be all right, Maurice. Just believe it."

She kissed me tenderly and left, but when the door closed it was impossible to believe anything except that some final horror was lurking in this place, waiting to claim me. What it was or when it would confront me, I did not know, but every nerve in my body had tightened against the threat I felt so strongly.

I took up my vigil at the window again. The last of twilight still hung in the air and the trees and grass and sky, drained of their own colors, had all merged into a deep gray, melancholy universe. Then I saw him. At first like a ghost and then more clearly as he approached, a solitary man, his shoulders bent, moving with a shuffling, hesitant step along one of the paths that led into the gardens below. He stopped frequently, half turning in his tracks, then he'd shake his head again and again in a lost, heartbroken way before going on.

"My God," I whispered aloud.

Suddenly my hands felt icy and the chilling cold spread to the very core of my soul. That pathetically finished man wandering through the grounds on a hopeless route to nowhere — was he some kind of eerie harbinger of my own fate?

I couldn't bear to watch him any longer. Blindly I turned and slumped into a chair, praying I could blot that disturbing image from my memory. But it wouldn't leave me. If I could just manage to sleep for a little while, at least that would be some escape from the terrors encircling me.

But when I closed my eyes sleep refused to come. Time after time I would get to its brink and then something seemed to pull me back. Hovering on the edge of my consciousness there was a sound, too soft at first to bring me fully awake, but too persistent to ignore. Finally I opened my eyes and strained into the blackness that had descended, struggling to identify it. For a moment it didn't seem to exist, and then it came again, soft and persistent and unbearably tragic. It was the sound of quiet, desperate weeping. And it was coming from a room somewhere inside this house.

Get used to it, I warned myself, it belongs here. And then despondently I realized that I did, too. Before long I would probably be no different from any of the other grief-haunted inmates who had lost everything except their capacity for sorrow and suffering.

"WHY do I have to tell it all again?" I asked unhappily. "Isn't it written in those papers?"

Dr. Robert Dubois glanced up from the thick dossier on his desk, and his gray eyes held a look of patient, understanding friendliness. "Papers aren't human," he said and smiled. "With every word you say, I look, I listen and sometimes I learn. We'll have these talks often, Monsieur Chevalier."

And so we did. Twice a week I sat in the sunny corner room he used as an office and answered questions and poured out my feelings and always the mild-mannered, intelligent man across from me took in my words and probed and made notes.

"I want you to sleep as much as possible," he told me. "And if you can't sleep, at least rest." Then, as if he could read my doubting mind, he went on. "Don't worry, you'll be tired enough to want to. Exploring the country roads around here is an exhausting business."

My doubts went beyond that. The treatment seemed almost too simple. "Talks, and walks and rest — that's going to cure me?"

"All I ask is that you give them a try."

But for one endless month the trying seemed completely useless. Hours of talking about my fears did nothing to break their awful stranglehold. They were at my throat every mile of country road I trudged and they returned to my room with me like an implacable enemy who never tired of battle. The small flicker of hope I prayed for, that ray of light in my personal darkness, never came.

And finally, one dismal afternoon, returning through the village from a long walk in the rain-sogged woods, I knew that my prayer had been a waste of time. I would never get better. Only worse. I stopped in the deserted street. I could see nothing ahead but an endless landscape of suffering and grief. Then slowly I looked up and saw something else glistening in the wet air —

a sign painted above the shop across from where I stood. The word beneath the proprietor's name seemed to leap out at me like a beacon: GUNSMITH.

My heart pounded wildly as I read it again. Then, almost as if I were impelled by some irresistible force, I was across the road and inside the narrow, musty shop, pulling the collar of my raincoat higher to partly shield my face and bending my head over a display case of revolvers as the small, pinched figure of the owner emerged from a back room.

I shoved my hands into my coat pockets so that their trembling would be hidden. Nothing must arouse this man's suspicions and threaten my vital purchase. In such a place one could buy a gun without needing permits or encountering complications, I knew that. But still I must make the whole thing appear casual and ordinary. Any hint that I was a patient in Saujon and my chances of walking out of here with a gun would surely be finished.

The owner had come around the other side of the counter to confront me. "Found what you want?" His voice was flat and unfriendly.

"Yes," I answered, forcing myself to meet his narrowed gaze. "The one in the left-hand corner will do." My mouth was so dry the words seemed to stick to my parched lips. I wanted to moisten them, but I didn't dare, because his gaze was still fastened on me, hostile and appraising.

"It's expensive." He made no move to take it out of the case.

"That doesn't matter," I said, and rushed into the lie I'd just invented, terrified that my voice would crack in the middle of it and expose me. "You see, I have a summer place not too far from here. Sometimes I have to go up to Paris and my wife gets nervous alone with no protection. So you see —" My throat closed and I couldn't force another word out.

He gave me an annoyed scowl. "Not interested in what you

need it for." He pushed open the sliding glass panel and reached inside. "Just wanted to know if you could afford it."

A few minutes later the gun and the bullets that fitted it were in my pocket and I was heading back to the rest home.

This time I would do it. The words kept repeating themselves in my mind. This time I would do it, and the time of grief was almost at an end. Within an hour the useless, suffering shell named Maurice Chevalier would be dead.

. . . *Quatre*

THE RAIN was coming down harder now. It hammered against the windows of my room and thunder rattled the panes.

I sat on the edge of my bed, carefully feeding the cartridges into the gun. Then I crossed to a massive armoire that stood in a corner, opened it, pulled out one of the drawers in which my shirts were stacked, and slid the revolver in beneath them. Slowly I removed my wet coat and carried it to its usual hanger in the closet. Like everything else I had done since I came in, it was performed automatically, without thinking.

Then I paused. The sonorous tones of a grandfather clock in the hall below were sounding the quarter hour. In fifteen minutes I would be expected to appear for dinner. When I didn't come down someone would surely be sent to look for me. I couldn't let them find me still imprisoned by life.

Until that clock chimed I had been going mechanically through each movement, moving step by numb step toward the final one without considering how close it might be. Now time had made my decision for me, the moment was here. Like a sleepwalker I took the gun from its hiding place. I put the black muzzle into my mouth and stood there ready to embrace death, my finger poised on the trigger.

And then, in that split instant before eternity, the hypnotic numbness shattered. I couldn't do it. I could not pull that trigger. Again and again I struggled to make my finger obey my command, but it was absolutely impossible. Finally I dropped the gun on the bed and, completely spent, sank into the chair beside it.

What had stopped me? Was it a question of not having the courage? Or was it some deep conviction about living — some instinct that refused to let me die? I didn't know. I only knew that I had been to the very edge. Now, sitting there staring at the gun, I realized that in a way I was almost lucky to have gone so far, because in the supreme test the obsession to kill myself which I had been carrying helplessly within me for weeks seemed suddenly to have been destroyed.

In the weary days to follow, however, all was still not good. Knowing that I couldn't take my own life didn't change the unspeakable sadness which bound me like a shroud. I had survived, I would tell myself, but for what? In one sense I felt more lost than ever, because the one possible exit from my futile existence was now permanently closed.

There was no way to keep my feelings out of my letters to Yvonne, and as I sat in a corner of the garden late one afternoon writing to her, I suddenly shoved the paper aside, wondering if I shouldn't break off this lamentable correspondence completely. For more than a month I'd burdened her with my dark thoughts, and though her answering letters were frequent and unflaggingly optimistic, what a struggle they must have been to create.

I thought about her in Paris, a young, energetic figure with her future still shining brightly before her. And what was I contributing to it but my own desperation?

I picked up the half-finished sheet of note paper. If I couldn't offer her the response she deserved for her touching devotion, I could at least spare her more of my woes. I creased the paper in two. I would throw it away.

"If that's for me, Maurice, you won't have to mail it," a voice called out happily.

I looked up and as if she'd materialized out of my reverie, Yvonne was coming through the glass doors and running across the few feet of lawn that separated us.

She was in my arms, smiling and speaking in a rush of words, and for a moment I wasn't quite sure she was real. She had written nothing about coming down to Saujon.

"When I decided, I just picked up and came," she said. Suddenly her smile looked a little crooked, as if she were having trouble keeping it in place, and I felt her trembling. "You see, I can't seem to stop worrying about you, and when your letters sounded so strange —" She turned away, trying to hide the concern that had filled her eyes.

"I didn't mean to frighten you," I said awkwardly. "I'm sorry."

"I'm not." She turned back to me and her voice was gentle. "It brought me." She hesitated. Then I learned she hadn't journeyed to Saujon merely to pay me a visit. She had quit the show and given up everything that tied her to Paris, because she wanted to stay here and share my dismal life.

I was so deeply moved I didn't know what to say.

"I want to be with you." She searched my face earnestly. "And I thought you might need me."

Need her? I had never felt so alone, and looking down at that sweet, solemn little face I suddenly realized how much having her near would mean to me. I wanted to tell her but still I could find no words. Instead I simply took her hand. She smiled in a way that said she understood. And from that afternoon, the loving tenderness and patience Yvonne Vallée was offering me became an intimate part of my life.

AUTUMN was in the sharp smell of the air and it crackled underfoot in all the country lanes where drifts of fallen leaves had gathered. I had continued to follow the monotonous pattern of daily life that Dr. Dubois had outlined to me. Walk, rest, talk. Talk, rest, walk. I heard it so often it had become a nonsense rhyme in my head, with no more meaning for me than the assurance he never tired of repeating.

"You don't have to like this kind of life for it to cure you," he would say. Then a twinkle of humor would light his eyes as he saw through my transparently polite agreement. "Even if you don't believe me till you're back on stage performing again, it *is* going to happen."

I didn't believe him. And I didn't believe Yvonne, who echoed his attitude, either. But my lack of faith didn't seem to upset either of them, or weaken their own. With the doctor it was perhaps not so unusual, because patience was part of his professional training and he'd had years of experience to draw on. But Yvonne was quite a different story. She had nothing for support but her own spirit, yet she was a small, incredible pillar of sweet-tempered strength.

Nothing disturbed her. If suddenly in midsentence I no longer felt like talking she quietly picked up the sweater she was knitting for me and began to work in peaceful silence. And when she sensed my need to pace our room in solitude, she would slip out to wander serenely through the garden, stopping to talk cheerfully with the other troubled people there as if she were living in an ordinary hotel with ordinary guests.

Sometimes she would go with me as I tramped the now familiar roads, and when I set off alone she was always waiting for me upon my return, welcoming me happily no matter what mood she found me in.

But one day I sensed a subtle tension in her greeting, and when I started toward our room, she touched my arm to stop me. The pressure of her fingers was strangely taut. "The doctor wanted to see you, Maurice."

I turned toward her curiously. "Now? Instead of tomorrow?" She nodded. "What for? What's the matter?"

"Nothing," she said with a laugh that seemed strained to me. "He just wants to see you, that's all."

When one has been teetering for months on the fragile chalk-line between hope and despair, a simple change in routine can be alarming. Fear must have shown in my eyes, for Yvonne kissed me suddenly before I turned down the hall toward Dubois' office. I was more than ever sure that something was wrong.

But the doctor's face showed nothing. I sat across from him and blandly he began to discuss a holiday celebration which was going to be held several days from now in the small village hall of Saujon.

"It won't be the biggest audience in the world, or the most important," he said casually, "but I want you to sing for them."

"Sing?" It came out of me in a shocked gasp. The thought of facing an audience — any audience — had made the blood drain from my head. Alarmed and angry I jumped to my feet. "How can you ask such a thing? You know what happened to my memory. I can't trust it any more, so I can't perform any more! It's completely impossible!"

He looked at me evenly for a moment without saying a word,

then gestured for me to sit down. I wanted to walk out, but something compelling in his gaze forced me back into my chair.

"That's no longer true, Maurice," he said quietly. "You can perform, and you must." I started to protest but he cut me off. "I'm not asking you to do it, I'm ordering you to."

"And if I won't?" I said tightly.

"But you will."

Our eyes locked. A long moment passed. Then curtly I nodded and walked out.

The week that followed was relentless, unrelieved torture. I'd returned to my room shaking at what lay ahead and it had grown worse with every single hour. I had arranged two numbers in which I would dance and sing with Yvonne, almost as if I had the need to feel her close to me as a protection against the terrifying moment when I set foot on that stage. But even knowing that she would be there beside me couldn't lessen my anguish, and a dozen times each day, as I sweated and stumbled over the words of the songs, I would stop abruptly, certain that I was back on the treadmill of disaster.

"No, Dubois is wrong!" I would explode. "Do I have to die in front of an audience before he'll admit it?"

Yvonne would wait till the storm passed, then like a gentle ministering angel clad in rehearsal tights, she would come to my side carrying a damp towel and gently blot my soaking forehead.

"He's right, Maurice. You must believe that."

"Why?"

"Because it's true," she'd answer. Then with an encouraging smile she'd add, "You're going to be wonderful," and wait quietly till with a weary sigh I'd tackle the number again.

But still the terror persisted. What guarantee would there be that my mind would not go blank again?

"There are no guarantees," Dubois said slowly, when I appealed to him. "But fear is never a reason for quitting; it's only an excuse. When a brave man encounters fear, Maurice, he admits it — and goes on despite it."

Was I brave? I doubted it, yet somehow I knew that no matter what the outcome, I couldn't run from this test, and all too soon the evening started. It was almost time to leave for the village hall, and I had come downstairs ahead of Yvonne, so tense and ready to fly apart that I couldn't stay cooped up in our room while she finished dressing.

If I could just get my mind off the trial confronting me, even for a few minutes, maybe my screaming nerves would give me some respite. But how? I headed past the reception desk. Walking in the raw air was probably no answer, but at least it was better than sitting still.

"Monsieur Chevalier?"

The voice stopped me as I neared the door and I turned back to the desk. One of the doctor's assistants was extending an envelope.

"This came for you in the afternoon mail."

A letter from Paris. The handwriting was bold and unfamiliar, and there was no return address. Frowning, I ripped open the envelope, then stopped short in surprise. There was no letter inside. Instead I found a folded theatrical column clipped from a newspaper and thought it odd that someone would send it along without a personal note. I began to scan the printed paragraphs, and suddenly sick I knew why it had come anonymously.

"The favorite topic of backstage conversation," it said, "remains the sad story behind Maurice Chevalier's absence from the Paris stage this season. According to sources who should know it comes down to this: One of the capital's greatest stars, reportedly destroyed by too much wine, women and the worst indulgence of them all, *drugs*, is now locked away, a wretched, finished hulk whose mind is as lost as his memory. The talk is that many friends who have made the long journey to visit him found it a waste of effort, for he neither recognized nor remembered them. The sad conclusion? The audience that loved him will have to live on memories. Chevalier is finished. He will never return."

Drugs? Unrecognized friends? I stared at these lies, too stunned to move.

Yvonne was behind me. "Are you ready?" she asked, and then as she stood by my side, "Maurice what is it? You look like a ghost!"

"Maybe that's all I am," I answered in a dead voice and held out the clipping.

She read it with a small heartsick outcry. "But it's not true! No one will believe it, you know that!"

Did I? There would always be people to believe scandal, to feed on the disaster of others. And though I could prove the lurid gossip about my personal life was a lie, could I deny the truth of that "sad conclusion"? Perhaps at this very moment other columnists would be writing other predictions that I would never return to Paris, and perhaps they were right. For could a man who was afraid to face a provincial audience in a tiny auditorium ever have the courage or the ability to win his way back to the top?

Half an hour later Yvonne and I were standing in the wings of the village hall. The upsetting blow of that newspaper story, added to the strain of facing this evening, had been almost more than my nerves could deal with and I was trembling so badly I was sure it would be obvious even to the people in the last row of the audience. Frantically I tried in vain to control it and wanted desperately to turn around and walk back out into the night to just keep walking until I dropped. But the amateur orchestra was playing the introduction to my first solo number.

"I love you," Yvonne said as the notes of my entrance cue sounded and slowly I moved out on stage.

I stopped and turned toward the audience. There was only time for one gulping breath, and then I must start to sing. I reached into my brain for the first line of my song — and somehow it was there. Then the second line and the third and the fourth until somehow I had gotten through the entire number. Searching, finding and producing each word had been a separate, sweating agony, but at least I was under way.

The two numbers I had with Yvonne and my other songs alone came no easier. Still, not once during that entire, seemingly endless performance did my memory actually play me tricks, and finally it was over. Then soaking wet and almost too drained to move I dragged myself back to the makeshift dressing room.

I slumped exhausted into the one rickety armchair while Yvonne went out to the car with the few props we'd brought for the show. The evening was behind me now, but there was no feeling of elation or joy in me. Was it possible only four months had passed since I'd walked off a Paris stage? The way I'd performed tonight it could have been four hundred years. All I wanted was to get out of here and forget the whole thing, but when I picked up my coat to leave a brief knock sounded and Dubois walked in.

He shook my hand as if I'd just scored a great triumph and a big smile was on his face. "Congratulations, Maurice."

He meant it sincerely, but it hit me as the capping irony to everything I'd suffered these past few hours. "For what?" I asked bitterly. "For managing to get all the words out of my mouth? Almost killing myself just to accomplish that?"

His face sobered. "You proved your memory won't fail you. That's part of the way back."

"You have to offer an audience more than rote, Doctor."

"I didn't hear anyone booing," he said.

"Only because you were sitting in Saujon instead of Paris," I said tightly. "Do you know the kind of tough, demanding crowds I'd have to please? They want a performance, not what

194

I gave out there!" I grabbed my coat. "You can save your congratulations, Doctor. The Paris papers are saying I'm finished, and all I really proved tonight is how right they really are!" With that I turned and walked out.

But an hour afterwards I was regretting the way I'd spoken to Dubois. And even before I apologized the next day, I had to admit to myself the truth I had angrily ignored: I had gone through an entire performance without an accident. I couldn't kid myself about its quality or the toll it had taken of my strength; still, I had gone through it.

It would be a long, slow, difficult road, I was thinking, yet if I took it one step at a time, in a year or so I actually could hope to make my way back. And for now I could take comfort from passing the first test and relax and concentrate on growing stronger without worrying about the distant future. There would be plenty of time for that later.

But "later" arrived in one brief week. "A visitor downstairs, monsieur," the voice called through the door of my room. "His name is Franck."

Franck! I wanted to see no one yet from my old life, certainly not a friend who could do nothing but pity me for my fall. Still it would be worse to refuse, so reluctantly I started down, determined to dissemble, somehow to hide the discouraging truth of my state from him.

I tried nonchalance. "Well, old Franck, what inspired you to show up in a place like this?"

He took his cue. "I heard you were loafing, Maurice, and I figured you'd been lazy long enough."

I felt my smile cracking a little. "What do you mean?"

"I came to talk business. Fifteen days at the top of my bill, old friend, what do you say?"

"At the Alcazar?" I was in a spin now. Surely Franck knew that I was in no condition to pit myself against an important audience, and certainly not that of Marseilles with its violent, unpredictable moods. And surely he had read what the newspapers were saying about me. What was he trying to do?

"Marseilles was the big step before Paris once before, Maurice," he was saying gently. "It can be again."

"I'm not ready for either one," I said tightly.

"Your doctor thinks you are." He saw my surprise. "He's on my side, old friend. You're outnumbered." Suddenly he was grinning again. "So how can you refuse?"

How could I? With Franck and Dubois adamantly overriding my frightened protests in the doctor's office, I put my trembling signature to a contract committing me to an appearance in Marseilles only eight short weeks away.

"Oh God," I said to Yvonne later, "what have I done?"

"The right thing, darling," she said and her hand closed over mine as if to give me strength.

And somehow, miraculously, it did.

YVONNE and I were driving slowly along the narrow streets of Melun. I looked at the shop fronts and houses and weather-bleached stone walls surrounding me. Only eight years had passed since I marched through these same streets on my way to war. It seemed an eternity ago.

Even Saujon, which I had left only eight days ago, seemed remote now and my first fearful day back in Paris when I had barricaded myself alone in my apartment against the unaccustomed noise and agitation and menace of the city. I had been terrified that day until the moment Yvonne returned, and then everything was suddenly all right again.

How often she had been beside me these past months when I needed her, I was thinking now, giving of herself with that beauty and grace that only those who give through love possess. I had felt its tenderness, I had known its depths. There were no doubts in me about Yvonne's feelings, but I had begun to wonder what my own were.

This gratitude which had grown deeper and stronger with every day we'd shared, which seemed at this moment to be filling every corner of my heart — was it love coming to live with me again? I had never known it to arrive so quietly, or to touch me with such a soft and delicate hand. Yet as I turned now to look at her — intent, gentle, lovely — I wondered what other emotion than love could be moving my heart so deeply.

We turned the corner into the main street and there was the movie theatre looking exactly as I'd remembered it. The manager was waiting for me in his office. "Now, what's this all about, monsieur?" he asked warily.

"Exactly what I told you on the phone."

"A star like Maurice Chevalier is willing to come to my little town just to perform in my little theatre?" He smiled like a man who is waiting for a practical joke to erupt in his face.

"That's right. This Friday through Sunday."

"But why?"

"I need a place to try out some new material."

"You? A tryout?"

"No one's ever certain," I said. Certain? This was my first professional step on the road back, and how far from certain I really was! I could hardly hold back a bitter smile as we made our deal.

Yet on the way out of town I began to feel a little sense of pleasure that I had carried this off so well. I was like an invalid learning to walk again. Helpless so long, I was now suddenly moving on shaking legs, but at least I was moving. Melun was set, in Paris I had already begun to study new songs with the happy surprise that I was not only able to learn but to memorize with a new facility; Franck had written that all was going to be well and I could honestly believe he was right. I had lived so long without optimism I had forgotten what fine flavor it could give to a day. Now, tasting it again, I felt pleasure expanding into a kind of elation.

A crossroads loomed ahead, marked by a single signpost: BOIS-LE-ROI.

Three simple words. Suddenly my heart contracted with pain and memory hurled me backwards so abruptly that for an instant I could see nothing but the image of the man I had been in the year of that beautiful spring when nightly I had turned down this road toward Mist and love. I had been at the peak of my powers, a man with dreams and strength and spirit. My entire world had been ahead of me then. Now it was behind me.

Elation, I thought ironically. For a moment I had found it in accomplishing a few pitiful little steps when I would really need the strides of a giant to get back to the place I had been.

"FIVE minutes, Monsieur Chevalier!"

I was sitting in the star dressing room of the Empire, a lavish new theatre whose curtain would rise for the first time tonight. In exactly five minutes I would be on stage before a mammoth première audience and all the fears for my comeback would be answered. Tonight I was finally facing Paris.

The journey to this crucial moment had been a weary grind from Melun through one small town after another all the way to Marseilles, weeks of agonized performances, steeling myself each night to stand before the footlights again and fight and sweat and learn that no matter how many times I got through in one piece, the terror for the next battle never diminished.

I could imagine the audience sitting out there now, exchanging clever, brittle remarks and knowing smiles, speculating on whether I was really as grave a wreck as gossip had it, enjoying the tragedy I'd suffered as if it were an added attraction on the bill.

Well, wasn't it? I asked myself despondently. If I thought

they had come just to watch an entertainer I was kidding myself. Paris had crammed this enormous theatre to its top gallery hoping to see the spectacle a crazy freak would make of himself on exhibition!

I blotted away the sweat that had broken through the mask of my make-up, then jumped up abruptly and headed for the door, swallowing huge breaths of air in a futile attempt to dissolve the tight knot that had locked my throat shut. Yvonne was waiting as I emerged.

"It's time, darling," she said quietly. "Are you all right?"

She was searching my face with that earnest, hopeful expression I knew so well. It was an appeal that was almost a prayer, and it seemed to say: Please, this time it must come true.

I looked down at her, lovelier than ever in the gown she would be wearing for the first of our three numbers together. Just once, I was thinking, spare her the pain of disappointment. I took another deep breath and forced a grin. "I'm fine," I lied and offered her my arm. "Let's go."

"They're going to adore you tonight, Maurice." Her smile had a radiance I'd never seen before. "You can't miss, darling, now that your old confidence is back."

My old confidence. It wasn't true. It hadn't returned, and it never would in just the way I had known it before. But at least I had found a kind of courage to take its place. Now, hearing the excited hum of conversation that didn't stop even when the house lights dimmed, I knew it would take all that courage to show myself before this crowd. I moved out to confront them, braced for their morbidly curious stares, certain that their response would come from hostile, coldly appraising hearts.

But the instant I appeared an incredible thunderous explosion of sound stopped me in my tracks. Applause rang and swelled until it seemed the sheer volume of it would surely crack the ceiling and still it continued. I stood there overwhelmed listening to Paris pouring out its warmth and love and encouragement in that prolonged ovation, and I knew that never in my life had I been so wrong about people.

I wanted to give back to them for that magnificent gesture of welcome every ounce of talent I possessed and more. I wanted them to share in the rich joyousness that was suddenly flooding me. I wanted to sing out in a voice stronger than I'd ever known, to make this as memorable an evening for them as they had already made it for me.

And like a miracle being granted, all that I wanted in that moment seemed to happen. From the notes of my first song, through the numbers with Yvonne, to the final beautiful curtain calls that threatened to last all evening, it was a triumph mixed with a rare and special magic. And coming off stage at last I felt a happiness I didn't think could possibly be richer, until I saw Yvonne waiting for me, her eyes glistening with tears.

I took her into my arms and gently brushed them away. "There's nothing to cry about now, little saint," I said softly. "I love you and the battle's won and all the bad's behind us."

She managed a tremulous smile, and I kissed her.

"I promise you, the best is still ahead," I said, and as I held her, I vowed I would make that promise come true.

... Cinq

"WHEN I make a promise, I keep it," I laughed, watching Yvonne move around the large, comfortably furnished living room, making little sounds of delighted discovery. I had brought her out to Vaucresson, a half hour from the center of Paris, to see the wonderful house set in the protective depths of rich green gardens that I'd rented for us. "How do you like it?"

"I love it, Maurice." She turned back toward me in a happy rush and I caught her in my arms. "And I love you, and it's even more than you promised. It's the most beautiful villa in the world!"

Perhaps it wasn't quite that, but I smiled down at her, happy that she liked it so well — happy, in fact, with life altogether and the way it was going.

The night of my opening at the Empire had been a turning point for me, a turning point away from the specter of failure. In that four-week engagement I broke every box office record for Paris. Moreover, with it had come a marvelous dividend, a rebirth of enthusiasm for work, bigger and stronger than anything I had ever known before.

It had carried me through a sweeping tour of Europe, back to a return engagement at the Empire and finally now to the highest pinnacle in the Paris sky — a three-year contract as the top star of the Casino de Paris.

Yvonne still shared virtually every hour with me, those on stage as well as the ones away from the theatre, but sporadically a tiny doubt over the wisdom of our almost perpetual intimacy would disturb my sense of well-being. I had never lived so closely with another human being in my life. In my nature there had always been a need for a certain amount of privacy, of time out to go at my own rhythm and in a way to renew my own spirit, and that kind of freedom was gone now.

Yet when an occasional sigh escaped me for its loss or a vague restlessness began to stir for former days that had held more variety and excitement, I had only to glance at that serene little figure beside me to dispel the mood and restore my happiness. Because the sight of her reminded me that out of my illness some gifts had come as well as torments. One gift was Yvonne herself, another a little more wisdom — enough intelligence to appreciate and savor the contentment I knew with her instead of seeking more violent emotional involvements which my appetites might dictate but my need for repose would never sustain.

The sweet peacefulness that had drawn me to this girl and to this place seemed to be filling the air, and I took her into my arms to tell her I'd decided on the name for our new home.

"What are you going to call it?"

"*Quand on est Deux.*" It came from a song I had introduced, about two people who together knew the happiness of being one.

Instead of the pleased smile I'd expected, her face was serious and there was a strange note of intensity in her voice. "Maurice, do you really mean that? Is it really the way you feel?"

"Of course it is," I said. But the urgent undertone of her mood was still in her eyes, and I kissed her, trying to make it go away without quite understanding what had caused it to appear.

It was a look I caught fleeting glimpses of many times again in the months that followed at Vaucresson, but I still kept silent because it was such a transient little cloud that it barely cast a shadow on all the good things that were happening.

"How does it feel, Maurice, being a star who can do no wrong?" Leon Volterra grinned at me one night in my dressing room at the Casino.

Quite honestly it felt a little fantastic, yet it seemed to be true. Everything I had to offer the public met with incredible acclaim.

Of all my songs in that lively era when stories of American bootleggers and gangsters filled the Paris papers and writers like Ernest Hemingway and F. Scott Fitzgerald made the Left Bank headquarters for literary exiles, none caught the public's fancy so strongly as a tune about an adorable creature named Valentine. But if I had guessed how soon that little darling was going to plunge me into trouble, I might not have sung out so gaily the story of her charms!

Soon after the song was launched a visitor arrived in my dressing room. It had been more than ten years since I'd seen him but I placed the quick Latin gestures and the slightly excitable manner immediately. It was the Spanish Ambassador who had brought me my first invitation to perform before royalty, and his call now had the same purpose. King Alphonso and his queen were again in Paris, and Yvonne and I were being invited to sing at a soiree honoring them at the Spanish Embassy. The distinguished guests would include Edouard Herriot, the prime minister of our own country.

"We'd be delighted," I said, remembering the very warm and friendly King of Spain. "What do you think Their Majesties would like to hear?"

The song he chose for the duet was fine, but when he proposed "Valentine" for my solo a warning bell of caution rang.

There was a problem with "Valentine." Along with commenting on her cute little chin and her cute little feet there was another of her charms which the song stressed repeatedly. To remove the reference to Valentine's cute little breasts would destroy the entire number, but one does not sing to kings and queens so candidly about these feminine attributes. How could I keep the ideas without keeping the very specific Parisian slang word in the lyric?

"I'm sorry," I said shaking my head, "but 'Valentine' is out of the question. I can't think of any way to get around those *tetons*."

He assured me with an expansive smile that there was no need to. "On the contrary, the King will adore that. *Tetons* — it's so French, so charmingly frank — Their Majesties will be delighted."

Would they? Reluctantly I agreed to do the song, but my worries about shocking that staid, dignified audience didn't abate. Instead they became acutely grave when the evening arrived and I was facing the heavy, silent formality of the Embassy drawing room.

It was too late to turn back now. The music started and with hollow enthusiasm I attacked the first chorus up to the moment of praise for those little *tetons*. When I heard the risqué word come out of me, I kept going, like a man running blindly, until the chorus was ended and the music forced me to wait silently before the second verse began.

Suddenly I felt I'd been insane to let the Ambassador persuade me into this impossible spot. What sounded charmingly frank in the Casino had surely fallen on those extremely sensitive regal ears as common vulgarity; I was sure of it. And probably if I had the courage to look up, I would see waves of distaste hanging in the air like tobacco smoke.

However, I couldn't risk finding out, for there were still two more choruses to sweat through. Then in the midst of the second one, feeling like a dying man who would never get to the last agonizing breath, I could stand the suspense no longer. With haggard eyes I forced myself to take in that array of important faces. My glance froze when it hit the corner where Edouard Herriot sat. I couldn't see his face. It was buried in his hands. I could imagine what it meant: "How does he dare? What kind of man is he that he can parade all those naughty *tetons* before the Queen?"

After that I couldn't force myself even to dart a glance at the royal couple. I was certain their outraged expressions would have paralyzed me where I stood. During the final chorus the only gaze I could hazard meeting was Yvonne's, and the compassion in her eyes was a reflection of my own agitation and suffering. Frantically I pushed on, wildly planning immediate flight for the two of us, and the instant I brought my catastrophe to an end I grabbed her hand and we fled for Vaucresson in a hysterical dash as if all the Spanish police were at our heels.

I paced the living room embarrassed and remorseful. "Just wait till the papers come out. 'Maurice Chevalier Insults Royalty' in big black headlines! How's that for a claim to fame?" Yvonne tried to calm me but it was useless. "And if I'm really lucky," I went on, "Herriot may even decorate me with the award for national stupidity!"

The days passed without either of my dire predictions coming true; yet it didn't assuage my fear that some painful repercussion would result. The sudden reappearance of the Spanish Ambassador in my dressing room one night after the show made me certain the moment had caught up with me.

But to my surprise he handed me a package with the compliments of the king. Inside I discovered an elegant cigarette case engraved with the royal signature. I looked at it for a moment, completely baffled.

"Mr. Ambassador, Their Majesties aren't angry with me?"

"Angry? Why should they be?"

"Because I shocked everyone with the *tetons* of Valentine."

Now it was his turn to be surprised. "But you didn't, Monsieur Chevalier. Everyone was delighted, believe me. The guests, the Queen and as for the King" — he darted a glance to either side and lowered his voice as if invisible spies filled the dressing room — "the King wants a copy of the song to learn for himself!"

The Ambassador left me in a marvelous mood. This was a wonderful story to share with Yvonne on the way home. As I looked for my car keys on the dressing room table, a polite little feminine cough sounded from the open door behind me. "I'll be right with you, darling," I said and glanced up at the mirror, expecting Yvonne's reflection. But the animated pretty face looking back at me with an impish smile was a strange one.

"Forgive me." I turned to face a lovely girl holding a theatre program in her hand. "I thought you were somebody else."

"I'm sorry I'm not," she laughed and asked me to autograph her program.

A moment later she was gone and I looked for Yvonne but her dressing room was empty and when I got to the car she was already inside waiting for me.

"Wonderful, the way it went tonight," I said happily.

"Was it?"

It sounded flat and measured and somehow almost angry and

I glanced at her surprised, but there didn't seem to be anything unusual in the look of her face except a few tiny lines of strain. Being tired had probably accounted for her tone, I decided, and launched into the story of the Spanish Ambassador's visit to lift her spirits.

It didn't elicit the laughter I'd imagined us sharing and almost everything else I mentioned during the drive drew no reaction from her but withdrawn silence. I could still feel the tension after we'd reached Vaucresson. It hovered in the air above the supper table like a crackling electric charge. I looked across at Yvonne. Her plate was untouched and her eyes were on me intently.

Irritation began to rasp my nerves. I knew it wouldn't help matters, yet I couldn't prevent it. This taut, mysterious reaction that had taken the edge off what should have been a charming evening was finally getting under my skin. "Will you please tell me what's going on?"

She looked at me levelly for a moment without speaking. "Why didn't you tell me about your other visitor tonight, Maurice?"

"What other visitor?"

"The girl. I saw you together when I came up to your dressing room."

I looked at her surprised. "What was there to tell? She was just a girl who wanted an autograph. By the time she walked out I'd completely forgotten her."

"If you say so." She stared at me evenly and her eyes suddenly seemed filled with the too-bright glow of jealous accusation. I read it with shocked disbelief.

Jealousy couldn't exist without an honest cause, I told myself, and there simply was none. I struggled to push down my annoyance and straighten out this almost ludicrous misunderstanding before it went any further.

Going to her side I pulled her up into my arms. She didn't resist but I could feel the tenseness of her body, the holding apart even when we touched.

"I've told you the truth," I appealed. "Don't you trust me?"

"Of course I do," she answered, but the rigidness didn't relax and I released her unhappily, realizing that she didn't. The fact that it made no sense only added to my upset.

A few minutes later she paused at the foot of the staircase. "Are you coming up, Maurice?"

There is a terrible kind of restrained politeness that only a man and woman who live together can know. It comes when they are facing bed and at the same moment closing themselves off from each other, and I could feel that between us now.

"You go ahead," I answered. "I'll be up later."

She turned without another word and I watched her go, the line of her back unnaturally stiff, till she rounded the landing and disappeared from sight.

Alone, I couldn't throw off the feeling of unreality that seized me. This couldn't be happening with Yvonne, I kept repeating. She had the greatest gift for perception and understanding of any woman I'd ever known. She'd proved it in a thousand difficult moments during the months at Saujon and the even more trying time of my struggle to make my way back. Surely with a gift so strong and fine — one she'd offered generously when my need was so desperate — she couldn't misunderstand something as innocent and trivial as what had gone on tonight. Yet, incredible as it seemed, she must have.

Could understanding between two people disappear that suddenly? It didn't seem possible.

The living room drapes were drawn but they didn't shut out the low moaning wail of the wind. It was an augury of winter coming and its heavy chill seemed already to be invading the room. I pulled my chair closer to the fire that burned in the grate and glanced across to where Yvonne usually sat facing me every night, sharing what I had always thought was the quiet happiness of this hour.

Now I wondered if those nights had been an illusion. Had the silences I'd read as contentment been filled for her with wordless suspicions and doubts? Was lack of trust behind the urgent, intense look that I'd dismissed so often when it passed across her face?

Suddenly fragments of tiny, puzzling incidents were leaping up from buried memory. "Can't we leave now, Maurice? I'm tired." I'd heard the words and seen the odd, tense frown that went with them a dozen times when, in the midst of enjoying herself at the rare parties we'd attended, unexplained fatigue would possess Yvonne.

But now that I thought of it, hadn't it often come when politeness dictated that I ask another woman for a single dance? Or those carefree strolls along broad, pleasant boulevards that sometimes had abruptly lost their charm for her. Hadn't this coincided more than once with a casual comment on my part about an attractive woman passing by?

Angrily I got to my feet and prodded the dying fire. "But I've given her no reason not to trust me!" I protested aloud. Then as quickly as it had come my anger left, because I knew that trust isn't extended like a payment simply because one has earned it. It's a natural force of love, a response of the heart that must come as freely as tenderness or laughter. I couldn't demand it of Yvonne. I could only pray that she would be moved to offer it. We had gone through so much together, and more than anything I wanted her to have the happiness she deserved. Yet I was helpless to give it to her. No, what happened with Yvonne and me rested in her hands — and hers alone.

I HAD agreed to star in a London revue called *White Birds*, and with Yvonne beside me as the train neared Victoria Station I felt the uneasiness mounting in me that I had resolutely pushed down from the day I signed the contract for this appearance.

Some instinctive voice warned me when Lew Leslie, the American producer who had captured Europe with his Negro revue, *Blackbirds,* asked me to head the bill in this new production. I was worried about London. In my one appearance there eight years ago I had really been under Elsie Janis's wing, while this time I was to be the top attraction in a language that still knotted my tongue and I would be pitted against the best English and American entertainers. But Leslie had lured me with a tempting offer, and here I was.

For the hundredth time I practiced that English combination of *t* and *h* which is so difficult for every Frenchman. "The thirty thick-throated thugs thought that they were thirty thin-throated thugs."

As I muttered the words, Yvonne's hand reached over and covered mine. "They'll not only understand you, but they'll love you," she said.

Yvonne had been wonderful. She had sensed my nervousness about this engagement and she had quietly offered cheer and support. After the strange night when her lack of faith had stood silently between us, I had tried not to think of it any more, and there had been good and warm times since. Yet I knew it was not the same as if it had never existed.

The train was pulling into the station, and Yvonne glanced out the window in surprise. "Maurice, what's happening?"

Her reaction to the scene on the platform was no more astonished than mine, for a platoon of beautiful girls was surrounding the car and shouting my name, and as we emerged they engulfed me in a giggling wave to pose prettily for a battery of newspaper photographers. I didn't know it at that instant, but this was only the first step in a monstrous campaign of ballyhoo for the show.

Using methods which were commonplace in America but

completely foreign to London, Leslie began to publicize *White Birds* in a kind of carnival manner. Every day the papers blared stories of the greatest performers, the best dancers, the most expensive and luxurious settings, the most beautiful women in the world.

"Wait a minute, Lew," I protested. "Suppose we don't live up to this advance publicity? The audience will murder us!"

Leslie only smiled and pointed out that as producer and director of the show he knew exactly what he was doing, then proceeded to dream up some new stunt.

Opening night was postponed twice, but finally the day arrived. By this time there had been rumblings in the columns that perhaps our show had been touted to be more than it was, and people were saying a little belligerently that we had better be good or else. Tension had swept over the entire cast on this last day, for we had all begun to sense that the spectators tonight might well be an enemy instead of an audience if we didn't sweep them off their feet with the brilliance of our show.

Yvonne and I were not to appear until the waning moments of the first act, but I waited in the wings to test the temper of the house. It was bad. From the opening lines of the evening it was apparent that London had seen better than this and was far from pleased. An angry muttering could be heard above the music, almost the sound of a crowd gathered for a world championship fight. It was the sound of a horde wanting blood.

By the time we went on it was to face a thoroughly enraged audience. Somehow we managed to divert them first into silence and then applause for our duet and afterwards for my solo which ended the act. But the tide of resentment was too strong to stem thereafter. The second half of the show disintegrated into a chaos of piercing whistles and objects hurling through the air to rain down on the stage. And finally, with most of the theatre empty and only the howling, catcalling gallery remaining to enjoy the bitter slaughter to the end, it was over.

I sat in my dressing room, crushed with the greatest disaster I had experienced in the theatre. Behind me I heard the door open and I looked up to see Yvonne, her eyes filled with compassionate tenderness.

"It's not the end of the world, darling," she said gently.

"It feels that way."

"But it won't tomorrow." She was smiling in that wonderfully quiet and patient way I had known when we first met. "We'll read the reviews that are sure to be awful, and then we'll concentrate on next year's hit. All right?"

I had to smile. And then I kissed her because once more she had managed to bring a gleam of hope into my life.

And the next morning when the newspapers, though personally kind to me, were pitiless in their criticism of the show, I could reflect that at least one comfort had emerged from the debacle. Somehow in the midst of all this trouble my little saint seemed to be back again, sensitive and sweet and infinitely understanding.

It was summer and the Riviera sun reigned supreme in a cloudless sky. Yvonne and I were at the little town of La Bocca in the hills above the resort city of Cannes. We were sitting on the terrace of the new villa I had built, the first home I'd ever owned. Gazing down at the broad sweep of the Mediterranean I was thinking how happy my mother was going to be with this beautiful place I had named in her honor, "La Louque."

It hadn't been possible to bring her here yet. There still remained a few finishing touches of construction. But I was enjoying a happy daydream of the moment she would finally arrive and we would make a tour of the sun-drenched grounds together.

The shrill ring of the phone from the house brought me sharply awake. "I'll get it," I said. "I'm expecting a call."

It was the lumber dealer in Cannes. There was going to be

another delay in a delivery, the third such postponement. It would hold up work for days, and I was annoyed.

"Was it the call you expected, Maurice?" Yvonne was saying behind me as I hung up.

"Yes." I started back outside.

Her voice stopped me short. "Well, aren't you going to tell me who it was?" The question itself was completely innocent but there was an edge to it. "Was it a woman you were talking to?"

Her implication took me by angry surprise. "Must it be a woman?"

"Why else would you refuse to tell me who called?"

I felt resentment hit me in one sharp sting. "It so happens I didn't refuse," I said tightly. "But now I do." I started for the door without looking back.

The whole flare-up was so ridiculous that I hadn't reached the terrace before regret caught up with me. If I hadn't been irritated with the lumber dealer, I would have answered Yvonne's first question properly, and this little misunderstanding wouldn't have happened at all.

I moved back inside. Yvonne stood before a vase of flowers rearranging them. "I'm sorry, darling," I said going toward her. "It was the man about the lumber. I was angry at him and I guess I took it out on you."

So the incident passed, but I couldn't help being troubled. Obviously doubt still lived in some recess of Yvonne's heart. What fed it I couldn't understand. All I knew was that there were moments, as recently as London, when I lived with a devoted woman in sweet harmony. And in one second of suspicion that person could disappear, leaving in her place a stranger. Suddenly I was wondering if within the same graceful body two completely different women could exist.

. . . *Six*

THE THOUGHT haunted me for weeks. It was a bizarre and improbable idea, yet I couldn't dismiss it from my mind.

"If we were sitting in my Paris clinic right now, Maurice," Victor Pauchet, a close friend and my neighbor at Vaucresson was saying, "I'd diagnose the trouble as love suffering acute threat."

I looked at him, startled. "Threat?" He nodded. "But Yvonne has no reason to feel that way," I protested. "That's what's driving me crazy about the whole thing. It's so illogical."

"Perhaps it's illogical to be in love with a man who never gets around to proposing." My eyebrows must have shot to the top of my forehead in astonishment because he went on with a wry grin, "I see you've at least heard about marriage. Now, maybe you should consider trying it."

Marriage. Strangely enough, until that moment I had given it no thought. Just why, I wasn't sure, but part of the reason might have come from my own experience of growing up in a house where it had failed. Some remote corner of my heart had never forgotten how the shattering of a marriage had brought my mother a cruel and separate grief, or forgotten that she had never completely recovered from the betrayal of its vows. So maybe in a subtle way marriage itself had become linked for me with suffering instead of happiness.

It had surely been no part of the happiness of loving Mist, I was thinking, walking slowly back to my own house. She belonged to Paris and life and me all at the same time, and to limit her loyalties and bind them into matrimony would have been as unnatural as trying to wed the wind.

"Quit dragging your feet," I told myself sternly, "and ignoring the issue. Yvonne is not Mist." Suddenly I stopped short, frowning, a little baffled to find myself playing the role of both prodding adviser and slightly hesitant suitor.

Pauchet was right. Why shouldn't Yvonne feel insecure? From our first afternoon together her every gesture and word and breath had shown me her devotion. Yet how could I expect her to believe mine without proving it by offering her my name?

A hundred tender images of her flooded my mind and I knew in that moment that I did want her to have the position she deserved before God and the law as my wife, to be honored and cherished. And loved? I faced the question honestly. Surely what I felt now was not what I had known with Mist, nor was it so engulfing as some of the violent passions I had been racked by, but it was a feeling that came fully from both my heart and mind. It was a less tempestuous, but in one way perhaps a stronger kind of love — a kind that carried a deep spiritual appreciation for all that she had offered me and a genuine desire to dedicate myself to her happiness.

"Then what are you waiting for?" the prodding adviser demanded. "The girl can't say yes until you ask her!"

I had started for home slowly weighing the possibility of marriage. Now, with my spirits sailing, I found myself racing the last twenty feet across the lawn, to propose it.

I found Yvonne at the end of the terrace, heading into the house, and swung her around to face me. I knew there were many things we should discuss and I was planning to lead up properly to the moment. Instead, everything came tumbling out in one happy rush. "Yvonne, I want you to be my wife. I don't want you to have to work any more, darling, or worry about anything — except maybe feeding me and kissing me good-by when I leave for work and greeting me at the door when I come home — and living happily ever after. Will you marry me?"

In my mind I had imagined so vividly her soft answering "Yes" that an instant passed before I realized with shock that she'd said nothing. I searched her face expectantly, and finally she spoke.

"But I want to go on working with you, Maurice."

"Yvonne," I said hesitantly, "you can't in any case." It was a difficult thing to tell her because she had been such a close and very good partner to me. Still, the problem of making a change had been coming toward me for a long time now and I explained as gently as I could that no matter what we decided to do personally, this issue had to be settled and there was only one realistic solution. A candid critic had made that clear to me in my dressing room a week ago.

"It's time you found a new girl to work with, Maurice," he had said. "Variety is the lifeblood of every successful act, and you're too good a showman to ignore that. But even if you do,"

216

he'd gone on, overriding my protest, "believe me, the audience won't!"

It hadn't been the first time I'd heard it, and I knew it wouldn't be the last. Also, I knew he spoke the truth. I had never worked with the same girl for so long as I had with Yvonne, and already I had begun to feel in the public a growing restlessness.

"The part I'm asking you to accept now, darling, has a much better contract," I grinned, trying to tease her out of her solemn mood. "The show runs forever, and I promise to be your loyal and dedicated one-man audience. So what do you say?"

"I don't know, Maurice," she said slowly. "I'll have to think about it."

My sailing spirits collapsed in an abrupt heap. It was the last reply I could have imagined to the first proposal of my life.

Nevertheless she meant it. And the question that had originally come out of me in such a spontaneous burst hung unanswered in the air for days that passed in long, searching discussions.

But still I couldn't persuade her. Was she afraid, I asked myself, of what might happen once she gave up her place beside me on stage and devoted herself to running my house? In the back of her head could there be the fear I might use my liberty to pursue those delicious little adventures that are so often encountered in the life of the theatre? But those tempting episodes were a fruit I had already tasted too much of in my life, and ironically all I wanted was to be as faithful a husband to her as I had been a lover.

As the days dragged on and I struggled to make her realize this, I began to think that no man had ever tried so hard to get married. Then finally, on a spring morning made of pale gold, the "Yes" I had waited so long to hear came softly from her lips and we stood before the village priest and were married.

"She's a nice girl, Maurice," La Louque said to me later, her happiness showing in her gentle eyes. I knew she was right. And I felt the promise I had made so long ago to Yvonne — that the best was still ahead of us — was at last coming true.

BUT I was completely mistaken. In the new revue at the Casino I had decided to try working without a partner at all, and the freedom I felt was like an injection to my spirit. A kind of contagious gaiety seemed to flow back and forth across the footlights between me and the audience and those few hours in the theatre were almost a feast of joy. The feast came to an abrupt end each night, however, the moment I returned home.

Marriage hadn't really changed a thing between Yvonne and me. Sadly I realized that being my wife had brought neither security nor confidence to her heart. Her lack of faith seemed now more intense than ever. Those hours we spent apart, which should have added to the sweetness of homecoming, were for her a time to entertain fantasies about a thousand things and brew storms of doubt that sometimes raged from the moment I came through the door to the time I left the next evening.

It takes two people to create strain in a marriage, just as surely as it takes two people to create harmony, and I couldn't pretend that I hadn't contributed to our difficulties. I had never kidded myself that I was an easy, uncomplicated man to live with. There was a nervous streak in my temperament that often made me lash out when it would have been more intelligent to remain calm. But the problem now was not where to place the blame but how to find a solution.

I smoked my way through dozens of sleepless nights searching desperately for some answer to this impossible situation. Divorce, I asked myself gravely? No, we had entered into our marriage for a lifetime. Yet I knew something must be done.

I thought about close friends I might appeal to for advice, then rejected the idea because even when a man and woman are suffering a kind of hell inside their marriage it's still a very personal thing between them. And they are the only ones who can change it.

So it was obvious that Yvonne and I would have to tackle our problem together, for it could never be solved without honest discussion. But when? When would we ever be able to speak reasonably of our bitter differences without that very bitterness turning the words into still another battle?

Not long after that our lives did change, however, and we became much happier. But it was destiny, not discussion, that supplied the reason. One afternoon Yvonne told me that we were going to have a baby.

Almost from that moment tension disappeared and soon a new grace was blossoming in her spirit. I watched it flourish and a serene contentment touched us now. Her mood seemed always to have a bright edge and there were moments of sudden gay enthusiasm and that very nice kind of tender silliness when she would rush to me to discuss plans for the baby that projected at least twenty years into the future.

Every night when I left for the theatre I whistled my way happily into Paris because I carried with me the marvelous knowledge that every turn of the road coming back was no longer a threat to my spirit.

One evening that whistle broke off in puzzlement as I came through the stage door and turned into the corridor leading to the dressing rooms. Usually it was completely empty at this hour while everyone dressed and got into make-up. But tonight it looked like a crazy pageant. The entire company was clustered in knots or milling up and down the hallway, and excited talk charged the air. Moving among them I heard the same word on every tongue. "Lindbergh." And quickly the puzzle was solved.

For this was the night of May 21, 1927, and all of Paris was waiting for the moment when the young American would swoop down from the clouds to become the first man in the world to fly alone, nonstop across the enormous expanse of earth and water that lay between New York and Paris.

Nobody could predict the exact moment of his arrival. But if the fever of anticipation is already running this high backstage, I was thinking, I can imagine what will be going on by the time the audience arrives! And it was that way. Moving out on stage I could feel a kind of tension in the people, as if they were sitting on the edge of their seats straining to hear the motor of a tiny airplane in the sky.

Before the final curtain fell Lindbergh had landed, and as the news spread from those thousands who watched him climb from the cockpit at Le Bourget airport to thousands of others in every corner of Paris, the fever turned into a hysterical celebration of welcome for the world's newest hero.

Driving back to Vaucresson alone, I realized that I was grinning the same happy grin I'd seen on every other face tonight. It was something you couldn't resist feeling pleased about, this great moment when all the vitality and daring spirit of America seemed to have touched France in the symbol of one boyishly appealing figure. I thought about the country he had taken off from less than thirty-four hours before he touched French soil, and felt again that warm affection for a land that had begun to claim my heart when I was a kid and had first heard its wonderful syncopated music.

Putting my key in the door, I was humming an American tune I was doing in my current show and toying with the pleasurable idea of possibly making another trip to the States.

But a moment later it was forgotten along with everything else that had happened tonight because I was sitting anxiously beside Yvonne, who lay on the couch trying to reassure me with a smile that didn't change the haggard look in her eyes.

"I'm just tired, Maurice. It's nothing to worry about."

I looked down at her, disturbed. Her face was like a mask,

drained of all animation and even her voice sounded lifeless. It didn't seem possible that fatigue alone could account for such a shocking change in the few hours since I'd left. "Darling, please," I said, starting to rise, "let me get Pauchet. I can have him here in a few minutes."

She caught at my hand. "No, honestly it isn't necessary. I'll be all right."

But next morning she wasn't and I waited concerned, an hour after I'd summoned him, for Victor Pauchet to emerge from our bedroom. His face was grave as he gestured me to follow him downstairs.

"Well?" I said anxiously.

"I don't know, Maurice." He shook his head thoughtfully. "There may be trouble with the baby. We'll just have to watch her and see."

I stood on the terrace looking after him till he disappeared from view, feeling the terrible helplessness that comes when suddenly there is a danger threatening which you are powerless to fight. I could only hope that somehow Pauchet would be wrong.

It was a futile hope, for he was right. There was going to be trouble and one day it became critical. Minutes after I had put through an urgent call, I had Yvonne beside me, small and white and silent while I concentrated on covering the road between Vaucresson and Pauchet's Paris clinic faster than I had ever risked driving it before.

In the waiting room of the hospital I rose abruptly as I already had a dozen times earlier and moved past wicker chairs and potted ferns to search the empty corridor again. Then a frosted glass door opened and Pauchet was coming toward me. He paused when he saw me, like a man in a pressing hurry who is reluctant to be detained.

"I've had her prepared for surgery, Maurice. We should operate immediately."

"Surgery?" I shook my head trying to clear it. I had been waiting long and anxiously for some word, but now what he was saying seemed too sudden to grasp. "But what about the baby?" I said, bewildered.

"I'm sorry, Maurice, there isn't any question of saving the baby any more. I'm operating to save Yvonne."

A few hours later I stood beside her narrow hospital bed while her nurses silently left the room. It shook me to see her face, pale against the pillows. She looked so vulnerable and lost and even in sleep so poignantly sad. My heart ached for the moment she would awaken, because that sadness would come awake with her and grow even sharper. I didn't realize the moment had already arrived until I leaned over to kiss her gently and saw the tears that had slipped silently from beneath her closed eyelids to run down the curve of her cheeks.

"Darling, it's going to be all right," I said softly, searching desperately for words that could comfort her.

She opened her eyes and they were filled with loss. "You don't have to pretend." It was a choked murmur. "I heard the nurses. I know about the baby." Her eyes closed again and she turned her head away.

"Believe me, darling," I pleaded and I meant it earnestly. "You'll be well again and everything *is* going to be all right." Like a ghost from the past the words echoed in my mind, and I realized they were the very ones Yvonne had appealed to me with one long-ago night in Saujon.

But my saying them and meaning them was not enough. Maybe if the baby had lived they would have come true. A child might have changed many things for us and given us a whole new foundation on which a strong happiness could be built. We would never know, because that chance was not to come to us again, and within a few months it was almost as if it hadn't happened the first time, because life reverted to the same bitter pattern of battle and strained truce.

I WAS at my dressing room table one night wiping the last traces of make-up from my face when the page announced that a man had come backstage at the Casino asking to meet me. I was tired and in no mood for strangers.

"Who is he?"

The page repeated the information he'd been given. A Mr. Irving Thalberg from a Hollywood studio called Metro-Gold-wyn-Mayer. He was in the corridor with his wife. "You should see her, Monsieur Maurice. American — and so beautiful."

His admiration was so candid I couldn't repress a smile, and, though I had no idea who they were, agreed to having them shown in. But as I rose to shake hands with the thin, somber-eyed man I was thinking he was much too young and almost shy in his manner to be anyone very important, and while his wife was indeed beautiful with her dancing, vivacious eyes, I hoped these two charming youngsters would be done with exchanging pleasantries with me soon and go.

"Your English is very good, Mr. Chevalier," she said warmly.

It was a compliment Americans seemed moved to offer any Frenchman who had gotten through a few sentences in their tongue without stumbling. It was a very nice and gracious thing to say, even if it wasn't always very true and I took it the way I thought it had been offered — not very seriously.

"That's very important now that pictures are talking," the man added soberly, and I nodded my agreement, a little at a loss. He looked at me for a moment, a strange appraising look. "If you'll make a screen test for me and it turns out well, I'm willing to offer you a Hollywood contract, Mr. Chevalier. Interested?"

It came out so flatly it sounded as if he were proposing a lunch date he didn't care too much about keeping, and I regarded him doubtfully. Hollywood had become the dreamed-of ultimate goal for thousands of performers all over the world. To succeed there was to arrive at the golden pinnacle of acclaim.

And surely those in a position to offer such a chance, I was thinking, would have more force and authority than this young stranger. Suddenly the notion hit me that someone had put him up to playing a clever practical joke on me and I decided abruptly to expose the bluff.

"I'm sorry, Mr. Thalberg," I said a little shortly, "but a screen test is out of the question." From the corner of my eye I caught sight of Max Ruppa, my secretary, in the doorway. His expression seemed a little strange but I was too intent on carrying out my plan to pay attention. "Either people are interested in hiring me or they're not. I don't audition any more!"

Very calmly he expressed his regrets and with his lovely lady turned and left. The instant they had cleared the door, Ruppa closed it and faced me with the agitation of a man on the verge of apoplexy.

"Maurice, what kind of game are you playing?" Then in an upset outburst he informed me that I had just turned away the king of the entire American film industry who had walked out of here with the new young queen of actresses, Norma Shearer!

For one frozen moment all I could think of was that I had better start going to the American films as often as my secretary obviously did. Then I opened the door and sent Ruppa rushing after Thalberg to offer whatever explanations he could invent en route. "If necessary tell him you work for a madman, but in any case tell him I'll be there for the test!"

And I was, the next day at a studio in Vincennes where I discovered, when the film was later run off, that despite my earlier doubts my face was what Hollywood deemed "photogenic." But then finally, after the mix-up had been straightened out and all the other hurdles cleared, Thalberg and I couldn't make a deal we both thought was fair. I had been given a copy of my screen test to keep and it looked as if it would be my only souvenir of a Hollywood film career, one I could put in a drawer and forget.

But it was back out of the drawer one morning only two short weeks later. I had had another Hollywood visitor in my dressing room, a wonderful man I was later to know well and love. Jesse Lasky was one of the heads of Paramount Studios and this time my response to the offer of a screen test as the preliminary step to a contract was quite different.

"Thanks to one of your confreres," I grinned, "I can save us both a lot of trouble." Then I explained what had happened with Thalberg.

"Good." He gave me his warm smile. "You bring the film to me. Eleven o'clock tomorrow morning. We'll look together."

WE HAD. And now with the chimes of an ornate mantel clock striking noon I took the cap from my fountain pen. Just sixty minutes ago I had walked into this room never dreaming that before I left it I would be signing a six-weeks contract with options to go to Hollywood under the auspices of the friendly man seated across from me.

After an enthusiastic parting handshake I left Lasky and with a copy of the contract crackling in my jacket pocket at every turn of the wheel, I drove eagerly toward Vaucresson, my happiness almost too much to contain. It kept spilling out of me in that wonderful kind of laughter that only comes when you feel the whole world is one enormous glass of champagne.

"It's a door opening for me that can lead to the absolute top of the sky," I heard myself telling Yvonne exuberantly. She was scanning the contract I had thrust into her hands a moment ago, but suddenly I couldn't wait for her to read through the paragraphs. I was too carried away with the wonderful elation I felt and my desire to have her share it with me. "Hollywood, signed and guaranteed! What do you think of that for an hour's accomplishment?"

Slowly she raised her eyes from the page. No trace of joy for the news I had brought showed in her gaze. Instead I saw doubt and suspicion. "Are you taking me with you, Maurice?"

The question hit me like a sharp knife. "Of course I am. Passage for both of us is part of the deal I made."

Now the smile I had been anticipating so eagerly came into her face. But her response was too late, for my own elation had suddenly dissolved.

I put the contract that was going to carry us to Hollywood back in my pocket, and I wondered what would happen to us in that strange city six thousand miles away. The way things were between us, how long could our marriage survive there, I asked myself. In fact, how long could it survive anywhere?

... *Sept*

THE *Ile de France* lay majestically at the dock in Le Havre.

Yvonne and I entered the best suite on her top deck and took in the incredibly opulent surroundings Paramount had arranged for us. I couldn't be sure for an instant whether this floating apartment, almost buried under an avalanche of bon voyage baskets, huge floral bouquets and endless stacks of wires and cards, was real or a hallucination of the fever I had been battling along with my other concerns: these past few hectic weeks.

Already I had begun to feel there might be more to worry about on this Hollywood venture than my personal difficulties with Yvonne. Soon after I had signed the contract

227

the studio's publicity department had taken over and my departure had been built up almost into a national event.

One interview after another was arranged and I faced a barrage of photographers daily. Beyond this, Paramount had given lavish dinners for actors and critics in my honor, and I had smiled through them all while a persistent question kept nagging at me: What honor? Despite this publicity I was really only sure of making a single picture. If my option wasn't picked up, that's all there would be. All, that is, except the ridiculous figure I'd make returning after the bubble had burst.

An hour out of harbor the perpetually enthusiastic public relations man who was sailing with us cornered me in the ship's bar as I waited for Yvonne. He looked a little bit the way a fight manager does when he steps into the ring to give his boxer last-minute coaching.

"It's all set, Maurice, you're at the Captain's table with everybody who matters. And I'm expecting you to win over every last one of them."

"Is this to be dinner or a performance?" I said a little apprehensively.

"Both. But you've got nothing to worry about. Just relax and be sophisticated."

"Sophisticated?" I looked at him, puzzled. "It's a word I've never heard. What is it?"

For an instant he seemed amazed, then he began to laugh. "Quit ribbing me. There isn't a Frenchman alive who doesn't understand that word!"

"Yes, there is," I said earnestly. "You're looking at him."

It was true, and I'm afraid, despite all the vague explanations he poured into my head, it still is today. If sophistication means knowing how to live, how to behave and things like that, then I suppose by now I am sophisticated because I have been through many experiences. But if it means being the kind of man Cole Porter writes about in his songs or Noel Coward portrays on the stage, then I have never become a sophisticate at all. Yet from that moment on it was a word which would hound me, because for nearly a decade I was not only supposed to understand sophistication, I was expected to give off great waves of it practically on command.

I began to wonder if all I had in common with the personality Paramount had signed was the same name. If they didn't want the Maurice Chevalier I had been in Paris, how could I hope to make the grade? Whatever success I had built had been won by honestly offering my own quality to the public. I was determined that somehow before I ever walked in front of a Hollywood camera I must convince the studio that my genuine self was surely more solid than a masquerade.

But my determination wavered before the ship had gotten halfway to New York.

The sun was low in the afternoon sky as I strolled toward the prow. It was my third time around the deck on this solitary promenade, and twice before as I'd passed, I had exchanged friendly salutes with an American journalist I'd gotten to know and like on the journey. His name was Mark Hellinger, and as I neared him again he fell into step with me. He had told me earlier that he'd come to see me with Al Jolson and his lovely young wife, Ruby Keeler, at one of my final performances in Paris.

"Look, Maurice," he said suddenly after we'd strolled in silence a few minutes. "There's something I've got to tell you." His amiable face furrowed with a concerned frown. "After I saw you in Paris I cabled New York that compared with Jolson you were a little anemic — and that I thought you'd flop in America."

His words took me by complete surprise and I stopped in my tracks, not knowing what to say. He drew me over to the rail and the frown seemed even deeper.

"Mind you," he went on with unhappy candor, "I still think

so. But since I've gotten to know you personally, I like you and I'm sorry I had to knock you. Yet how can I go back on my own judgment?" He sighed morosely. "I'm awfully sorry, Maurice, but what can I do?"

I gulped before I could find my voice. His honesty in his dilemma was so compelling it deserved as much in return.

"Well, Mark, it's not so grave." I struggled for a note of jauntiness which I didn't quite manage, because the truth itself was enough to deal with. "If what you wrote was right, I'll be in America such a short time it won't matter. And if you're wrong, let's say you owe me a column admitting it publicly."

Much later Mark Hellinger wrote that column and we became good friends, but as he left me at the rail that afternoon, I glanced down at the darkening water and wondered if maybe I should just jump now and save myself a lot of problems. The comforting thought that what I had offered audiences in Paris could win me success in America was no longer so comforting. At least where one American was concerned, my talent wasn't anything to write home about — except disparagingly.

The last night out I slit open a cable the cabin boy delivered to our suite. It was from Doug Fairbanks and I translated the warm, affectionate message to Yvonne. But when she'd gone back to her packing I read the words of welcome again, trying to ignore the nervous question inside of me. Welcome to what? Professional disaster, maybe?

But soon after dawn broke the next morning it more closely resembled a welcome to bedlam.

A tender packed with more than fifty reporters and photographers along with a handful of Paramount representatives had cut across New York Harbor to board ship and the power of the press was hitting me with such impact it was literally knocking me off my feet.

I felt I had been captured in the midst of a combat assault.

230

Photographers grabbed my arms and legs and in the spinning melee it looked as if the entire world had somehow crowded onto that single deck.

A thousand cries seemed to be ringing in my ears at the same instant. "Come on, Maurice, let's have that big smile!" "Wave your hat in the air!" "Where's Madame?" "Give us a big, 'Hello, New York' look!" Again and again and again. And through it all the cameras never stopped clicking. Yvonne was swept up and perched on the rail. Smiles. Waves. Handshakes. For a solid hour the carnival continued and then as much of the human tide as could wedge itself through the door flowed into our suite for champagne and questions. On land prohibition was still the law in 1928, but aboard ship it didn't apply. It was an interview vigorously punctuated by the sound of popping corks.

During the next few days, carried on a whirlwind round of receptions and the high spots of New York, I marched to the ceaseless rhythm of publicity drums. Then the most exaggerated drum roll of all ended with a band breaking into the "Marseillaise" at the end of a five-day train ride. With the French national anthem blaring in my ears, as if I were a war hero approaching the Arc de Triomphe, I stepped onto the station platform to face Hollywood.

THE first film I was to make was called *Innocents of Paris*. There was a song I'd be doing in it that was going to be my first big popular hit in English, and as it had been with "Valentine," now another girl was coming into my life to stay with me for the rest of my career. This time her name was "Louise."

Talking pictures were just beginning to get under way and a full roster of silent films had tied up all the huge shooting stages at Paramount by day. So, a little like the new baby brother in the crowded family, our picture was being squeezed into the schedule in the only space left. We would have to shoot at night.

But before the filming ever began I was brought to Paramount for my first look at this bizarre new world and to meet some of the giants who labored behind its imposing grillwork gates: Adolphe Menjou, so warmly amiable; Emil Jannings, the eccentric German whose brilliant power as an actor had already made him a legend; Clara Bow, with her tousled mane of red hair and intense black eyes, who generated sex appeal and excitement with breath-taking ease. Hollywood had brought each of them international fame, yet this did nothing to bolster my own hopes for achieving it.

At least for the moment my worries about having to play a "sophisticate" had been assuaged, because there was surely nothing sophisticated in the role of the simple Parisian ragpicker I would soon be portraying. But another fear had cropped up to replace it. Except for a few already established stars, all the Hollywood actors seemed so handsome and young. I was nearly forty and I had spent enough hours making up my face to know what it looked like. I doubted that I was as youthful and dashing as I'd need to be for my Hollywood camera debut.

I had confided my fears to Emil Jannings.

"Just forget there is a camera." In his dressing room he emphasized his words with intense gestures, speaking in an almost unintelligible Teutonic accent. "Forget wrinkles and double chins and profiles. The movies need more true personalities. Less empty beauty. Forget everything except playing sincerely."

Three months later that accent which I had found so difficult to understand had cost Emil Jannings his eminence in Hollywood. He had conquered the heights in silent films but his battle with English for the talking screen would never be won. Soon after he had collected an Oscar as the outstanding actor of 1928, the studio let him go and he returned to Germany forever. I didn't dream that afternoon that fate had a strange and frightening sequel planned for Jannings and me more than a dozen years hence. All I knew then was that he had offered me a valuable piece of advice and I was grateful.

Determined to practice it I faced the first night's shooting with fewer qualms than I had expected to be suffering.

The one who seemed strangely nervous was Yvonne. When it was time for me to leave for the studio I came through the living room of the delightful little house we had rented, to say good-by. It was perched on the mountain overlooking Beverly Hills and I found her standing at the window watching the winking lights coming on in curving patterns below.

She turned abruptly as if she had been waiting for me and I saw that she was dressed to leave the house. "Are you ready, Maurice?"

"Yes," I said a little surprised, "but where are you going?"

"With you."

She hadn't mentioned a word about it until now and my startled reaction must have shown in my face. "Yvonne," I protested, "that's ridiculous. I'll be working all night."

"I don't care." Her voice was a little breathless and I saw her hands tighten in strain as she clutched her purse. "I still want to go with you."

It seemed almost like an urgent appeal and I looked down at her, suddenly wondering if the prospect of staying alone in this house was at the bottom of her taut mood. She was never frightened at Vaucresson, I was thinking, but this is still a strange, unfamiliar land. In the few weeks we had been here, more than once I had known that sense of being lost and alien myself. Yvonne would have to adjust to her new surroundings, but I wasn't going to ask that of her tonight when she seemed so tense and unsure.

As we drove down the twisting mountain road together her

face was enough to tell me she was completely relaxed now. And my own mood was lifted by the thought that I was en route to making my first Hollywood picture, liberated from the fear of what the camera could do to me.

But I soon learned that all the dangers in making a film are not mechanical.

It was a lesson taught me by a six-year-old professor with a face of such enchanting innocence that at first glance you would surely think the angels themselves had loaned him to Paramount for the picture.

He was playing a small waif I had adopted after I had fished him out of the Seine. His mother had jumped in with him and the script dictated that the poor lady drown, leaving the tot to face life with me in my garret. The scene we had come to in the shooting called for him to be overcome with despair as he remembered his mother and to weep inconsolable tears. I was to put one hand around his neck paternally, rest the other on his thin little shoulder, and speak tenderly in an effort to comfort him. But still the tears were to pour until, beside myself to stem his grief, I was to sing him a funny little song which miraculously would turn the trick. The scene wasn't exactly written by Victor Hugo, you see? Still, we had rehearsed it until the director was satisfied it would play and he called for a take.

With the cameras turning I kneeled and began to speak into his small wet face.

"Cut!" the director shouted.

I got to my feet and a moment later a second take was called. Again at the place where I put my arm around the boy, the director abruptly halted the scene. This time I moved off camera and faced him, upset. "What's gone wrong?"

He took me by the shoulder and walked me over to a remote corner. "Maurice," he said gently, "the kid is taking you over the hurdles." I looked at him, baffled. "That little pro is pulling the oldest trick in the business on you. He's backing away just far enough so you'll have to turn away from camera to speak. On the screen it'll be a scene between his tear-stained face and the back of your neck."

I shook my head, finding it hard to believe that after nearly thirty years in the business I could be taken in by such an appealing little crook. And when he had been called to account by the director and protested his innocent regret in quite a beguiling way, I began to think surely it was just a lack of concentration that had made the child's feet wander and pull me out of position.

I was surer of it than ever when we went through another rehearsal in which he stood absolutely still and all was perfect.

Then the camera started again, and once more on my knees with my hands about his neck and shoulder I was speaking tenderly when suddenly I felt that I was trying to hold on to an octopus. The little rascal had begun to side-step his way into upstaging me again. Now all my doubts as to who was innocent and who was the victim fell away. Without permitting a single note of the tenderness in my voice to change, I nailed him to the spot with a viselike grip. It was a pitched battle with a tiny, squirming monster, but I managed finally to complete the scene with at least my profile showing.

When shooting ended and I followed Yvonne beyond the heavy metal door of the sound stage, the sun had just come up and the morning air was still wetly cool. As I wrapped a coat around her shoulders I saw the lines of fatigue in her face. She had sat in a corner of the enormous drafty interior where we worked for the whole night, and there is nothing more tiring in the making of movies than simply sitting.

Yet for five nights now she had insisted on coming to the studio with me. She was wearing herself out staying up all night with me and then half the day with arrangements around the house. "Yvonne," I said gently as we drove away from the lot, "this is silly. It's not good for you to be on the set all night; you should be asleep."

"I'm all right, Maurice. Please don't worry about me."

"But I do. You look so weary."

"I'll get used to it," she said tightly.

Used to it? The words had come out automatically without any thought, and it chilled me. Suddenly I realized that Yvonne apparently had no intention of staying home, even after Hollywood ceased to be an unfamiliar place. This was to be a permanent arrangement. I was to go on working night after night with her small, implacable figure waiting in the shadows, her eyes fastened on my every move. This was her motive, I was thinking with helpless anger. Suspicion. Whether we were in France or America it was still the same.

Silently I drove through the streets that were just coming to life, biting my tongue to keep back the resentment I felt. We had been in this new country so short a time and already the rancor was beginning. Somehow we must try and hold it back.

Two days later Paramount notified me officially that they were exercising the option in my contract. This meant that after I completed this first film I would begin a full year for them with better terms. They had viewed the first rushes, those chunks of unedited film that contain each day's disconnected scenes, and though they couldn't know now how the picture would be received, they had considered me promising enough to take a gamble. At least I wouldn't return to France a complete failure.

But I was still a long way from success, I was thinking, as I walked across the lot to begin the night's shooting. Even in this medium where one performed in front of a machine instead of an audience, it was nonetheless up to an eventual audience to decide if you had anything worth applauding. For that decision I would have to wait till the picture was finished and judged.

At last the night arrived. In a large theatre in downtown Los Angeles *Innocents of Paris* was being previewed before an audience of regular movie-goers along with a sprinkling of Paramount stars and executives, all eager to learn how I would fare in my Hollywood debut. I paused for an instant on the sidewalk for a last nervous puff of my cigarette, tensely aware that before I emerged from this ornate movie palace I would have the verdict: Good enough — or not good enough.

I had found seats for Yvonne and me in the middle of the orchestra, apart from the studio group.

"If it's going to be bad," I whispered as the titles appeared on the screen, "I'd rather be among strangers." This way I would at least be spared from somebody leaning over to tell me the harsh truth before the film had ended.

It was dim comfort and it didn't last long. In a cold sweat I had been watching the film for only five minutes when I discovered I had my own personal critic seated directly in front of me. He was a large fellow physically, and though his clothes and accent were American, he was certainly related in type to the rough, burly dockworkers I'd played to in Marseilles.

Suddenly he shifted his large bulk and turned to face his pal beside him. In a hoarse stage whisper he rendered his capsule review of what he'd seen so far. "Lousy."

From that moment on I was mesmerized. No matter what happened on the screen I found my eyes glued to that huge frame, holding my breath, trying to read his reactions. All I got for my efforts were a few grunts until, a little later in the picture, one of my songs apparently was more to his taste, and he gave his pal a hearty shove in the ribs to indicate his approval. Then still later he nearly knocked me out of my seat when he responded to a little joke I had just made with a sudden jolting belly laugh. And finally, when he and the rest of the audience applauded after I had sung "Louise," I found that at last I could breathe a little more normally.

But *Innocents of Paris* was no epic, and as I followed Yvonne across the lobby when it was over, I was worried.

"Maurice!" It was a familiar voice and I turned to see Adolphe Menjou trying to catch up with me in the crowd.

In a moment he was at my side, shaking my hand warmly. "I won't kid you, Maurice," he said with his genial smile, "the picture's not the greatest. But you!" His eyes were dancing with enthusiasm. "You are going to be the greatest French success America will ever see!"

He meant it genuinely and I found myself swallowing hard trying to thank him. What a swing the pendulum had taken! In a little over an hour I had graduated from that flat, growled "lousy" to this glowing prediction. It wasn't conclusive proof yet that I had made it, but my notices were certainly looking up.

Menjou's response wasn't the only optimistic one I encountered after that preview. A few days later, as I was coming out of one of the executive offices at Paramount after a conference over my imminent trip to New York, where I was to combine a four-weeks personal-appearance stint with advance publicity for the picture, a small round figure accosted me in the hall.

He looked a little like a droll, cigar-smoking cherub but I already knew from his reputation that Ernst Lubitsch was one of the most brilliant directors in Hollywood. He was a man of strong, positive opinions delivered in a deceptively mild fashion, and I listened attentively to what he thought of my work in *Innocents of Paris*, happy to have earned this man's praise.

"I am walking around with a film musical in my head, Maurice. Now I will put it on paper." He pointed his finger at me to underline his decision. "I have found my hero."

The possibility of working with Lubitsch filled me with happy anticipation which increased when he told me that this first large-scale musical operetta the studio would be undertaking was based on a French property. There wouldn't even be the problem of trying to play a role too far removed from my own personality, I was thinking. But when he began to outline the story which would be called *Love Parade*, my hopes fell down to my feet.

"The hero is a prince?" I said, dismayed. "You see *me* as a prince?"

He nodded and I shook my head in practically the same instant. "I'm sorry," I said. "I'm flattered, but it's impossible. A fisherman? Yes, that I could play or any other kind of man from a simple background. It's what I am and it's in the way I talk and the way I walk and everything I like and understand. But an aristocrat? Believe me, in a royal uniform I would make the most ludicrous-looking prince on the screen!"

He smiled at me blandly. "All right, Maurice, I'll believe. If it's true." His smile became more persuasive. "Otherwise, I still have my hero. Agreed?"

Lubitsch proposed a test I couldn't turn down and I set off on a whirlwind tour with him of the make-believe land that is Hollywood. Our first port of call was the costumer's, and he steered me into a vast, crammed building where iron racks and drawers and boxes overflowed with all the trimmings needed to turn an ordinary man into a cowboy, a fire chief or a knight. But an outfit that could turn me into a prince? I seriously doubted that all the trappings of this entire establishment could pull off that trick.

The single-minded director, however, didn't share my qualms, and he kept returning to where I was trying on various combinations of elegant riding trousers and boots and coats to evaluate, frown and return for still another assault on the racks. Finally I buttoned myself into a garish tunic that earned his approving nod and took the royal shako a wardrobe man handed me to crown the regal image. It was a foot and a half high.

Balancing it a little shakily on my head I turned to survey the results in a full-length mirror. "Perfect," I told Lubitsch wryly. "Now I'm ready to play the part of an overdressed extra."

"We'll see," he said cryptically. "Come."

The next stop was a session with a photographer. His assignment was to shoot me from every angle in my strange getup, and the decision about how princely I could look would lie in the pictures. As I creaked around in my stiff leather boots while he clicked away, I was thinking how admirable his self-control was. He hadn't so much as smiled. And I was sure that in his position I would have broken down in helpless laughter at the comical figure I must be cutting.

Approaching Lubitsch's office the next day, certain that the still pictures would have proved me right, I was already framing a little speech of regret in my mind. Suddenly his door burst open and to the astonishment of everybody in the corridor, he rushed toward me triumphantly brandishing a batch of photos, shouting in glee for all of Paramount to hear: "Splendid, Maurice! Marvelous! *You are a prince!*"

I looked at the shots and shook my head in amazement. The proof of what Lubitsch had been able to see all along was there now before my eyes. We shook hands on the deal and I grinned down at the small man whose imagination was big enough to turn me into royalty.

From the first day of rehearsal under Lubitsch's talented guidance I found him an almost magic man to work with. He was supposed to be a very difficult director with American actors, but for me he seemed the easiest person in the world to understand. Just from the expression in his eye I could see what he wanted and somehow always produce it. And that bond of creative respect and sympathy seemed to affect the rest of the company as well, including the charming young red-haired beauty named Jeanette MacDonald he had discovered singing in a Chicago musical comedy and brought out to be my partner.

When *Love Parade* was finished, Lubitsch promised to cable me the results of the preview, and Yvonne and I left immediately for Paris. From the moment we arrived the front pages of the papers were filled with the news of my homecoming, and if I had voyaged to Mars and back the excitement couldn't have been greater than on this first return to my native soil from Hollywood.

Innocents of Paris had opened here, and it seemed as if everyone in the city had seen it at least once and emerged from the theatre to join in the incredible festival of acclaiming my success. It felt a little out of proportion as crowds thronged to greet me everywhere and a host of banquets and receptions were organized in my honor, but I was tasting again and again that marvelous special joy of the man who has come home after making good.

My head might have been in danger of spinning around completely, because the intoxication of finding yourself suddenly the idol of your own people can make you giddier than a hundred glasses of champagne. But one thought in the back of my mind kept sobering me for balance. No falling star can plunge into oblivion faster than a one-picture movie star whose second film is bad. It was something that nobody else in Paris seemed to be worrying about, however, for the extravagant welcome the capital was offering me continued undiminished for weeks.

"It's no more than my son deserves," La Louque said and the gentle familiar smile I adored was on her face, but her voice had a remote, faraway quality in it now.

"You're a lovely prejudiced lady," I teased and kissed her serene forehead, but when I looked into her eyes there was no answering spark of humor, and I realized a little poignantly that my beloved La Louque was older now and tired, rather like a lamp that is beginning to dim.

The final two weeks of my stay found me again occupying the same dressing room at the Empire from which I had stepped forth one night fearfully to face my first Parisian audience after my nervous breakdown, when Yvonne had been my shield against anxiety. Now I looked around the flower-crammed room in the midst of this special sellout engagement and it hit me with bitter irony that all the problems that had seemed unconquerable that long-ago night had been licked, and it was the girl who had seen me through it who had become the gravest problem in my life.

"Cable, Monsieur Chevalier," the page called from the doorway and an instant later my eyes were racing across the words Ernst Lubitsch had sent from half a world away. The message seemed to have too many superlatives to be true, but there was no doubting the success he was reporting. It ended, "You are sitting on top of the world, Maurice."

I read the last line aloud and liked the sound of it. Maybe if *Love Parade* did as well at the box office as seemingly it had at its preview, I wasn't going to be a one-picture star after all.

. . . Huit

LOVE PARADE was released to break box-office records around the world and Paramount, which had already tripled my salary after *Innocents of Paris*, voluntarily ripped up my contract once more. Suddenly, after just two films, I was earning what the greatest, long-established stars were being paid, and I could only shake my head and wonder if fate were working out some kind of strange balance providing more than full measure of reward in my career to compensate for the lack of joy in my personal life.

Yvonne and I had just returned from New York where we had shot my third picture. Still being edited, it was to be called *The Big Pond*. The studio had decided to make two versions, one in English and the other in French, so

243

we had to find a bilingual actress to play the feminine lead. In a Broadway theatre I watched a young woman on stage who I was told had been born in France but emigrated with her family to America. She was lovely, brunette, talented and a delicious comedienne, and her English was perfect. So far, so good.

In her dressing room between acts I chatted with her in French. It too was marvelous. I had found my partner, and she signed the next day. Soon afterwards we began shooting, and from that first day on the set it was apparent that a charming new star was on her way to the top.

Her name? Claudette Colbert.

I was to make another film with Claudette, but time and work and exciting events would intervene first, for my life was racing at a breakneck pace these days. On the train back to Hollywood I had viewed the magnificent breadth of America as it moved past my window, trying to comprehend the immensity of what had happened to me here in one short year. Though I honestly didn't think I deserved it all, I had soared higher in that brief span than in my twenty-eight earlier years as a performer. Ah, what a fabulous country, I was thinking, fabulous!

Seated opposite me in the compartment Yvonne was reading, and I glanced at her face which even now didn't seem completely relaxed. This new life of ours was obviously filled with a relentless tension for her, yet she seldom tried to talk it out with me, just as I had practically ceased to share my hopes and fears with her.

It had not always been so. I remembered the early days when she had stood beside me, when I had needed her so much, and I couldn't help reflecting that our relationship had gradually weakened and wilted as each day I required her strength less to sustain me. It saddened me to realize that though we had never had a powerful, compelling love, now we had little or nothing left of what once had at least been a friendship.

And friendship must be a part of an enduring marriage. If

you can have a woman that you like in your arms and at the same time a woman that you like to have in your heart, then you're very rich. When you have both the physical happiness and the spiritual happiness, a good friend to run to for understanding and response, then you're truly blessed. It seemed to me, as I gazed at Yvonne silently, that I had none of this and I regretted it achingly.

I doubted that strong love could ever come to us now. But could we at least revive some measure of friendship? If we found a common meeting ground, an interest we both shared, it might help. Work, I was thinking. Yvonne had a career once, why not again? There would be professional problems for her to solve, and if we tackled them together, perhaps it would bring a little amity between us. I said nothing aloud, but I determined to find a part for her in my next picture.

In the French version of *Le Petit Café*, I found it, but the attempt to use work as a bulwark for our faltering marriage failed. Yvonne had little interest in a movie career. Waiting for a set to be struck the first day of shooting, I saw it clearly when I ventured the idea that this role could surely lead to others if her English continued to improve. She merely shrugged in response, and I knew that one more possible support had been pulled out from beneath us. I wondered how many were left before total collapse.

During this film the dressing room next to mine was taken over by a new tenant, a startling young woman with long, beautiful legs and feline grace and an entrancing, mysterious face. Marlene Dietrich had just come from Germany and a sensational success in *The Blue Angel*. Now she was at Paramount to make *Morocco* with Gary Cooper.

Every man in the studio was quickly aware of this ravishing girl. She sought no one's company, moved across the lot almost like a sleepwalker, looking neither to right nor left and speaking not a word. She was not unfriendly, you understand, she was simply not there at all, and though I was tempted to talk with her, it was better not to risk her disdain or Yvonne's disapproval.

And in a few days she was gone, for their shooting had moved elsewhere. Marlene and I had never spoken, but she had been a lovely vision to brighten the day, and I was a little disappointed. I did not know then that one day we would meet again. And this time we would speak long and earnestly.

PUBLIC reaction to *Love Parade* had turned into hysteria. A kind of Chevalier fever had broken out everywhere, so that in theatres all over America professionals and amateurs alike were doing imitations of me and I was being deluged with offers, each more phenomenal than the last.

But in every fever there is a little distortion, a little bit of going away from the calm and reasonable. Every place I went now there were crowds and ovations and receptions and autograph seekers, and suddenly it seemed to me that I was living in a goldfish bowl. The movies had made me familiar to millions, but they had also robbed me of any semblance of privacy. The walks I had always loved to take, wandering through busy streets to window-shop, were impossible. Mind you, in Paris it had once been a very warm feeling when the smiles or the friendly "hellos" of strangers who had seen me in the theatre marked my strolls. But it was something very different now. Something flattering and disturbing at the same time.

And London marked the peak of it. A few years earlier Yvonne and I had been greeted here with only the splash of Lew Leslie's publicity for his ill-fated *White Birds*. This time Victoria Station was a mob scene. Arriving to fill a two-weeks singing engagement, I was caught up in a tide of almost twenty

246

thousand boisterous, welcoming fans. A hundred mounted police-men and as many more on foot struggled to hold them back behind barriers.

I looked at the faces around me. Love, passion, worship seemed to be written there, and when I spoke a few idiotic phrases into the microphone to this assemblage, those emo-tions erupted into a frenzy. The police forced a way through the crowd for Yvonne and me to reach our car, and while some women fainted, others screamed endearments or begged me for a smile or fought just to touch me or tear at my clothes.

With today's animated teen-agers, this sort of demonstration toward a Frank Sinatra or an Elvis Presley is perhaps not so unusual, but these were not children caught up in this wave of madness. They were adults, and their outburst had me in a sweat until the car pulled away to leave this nightmare of pop-ularity behind.

I couldn't believe it a few days later when it appeared that the immortal George Bernard Shaw had joined my throng of admirers. My producer was so excited he was stammering. "He sent word that he wants to meet you, Maurice, and what a story this will make!"

This was a little too much adulation, I thought unhappily, and I tried to refuse the invitation.

"If you don't accept this honor," he said in a choking voice, "you'll insult the whole country, don't you realize that?"

So it was all arranged with full details, of course, for the eager newspapers. Columns were devoted that night to George Bernard Shaw and Maurice Chevalier, our names linked as if we were an acrobatic team or a soft-shoe act.

But I was worried. Shaw was a writer whose reputation I knew better than his works; yet with two shows a day, dozens of interviews and performances at charity balls, there was no time to cram those works into my head. He would know everything about me, and I would simply look like a fool where he was concerned. I began to dread our impending meeting.

In his house near Piccadilly we were introduced. Tall, thin, straight, white-bearded and with blue eyes of an unnerving intensity, he was a striking, superbly vital man. And this intellectual giant is one of my fans, I was saying to myself, it's unbelievable. But what happens when he discovers that I've never been a fan of George Bernard Shaw?

From the first I felt uneasy, because we were regarding each other in silence for a moment and I could think of nothing to talk about in order to get the conversation started. Then Shaw broke the ice to say that he'd read all about me in the papers, that he was interested in the qualities of a man who had warmed up the traditionally cool English crowds.

To this I nodded uncomfortably and we went on speaking generalities for what seemed an eternity. All the while I was perspiring in an agony of embarrassment, wondering how much longer before we would reach the subject of Shaw and reveal my ignorance. Then a sudden twinkle came in his eye and, horrified, I knew that in my anxiety I must have made some blunder.

"Monsieur," the great man said, "you look like a very nice chap, so I'm going to speak frankly and enough of this equivocation. I never go to the films and seldom the theatre, and I know absolutely nothing about you."

I'd heard of the Shavian wit, and this was surely a joke, so I managed a weak smile.

"I don't even know if you're a tenor, a baritone or a bass. But I'm a writer, and I was curious to meet the man who could stir up a broth in my country such as you've done. Now, tell me something about yourself."

He was not joking. For an instant my smile was frozen in place, and then I saw the humor of this whole episode. Shaw and Chevalier were no team, after all, for neither one really knew the first thing about the other. Though I said nothing aloud, I wanted to laugh and confess, "Monsieur Shaw, you've made things easy with your frankness, because now I can tell you for my part that I've never read a single one of your plays!"

Relieved and amused because all our cards had been set firmly on the table, I enjoyed the rest of my visit with George Bernard Shaw to the fullest. And I hadn't really lost a fan, I realized, for I had never had this one in the first place.

Success is a tenuous, precarious pedestal. You scramble and struggle and strive to reach it, and once there you must then fight to maintain the quality, that personal something which brought you plaudits, or you will topple back again. It is a delicate balance that keeps you there, believe me, and every performer must worry about it or lose.

I was feeling the tension of this concern the first Sunday night in New York after our return from England. Tomorrow morning, in a Long Island studio, shooting would begin on a new film. Lubitsch would direct it and that was to the good, and it was pleasing that Claudette Colbert would be in *The Smiling Lieutenant* with me and a new blond actress destined for important things, Miriam Hopkins. But the picture was riding on my shoulders, and it was a weight. Hours passed before I drifted off to troubled sleep.

The sound of knocking invaded my dreams and then brought me to consciousness. It was morning. Still groggy, I took the cable from the bellboy at the door, but the cruel words on the paper shocked me harshly awake as I read them. The message was from Paris. La Louque was dead. My gentle, sweet, adored mother had not been sick. The lamp had simply burned out and she had died.

I turned to Yvonne with a cry of anguish, and I felt drained inside as if half of my own being were dead as well. Waves of despair were sweeping over me and terrible sobs racking me as

I realized that never again would I see La Louque, and it broke my heart to think that in her last moment when she needed me most I had been three thousand miles away.

On the set I went mechanically through a confusion of gay, grinning scenes that went on for days. And at the end of each one I would stumble back to my dressing room aching with loss and helpless to hold back my tears. But of course grief finally is softened, and one day the tears came no more and a memory filled their place which has never dimmed since. Right now I can tell you truly that La Louque seems always close to me, just as she was alive.

When I returned to Hollywood it was to do still another film in the same genre with me in uniform, smiles and cute winks of the eye. And one more with Jeanette MacDonald, *One Hour with You*. "Cute." It began to be the perfect word to describe all my roles, and suddenly an old fear was reviving in me. From my early days with Mist I had been aware that no performer could simply stand still in his work.

Paramount didn't agree. "You're commercial, Maurice," they would tell me. "Look at the box office for the answer."

I should have expected it. Hollywood must depend on the support of the mass audience to make money, and apparently I had an appeal for that audience. But I was more than the *boulevardier* I was playing, a much deeper Parisian than that. To win the public on the stage in France, I had been forced to be more than a glib fellow with no real depth of emotion. Knowing this, I wanted to show Hollywood that I could do more than be a cute lady-killer.

But my contract with Paramount was far from expiration and they were calling the tune. So I went on singing in the key they demanded, unhappy that Hollywood and I didn't really understand each other.

It was not all I failed to understand one weekend at Pickfair, the magnificent estate of Douglas Fairbanks and Mary Pickford, where every Sunday a group of their friends gathered for lunch and later for tennis or a swim. Yvonne and I were here often, for Mary and Doug were our closest American friends.

I was standing at the edge of the pool while Doug, who was a marvelous athlete, went through a startling routine of dives from the high board and even the roof of the clubhouse. I was dressed rather nattily in a gray flannel suit from London, not exactly the attire for swimming. But Doug thought so. He grabbed me from behind and before I could protest tossed me headfirst into the pool. As I went under I heard a roar of laughter from the crowd.

All I could think of as I pushed myself to the surface was my ruined clothes and expensive wrist watch. Coughing and spluttering I floundered through the water to the ladder and out. Doug was almost crying from laughing so hard, but I had nothing to say. I looked like a wet dog and I began to shiver with a chill. Everyone was still laughing and I honestly wanted to join them, but I couldn't even smile.

This type of humor and my own brand of French wit were miles apart. I found nothing amusing in a practical joke like this, for I had known too much poverty to joke about wrecking a fine suit and a wrist watch I had dreamed for years of owning. True, I made enough money now to afford many of each, but still it could not be funny to a man who had lived through near starvation as a boy. Believe me, when you have experienced that, you don't laugh at someone who throws away bread just to be doing it or lights a cigar with a five-dollar bill.

But Doug, who was to remain my good, good friend until his death, slapped me on the shoulder and said with a grin, "Maurice, you have no sense of humor!"

And in the way he meant it, I had to agree. Yes, there were so many ways in which Hollywood and I did not exactly understand each other.

JOSEPHINE CHEVALIER.

The gold letters were engraved in the simple stone above La Louque's grave in the Cemetery of St. Vincent, and I stood in this tranquil corner high on a Paris hill drawing comfort from the woman who had helped me so often before.

This first time home without La Louque had made Paris seem a lonelier place, but at the same time I had been drawn more strongly than ever by my city. Now, leaving once more for Hollywood and a new film brought poignantly to mind how much I loved the trees and buildings and the streets and the sky of Paris. And loving America also, I was torn between the two.

I would not see Paris or this last resting place of La Louque again for another year, and I was saying *au revoir* to both this afternoon. There was still good-by to be said to Yvonne — unexpected, for after she'd had an operation this summer at Victor Pauchet's clinic I had assumed we would return together to Hollywood.

"If you're due back, Maurice," Pauchet had said, "you should go alone. Yvonne needs a few more weeks of convalescence before a trip like that."

When we talked of my going by myself, Yvonne's face had revealed nothing, yet I wondered if she felt as I did, that this first separation could have an enormous meaning for us. It would give each of us a chance to think straight without the subtle influence of the other. In the time we would be apart it would let us find out if there were truly anything at all left between us. Absence can make the heart grow fonder perhaps, but it can also make it wiser.

If La Louque had been alive this day, I would have been able to talk of this with her. But now I could only drop the flowers I had brought upon her silent tomb and say farewell.

ENTERING the studio restaurant on my first day back at Paramount, I glanced around the room for familiar faces. My eyes met the half-mocking gaze of Marlene Dietrich, whom I hadn't seen since her arrival so long ago, and surprisingly she gave me a faint, languid smile of recognition. She sat alone at a table near the center of the room, and as I nodded an answering hello, I had a sudden unexplainable and uncontrollable impulse to forego lunch for the moment and cross directly to this seductive woman's side and tell her how marvelous she had been in *The Blue Angel*, which I had just seen in Europe. I think she was as astonished as I when I exploded into raptures about her performance and how the audience was captivated, myself among them. But she shook my hand and thanked me and for an instant that challenging indifference of hers disappeared.

When I moved to my table I felt the curious stares of everyone on me and realized that I had probably taken the room aback with my enthusiasm. Still, I had no regrets for my whim. Instead I felt a sense of accomplishment and as light as a bird that I had done exactly as the spirit moved me. If Yvonne had been here, it would never have happened. I'd had my first glimpse in years, I was thinking, of the dangerous pleasure in leaping first and looking afterwards.

After that encounter Marlene at least lowered the barrier between us enough to exchange good mornings when we passed on the lot or met outside our dressing rooms which were separated only by Jeanette MacDonald's. And in a few days it was not surprising that we should have tea together. We had a great deal in common — our profession, reactions to America, my own country which she adored. It was inevitable that once we got to know each other we should be good friends.

We became exactly that, for Marlene was an extraordinary comrade, a woman of great intelligence and sensitivity, spiritual, kind, amusingly and charmingly unpredictable in her moods. In the weeks Yvonne was in Paris, we dined together in public and went dancing and found distraction in each other's company and conversation from the rigorous routine of work. It was simply camaraderie, but it was bound to be seized upon by columnists who needed choice items for hungry readers. We ignored the comments, for they deserved nothing more, but I couldn't ignore Yvonne's imminent return. From past experience I could surely predict her reaction to this friendship I had formed. Yet I'd had a taste of independence, and I was ready to fight before I relinquished it again.

The day I drove to the station the sky was cloudless and so blue it made you gasp with the brilliance of it, and in the distance the cragged Sierra Madre peaks shimmered in the thin air. But the beauty of this glorious autumn day had left my mind by the time I reached the platform and waited for the train to rumble to a halt. Suddenly the moment of encounter with Yvonne was upon me, and every nerve in my body was tense with the strain of it.

I moved along the cars, scanning each window for a glimpse of her, and then I saw her emerge near the end of the train and glance around hesitantly. She seemed a little drawn, but as we embraced I told her that she looked wonderful.

"Thank you," she said and then after a few restrained questions about her trip, we lapsed into silence while her bags were being brought to the car. Oddly there didn't seem to be very much to say.

We maintained the same uneasy quiet for most of the drive to Beverly Hills. It was like the moment of stillness before a big storm explodes, and I was sure by the time I pulled the car into the driveway that Yvonne had either read in the columns about my public appearances with Marlene or had been quickly told on her arrival in New York by that kind of good friend who loves to drop such malicious tidbits.

I had guessed right. We were hardly inside our house before Yvonne dropped her coat on a chair in the living room and turned to face me with a look that was empty of all sympathy and understanding. I knew the scene was coming, and helplessly

254

I felt my hostility rise to answer the inevitable attack. And so it began.

First reproaches, then angry accusations and when these were not stemmed there followed harsh, cold threats. It was all the unpleasantness between us that I had dreaded and more, and neither of us was sparing the other's feelings. Certain words should never be said between two people, for they are too cruel ever to be erased and you can never buy them back. They are the words that come when human passions rip through and shred forever the last veil of all pretense, and there remains only the naked, violent, ugly truth of your feelings.

Yvonne and I were doing this now; I knew it even as it was happening, yet we couldn't stop ourselves. The dam holding back so much of the resentment and incompatibility that had filled our years together had finally broken and we were drowning in the flood. As we shouted irreparable phrases back and forth, our marriage, which had been kept together without reason for so long, simply disintegrated in front of our eyes. The last support was gone. It was over, at last crumbled beyond repair.

Perhaps the original mistake was mine, for I had married Yvonne without a strong, complete love. But I had honestly tried to make it work because I had an immense gratitude to her for all she had done for me, and an appreciation for that time would be in me forever. She had been willing to do anything in the world for me when I needed her, but she wanted my soul in return and this unhappily I could not give. Now the moment of reckoning was here.

It was to be a painful process, this dissolution of a bond. Divorce is always painful, and ours was no different. In the days that followed our initial explosion there were long discussions of property and interests between us, meetings that resembled exactly the coming to terms in a contract negotiation. A contract for freedom. I accepted everything Yvonne asked, so that financially she would be taken care of for life.

Ironically, though our marriage had died in Hollywood, its death knell rang four hundred and fifty miles away in San Francisco, for I had agreed to play a week's engagement there and the date arrived before Yvonne and I had said our final words. In a hotel room that overlooked the city with the waters of the Golden Gate gleaming in the distance, we reached the end.

She was returning to Hollywood on a train that left in an hour. I stopped her at the door. We were two strangers saying farewell in the afternoon. "Yvonne," I said slowly and I meant it with all my heart, "I hope you'll find the man I didn't prove to be."

Her eyes met mine levelly. Then with a sad smile she turned and was gone. I closed the door and moved back inside the room, weighted with a kind of heavy regret at what had really been the only great failure in my life.

I would never marry again, I was thinking. I could not face the hazard of it a second time, though it was not marriage itself that frightened me. It was the fear that I might once more fail to find the woman with whom I could share passion and friendship, the woman who could respond to the gift of love I felt was within me to give. And a second such failure I could not endure.

No, whatever love had in store for me, it must surely never again be marriage.

If love were what the rose is,
    And I were like the leaf,
Our lives would grow together
    In sad or singing weather.
                    — A. C. SWINBURNE

III

In
Sad
or
Singing
Weather

. . . Un

HOLLYWOOD in one way didn't seem the same at all. Yvonne was in Paris, my lawyer had written from there about divorce terms and I'd agreed to them, and suddenly I was free. I had never been truly happy in the film capital, but in this moment of liberation, my relief was a kind of happiness.

It was soon to be tempered, however, for the first time I saw Marlene after my return it was obvious that our good and close friendship couldn't go on in the old way. Too much had happened, too many eager tongues had bandied gossip about in a town that fattens itself on rumor. The fact that my breakup with Yvonne had been fated, that trouble between us had been brewing for years, could be conveniently shrugged off by those who whetted their lips hopefully over a possible connection between that breakup and my admiration for Marlene. Further meetings between us would only give them ammunition.

"And you're worried about it," I said to her. "Because nobody knows where the talk will stop."

She made no reply, but the shadow that crossed her bewitching face with its delicate yet sensuous sculpture was answer enough. It was inevitable that from now on each time we met we would be less at ease, and I realized that the sooner it was finished, the better for both of us. Our amity was surely not over; it was simply to be packed away for moments of remembering.

And happily there was no dearth of other alluring women to encounter — Merle Oberon, Claudette Colbert, Miriam Hopkins, Kay Francis — stars whose intellect matched their beauty. And Greta Garbo, strange and unpredictable and ethereally lovely. Each time we found ourselves together at a party I would try to follow the famed Garbo moods which abruptly changed from gay, witty brilliance to deep sadness or a kind of mysterious despair.

The last time we saw each other in Hollywood, we were partners at a small, intimate dinner given by a director, and we chatted animatedly and easily about many things. As the evening progressed I began to wonder why I had ever found it difficult to converse with this fascinating woman.

"Do you like to swim, M. Chevalier?" she asked suddenly. "In the ocean?"

We had been discussing the theatre and it seemed an odd, disconnected question, but I smiled and nodded.

"Good," she said firmly. "Shall we all go now to the beach?"

"Now?" I was startled and the word popped out with dismay. It was almost midnight and the icy Pacific held little appeal for me, which I quickly pointed out. This apparently was my mistake, for instantly our warm, friendly conversation was over. The lady still sat beside me, but for the remainder of the party she was so remote and withdrawn and far away that I felt almost alone. I went home that evening more than ever convinced that the glorious Greta Garbo and I were miles and miles apart.

Paramount and I were still miles apart, too. I was still asking their top people why every picture I made must be in the same mold, why every character I played must be debonair and cute and devoid of emotional depth, and I was still receiving the same answer — that my films were making too much money to risk a change of pattern.

I drove away from the studio late one afternoon and headed for my house in Beverly Hills, dejected by my latest fruitless attempt to escape from a routine I feared would someday smother me. The first lights of evening were beginning to garland the hills above Hollywood, but today I was beyond noticing this favorite view. My mind was on a passage from one of the essays of Montaigne, the great French Renaissance writer. I had read it only the night before, but now it eluded me.

At home I turned the pages of the book and found the line I sought. *"L'utilité du vivre n'est pas en l'espace, elle est en l'usage,"* I read. The value of life lies not in the length of days but in the use we make of them. I was not using mine the way I would have liked, but my hands were tied.

Montaigne was becoming a friend of mine. So were Tolstoy and de Maupassant and a host of other immortal authors whose works I was meeting for the first time at the age of forty-three. I, who had never read anything outside of the daily papers, who with so little formal education was ill-equipped to be a scholar, had been turned into a student of great books by an actor newly arrived from France to make a French version of a Wallace

Beery film. Once here, he had decided to stay and try his luck in English, which he was studying night and day.

I had known Charles Boyer slightly in Paris, but in Hollywood we had become marvelous friends. Well-educated, cultured, intelligent, Charles had convinced me that a world of satisfying knowledge was waiting for me in books, and today in my library those first volumes he suggested I acquire sit alongside hundreds and hundreds of others I've read over the years.

When either of us was away from Hollywood, we would exchange long stimulating letters discussing our impressions of important literary works, and now I was tempted to write Charles how this essay of Montaigne, written more than three centuries before, was troubling me today.

The strident jangle of the telephone interrupted my thoughts. The voice at the other end of the line I had heard first in Paris, five years ago outside my dressing room, and then many times again in Hollywood when our paths had momentarily crossed.

"Irving Thalberg, Maurice," he said. "Remember the last time we met we were talking about a new kind of Chevalier on the screen?"

"Too well," I said ruefully.

"Well, how about lunching with me at the studio? Maybe we can do something about it."

We made a date, and I hung up thoughtfully. Had Thalberg, the great manitou of Metro-Goldwyn-Mayer, managed to borrow me from Paramount for a film in which I could really be an actor? What was on the mind of this young movie-making genius? Was I about to make better use of my days after all?

"Your contract's up in a few months, Maurice, right?" Across the table he was regarding me with his melancholy, intelligent gaze. "Then why not make a change?"

"I hadn't thought of it one way or the other, Irving," I said candidly.

"Then do. You come over with me, and there'll be wonderful parts, you'll make the kind of pictures you've wanted to, and I will personally see to it."

Make a change? In Paris, I was thinking, Thalberg and I had certainly not seen eye to eye, so could it be different in Hollywood? But now his earnestness was compelling. It was apparent that he understood the dissatisfaction tearing at me and was anxious to help. Suddenly it seemed to me that everything was going to be good in our relationship. Working with this charming and clever man who had produced so many fine films in his remarkable career would surely serve to right what I considered my present wrongs.

Perhaps Hollywood and I would become firm friends after all.

SUMMER at La Bocca. There was time to lie in the soft, indolent air and think. Weeks from now I would be crossing the Atlantic, boarding a train in New York, traversing the endless, majestic landscape of America and finally returning to deal with Thalberg's offer. But at the moment I was occupied with the evening that lay just a few hours ahead, and a meeting — my first encounter with Mistinguett in more than a decade.

A mutual friend had arranged this. When he had first approached me, I had thought it was a useless gesture for both Mist and me ever to come together again, even for a brief hello. The past was so far away, wasn't it better to leave it so? But she was living in nearby Antibes now, so we were almost neighbors, and if we didn't meet tonight we would probably run into each other ultimately anyway.

I found myself wondering if the years had been kind to her and hoping they had. I was sure the bright aura of youth had not clung to her as she neared sixty, but the magic of Mist would still be there, quieter now and warmer and gentler. Age would have mellowed that vibrant personality, and having grown with the years in understanding and tolerance, she would surely have a softer but still appealing glow.

It was almost dusk when I drove up to her house. Stepping from my car I heard a door open and she was standing there, her hands outstretched to greet me. Her voice was challenging as always.

"Well, Cio, you finally found the way."

I took her hands and they were trembling.

"Come inside. Let me look at you," she said and we moved into the house. When she turned to me, I could see that her face was drained of color, and for an instant I was afraid she was going to faint.

"We'll look at each other in a moment, Mist," I said and led her to a chair, but she shook her head and forced the smile I remembered so well. "You haven't changed, Cio, but neither have I, isn't that so?"

"Of course you haven't. You're as lovely as always," I said gently.

The color was returning to her face now. "You've done wonderful things, Cio. I've seen your films, they're very good."

"Thank you, Mist."

"I've stayed on top, too, you know." She spoke with a kind of defiance. "Nothing's really changed very much at all."

But a great deal had changed, and it pained me that Mist was admitting none of it. We talked for a long time, and I realized that she was still commanding the clock to remain motionless, that she could never accept the passage of years, for to do so meant to her a kind of withering and death. How sad, I was thinking, to demand a perpetual diet of moonbeams and youth and unreality.

"I've arranged a supper at a club in Cannes, Cio," she was saying and before I could protest she went on, "You'll know everyone and they'll be dying to see you."

264

When we arrived, I found myself dancing with Mist, her body lithe and supple and responsive as ever, and my memory was evoking the countless times we had danced in such harmony. I was aware that many eyes were upon us, but it really didn't matter, and in a way I was pleased that the friendly affection between Mist and me which had languished so long was now awake again. It would never go beyond a dance on a night-club floor, but it was pleasant to know that we were *en rapport* once more.

Suddenly photographers' flashbulbs began popping as half a dozen cameras were aimed at us, and I stopped dancing abruptly and led Mist away.

"What's the matter with you, Cio, are you afraid to have your picture taken?" she said.

"I don't want to be all over the Paris papers like this, and I shouldn't think you would either," I said, a little annoyed. "Don't you see what they'll try and make of it, Mist?"

"Who cares?" she shrugged, and as she turned to go to our table, the awful feeling welled up in me that Mist had planned it this way, that those photographers hadn't been there by accident, that somehow she hoped to profit by this ridiculous publicity. But I told myself that this was unfair and probably imagined on my part, and I pushed the incident out of my mind.

It returned a few weeks later when I went to see the baby daughter of Mist's brother. Playing with the child, with Mist beside me, a photographer unexpectedly emerged to take the picture, and this time I was angry.

"How did he get here, Mist? At your invitation obviously."

"People know you're here, Cio," she said placatingly, "and they knock at the door, camera in hand. What would you have me do, throw them out?"

This time I did not forget. I simply made a point of no more prearranged meetings with Mist, and the summer slipped by, and each passing week brought me closer to Hollywood and the road with Irving Thalberg and the big question mark of where it would lead.

Soon I had signed with M-G-M and Thalberg had chosen my first vehicle. We were to start with Franz Lehar's engaging operetta *The Merry Widow*, and immediately I suggested my very good friend Grace Moore, who sang so beautifully for the Metropolitan, for the title role.

I was talking to Ernst Lubitsch, who was to direct the film, and Thalberg and a handful of others. "Grace has the voice for the part, she's gracious and she's lovely."

"And plump," someone put in.

"Not any more," I argued. "She's lost pounds; she'll photograph perfectly, I know it."

"My dear Maurice," Thalberg said and Lubitsch seconded him. "She's not right. We're going to make this a truly great film, and we've got to find a girl to play the widow who's extraordinary and beautiful and dynamic and unknown!"

My arguments went unheeded, and the search was on for the new star. It became a world-wide exploration. The noise of publicity was intense, and I waited for the inevitable denouement: this undiscovered personality would turn out to be a well-established star in our own backyard. Of course it was the case. Thalberg and Lubitsch chose Jeanette MacDonald for the part.

Jeanette would be ideal as the merry widow, there was no disputing it. She was exquisite and talented, but we had already done three pictures together. Wasn't it time for each of us to have a new partner? Was this the "change" Thalberg had so glowingly promised that day at lunch? I wondered.

Our film was a great success, however, so no one could accuse Thalberg of having erred. Nonetheless, I joshed him later about his refusal to cast Grace Moore, for while we had shot *The*

Merry Widow, Grace had gone to Columbia Pictures to make *One Night of Love* and had skyrocketed to top stardom as a result. Overnight this marvelous woman had become an international sensation.

"And you turned her down," I teased Thalberg. "Has Columbia sent you a thank-you note?"

He shrugged. "Some days are just mistake days, Maurice. I guess that was one of them."

We both laughed it off, but a few months later I was to be professionally involved with Grace Moore in a way that lacked even a hint of humor.

Irving Thalberg and his charming wife, Norma Shearer, were my good friends. Each time I entered their luxurious house in Santa Monica to spend an evening — and there were many such times — I felt surrounded by a special aura of welcome. Even after all the years in Hollywood, I still felt completely at home in few places, but here it was almost as if I were a member of the family, the three of us drawn together by a shared respect and esteem for each other's opinions and aspirations and feelings.

This friendship made my meeting with Thalberg in his office that day doubly painful. I had just completed a film on loan to United Artists, *Folies Bergère*, and I assumed this call from Thalberg was to discuss my next picture on the home lot.

"How would you like to make a film with Grace Moore, Maurice?" he asked and I smiled, thinking this was more of the same joking. But he was serious, and I told him nothing would please me more.

"Columbia's willing to lend her to us, I've got a property in mind, and we'll break box-office records with you two as a team," he went on enthusiastically. "We'll get moving on it right away." Then almost as an afterthought he added, "There's one detail to straighten out, Maurice. Columbia insists on top billing for Grace."

I wasn't sure I'd heard him right. "It's not possible, Irving, you know that. My contract with you says I get top billing over everyone, man or woman."

"The important thing is to make a good movie, Maurice," he said earnestly. "And earn money. Isn't that right?"

"No, I'm sorry, it's not right," I said unhappily. "For almost twenty years I've been billed first, and I'd rather play that way in a cheap music hall than take second place at the Palace in New York."

"Pride."

"Yes, pride, and you understood it the day we signed a contract, so why not now?"

It was a question I need not have asked, for I knew the answer. Grace Moore, whom ironically the studio had rejected when I suggested her, was the current magnet at the box office. Thalberg was in a difficult position to obtain her now. Obviously he had to ignore my feelings. Suddenly I could see how precarious was one's position on the Hollywood ladder, how all must be governed by the law of business first, and I was thinking that if even such a man as Thalberg had to yield to that law, then what could I hope for in dealings with lesser men? Perhaps it was time to leave all this behind — to go home again.

Thalberg was saying some words, but I hardly heard him. It was time to go back to Paris. These had been seven extraordinary years, but the moment had come to terminate them. I remember a kind of calm settling over me as I decided this, and I was no longer upset but resigned and rather sad as I said aloud what I was thinking.

"Cancel your contract? With three years still to go?" he said startled. "Do you really mean that?"

"I'm sorry, Irving, but I do."

"This is your idea, Maurice. You're tough."

268

"Not tough, just a man who respects his word and his signature."

Impasse. It was apparent that neither of us was going to budge, and finally Thalberg said heavily, "You'll come back to Hollywood one of these days, bigger than ever."

"Maybe. Right now, I doubt it," I said and shook his extended hand.

So it was settled then and there in Irving Thalberg's office. Indemnified for a broken contract, I walked out of the building and took one last look around. In the distance I could see the vast, barnlike building that housed the stage where I had worked when I first came to this studio. The doors were closed, and a warning red light signaled that a scene was being shot inside. A wave of sadness engulfed me, a kind of regret at recognizing the end of an era, but I had done the right thing, of this I was sure. I was doing what my reason and my heart were telling me to do. It had always been that way with me. It always would.

And my mind was made up. Neither the new Hollywood offers that came in when my separation from M-G-M was announced nor chances to do revues in New York could sway me. The moment had come to pack up and sail for France, and once there I could review the course of my career and plot the next route.

"You'll never come back, Maurice," Kay Francis told me unhappily at dinner on my last night in Hollywood. "I know it."

Irving Thalberg had thought one way, this beautiful woman another. I wondered which of them would ultimately be right.

. . . Deux

I SAT ALONE in my Paris apartment sorting a host of thoughts that were dancing a saraband in my mind. On the train from Hollywood, even on the calm, leisurely voyage from New York to Le Havre, I had been thinking more of the past than the future, remembering and reviewing my seven crowded years in America. It had been enough then simply to accept the fact that I was finally going home. But now the future had suddenly become the present, for being home was only half the answer. Now that I was here, what was I going to do about it?

The easy route would have been to go on making films. I had contracts to do so — one in England and two others subsequently in France — and there was surely less risk professionally for me if I continued only in movies. But always in my heart there was the desire and the need to return to the stage, to stand alone before a theatre full of living, breathing people with the footlights blazing in my eyes and to sing and dance and hear the beautiful sounds of laughter and applause roaring up from the audience. It was a kind of nourishment I had been starving for, and I wanted to savor that marvelous taste again.

Yet what if I stepped out on that stage and performed and met with indifference? Europe's music halls and I had shared a long, happy love affair, but the lover had been away for seven years, and the spark of the romance could have died as it so often does in the case of love itself. My straw hat and pouting lower lip had filled movie screens in thousands of cities and towns and hamlets. Perhaps I had worn out my welcome with overexposure.

But I knew that ultimately I would choose to return to the stage. First I would find myself a group of new songs and sketches, rehearse and polish them, try them out in a little tour of the provinces just to get my hand back in, and finally come to Paris to stand or fall.

It was already late afternoon. I had been at this debate with myself for hours, and now with my mind made up I could go and dress for dinner and the theatre. With some friends I was seeing the French version of *Broadway*, which had been a hit some years before in New York and London. The leading man and woman were familiar to me, but I'd never seen the ingénue, a new young actress, before. Her name was Nita Raya, and my friends, who had already seen her perform, had said she was not only capable but very pretty as well.

It was less than half the truth, I was thinking, as I watched Nita Raya on the stage. She moved with an extraordinary grace and played her part with disarming sincerity, and more than that she had a youthful charm and beauty that won every heart in the theatre. Including my own, for once the show was over I found myself knocking at the door of her dressing room to tell her how good I thought she'd been.

For an instant she said nothing but regarded me with wide, guileless eyes and finally managed a shaky reply. "Did you truly think I was all right? I mean, I'm not Bernhardt or Duse and I know it, so if I try and it really comes across, well, I can't help being surprised."

"Maybe they felt the same way at your age," I said, trying to repress a smile at her ingenuous candor. "How old are you, Mademoiselle?"

She hesitated, then said ruefully, "I might as well admit it, I guess. Nineteen."

I was a little taken aback. I'd come backstage to see this adorable girl, I had to confess to myself, because I'd been attracted to her, and now I was learning that she was even younger than she looked. With her informally styled brunette hair and long, shapely legs that gave her a kind of coltish air she did have a child's quality. But nineteen? She was indeed a kid, albeit a winning one.

There was but one thing to do considering my own forty-six years. I extended my hand. "Good-by, and good luck."

She shook hands solemnly. "I — I don't think I'll ever forget this, Monsieur Chevalier. Truly, I won't."

When I returned home that evening, I found myself thinking a little regretfully of Nita Raya. I had never met anyone with quite her charming unspoiled humor, and it seemed a pity that now when I really wanted such a lively spirit near to help light the way ahead I had found her, but just a bit too young.

Late the next afternoon the postman knocked at my door to deliver a *pneumatique*, the swift and unusual special-delivery service found in Paris where mail is sped from post office to post office through underground pneumatic tubes. The handwriting was unfamiliar, but the name at the bottom of the note was not.

"Did I tell you last night," it said, "how moved I was that you should come backstage to see me? (I was so flustered I probably forgot!) But I left the theatre in a wonderful glow, Monsieur Chevalier, and I'm grateful, and I say it now. And I hope, I truly do, that I will see you again. Sincerely, Nita Raya."

I remember smiling gently at what she had written, for her personality was in every line on the page — open, honest, almost naïve, altogether delightful. And then a quiet decision formed in my mind. Where it would lead I surely didn't know, but I would see Nita again and listen to her bubbling laugh that crinkled her eyes and talk of whatever nonsense that came to mind and be younger than I had been in years, for somehow I felt that this girl would lend a freshness to my days and a vivacity and a spark.

And I was right. I had always loved to ramble aimlessly along the boulevards of Paris and the winding side streets, peering into shop windows simply for curiosity and amusement, but never had I done this with the women I had known. Neither Mist nor Yvonne had had the temperament for such a simple pleasure, but Nita was the perfect companion. Hand in hand we wandered, and she would press her nose to the glass and make a game of choosing her favorite item in the window, whatever the display — shoes, furs, office supplies, sea food, it didn't matter.

We passed a *pâtisserie* with delectable pastries on view and suddenly we had popped in, bought two éclairs and emerged to munch unashamedly on them as we meandered. Never had an éclair tasted so good to me or a late summer afternoon been more enchanted, for I was finding a zest to living that had been absent so long, a kind of abandon and ebullience.

Yes, Nita was the perfect companion, whether for onion soup

at dawn in the vast, sprawling market place of Les Halles or a drive in the country or any adventure anywhere. She took me to meet her parents. They were Jewish, a nice old couple who had left their native Romania four years before and who now depended on Nita for their livelihood. Starting as a dancer, she had gone on to become an actress, and they were proud of her. When they spoke her name, their eyes glowed.

Later, back at my apartment, my own eyes were glowing, for Nita was in my arms and I knew that love was coming into my life again. I had told myself that I was through with marriage or even serious affairs, but this girl had become too important to me. This was to be no casual romance. It was a joy we were going to share.

I HAD left Nita in Paris, traveled to La Bocca to ready my new act and opened with it in Nice. Then Cannes and the other important southern cities and all had gone well, but the big test was always Paris. Now I had returned, prepared to reintroduce myself on the stage of the last theatre I had played before leaving for Hollywood — the Casino de Paris.

"Of all the nights for me to be in a play," Nita wailed. "I'm tempted to be sick." She grinned mischievously. "And then I'll recover just in time to see you at the Casino."

She was joking, of course, yet not altogether, for Nita didn't take her career so seriously at the time, and I think if I had told her just to stop working and be my girl entirely she would have quickly agreed. But I had other ideas. Once she left the cast of *Broadway*, I planned to add her to the revue I was going to mount and together we would tour the great capitals. It would be a marvelous life, full of gaiety and excitement and love.

When I arrived at the theatre — a little late, because my solo appearance was to be the second half of a two-act revue —

crowds were thronging at the entrance. Backstage I stole a glance at the audience through the curtain, and I saw Charles Boyer with his young English wife, Pat Paterson, in a box. I wondered what he was thinking. Having decided to remain in Hollywood permanently himself, he may well have thought I was wrong to renounce my success there. I was convinced though that I was right, and even if it went badly here tonight, I would have no regrets, nor would I hurry to accept the new American offers I'd had since my return. I was home — and comfortable — and now that Nita was in my life, very happy.

The first act seemed forever, the intermission longer, but finally I was onstage, and it all went well. It was almost as if I hadn't even been away, the old enthusiasm, the laughter, the joyous response, and I'm afraid I stood there with a foolish, elated grin on my face long after the curtain finally closed. I was back in the fold at last.

"What will you do now?" Charles asked in my dressing room later.

"Live," I said simply, but what a world of meaning lay in that single word.

Afterwards, over supper, Nita's eyes sparkled at me across the table as she talked excitedly of the places we would visit on our tour, the sights we would see, the adventures we would have.

"Wait a minute." I laughed. "I have to finish at the Casino first, then do a film in London. It'll be four months at least."

"Just in time for my birthday," she said delightedly. "What a wonderful present!"

Birthday? It was a painful word. I wanted no reminders that this girl I adored was less than half my own age. I had thought of it often after our romance began, even considered stopping this untimely thing I had allowed to start, but the thought had hurt so much I had pushed it away. I hadn't the strength to deny myself this new miracle of love.

275

"Then make some other sacrifice," my conscience demanded as I lay awake that night. "Life shouldn't be so soft and sweet and delicious, it's too much."

It was true; I had to admit it. I should pay for all this pleasure with some kind of denial, almost as a monk would do to humiliate himself. Abnegation would prove that I had a measure of self-control. But what should I give up?

The answer was so startling I sat bolt upright in the darkness: *Smoking!* If I, who smoked three packages of cigarettes a day, could give them up completely, what a marvelous show of will power that would be! I had been unable to resist the lure of Nita, but if I refused the temptation of smoking, whose slave I had been for over thirty years, wouldn't it be impeccable proof that I was still master of myself?

I fell asleep with a kind of satisfaction and an eagerness to face the morning and my test. But daylight brought a few reservations. This proposed bout with tobacco was no new struggle for me. I had started smoking with my first job as an entertainer on a regular ration of two cigarettes a day, then with each new rung on the upward ladder I'd increased the daily total till finally I had arrived at sixty. From the moment of waking till that of sleeping I smoked. At work I had come to need one final puff an instant before my entrance on stage and an immediate one at my exit. And, aware of my total enslavement, I had tried to stop in the past — not once, but at least a dozen times.

In prison camp I had lasted thirty-five days, and during those harrowing months which led to my breakdown I had stopped smoking as a possible cure and started right back again when the cure didn't happen. Another time I had renounced cigarettes for three months and took just one to prove I was free. One led to one more and then another, and suddenly it was three packs a day again.

Now, here I was about to embark on the same tired old road, I told myself as I took a deep, satisfying drag on my first smoke of the day. Perhaps my decision of last night had been a bit hasty, perhaps I was ignoring my passionate temperament, my unwillingness to love with only half my heart. And I adored tobacco, there was no use denying it.

I took a deep breath and resolved to postpone my fight until I left for England and the film I was to shoot there. Away from Paris, with Nita and home and friends behind me, I would buckle down — and win. I could not meet my eyes in the mirror as I settled for this rationalization.

But in London, as filming began on *The Beloved Vagabond*, another actor and I took the pledge together. I smoked my final cigarette on a Sunday night, awoke to a tormented Monday with a hundred moments of overwhelming longing, survived, and after one week of abstention was sure that at last I had conquered the habit. Alas, how weak is the human spirit! Late that night I returned to my hotel room, aching for the smell and feel and taste of smoke in my lungs and heard myself saying, "Maurice, life is so short, you could be dead in two days, so why be so hard on yourself?"

In a kind of strangling voice, I was on the phone to room service, and a few moments later I was opening my precious pack with fingers that trembled as I made my last, futile arguments. Shame, I said, and I continued to peel off the paper. To smoke like a thief in the night, I went on, and drew a beautiful cigarette from the package. Resist, I pleaded with myself, and promptly applied a light to the tip.

It was too late now, I was smoking again. But with my hunger satisfied for the instant, I was sick at my desertion of the good cause and opened the window and tossed out the remaining nineteen cigarettes. The pack fell among a group of chauffeurs waiting outside the hotel, and as they glanced up, I drew back ashamed from view. I slept with a heavy conscience that night, and said nothing to my friend the next day. So far as he knew, neither of us had smoked for eight days.

And the game went on. I bluffed all day, and each night on returning to my room went through the whole disgraceful comedy: one cigarette from the pack, open the window, throw out the rest. Now the chauffeurs were waiting, eyes on my room, for their nightly gift from the eccentric on the fifth floor.

Then one day I could hide the truth no longer. The cast broke for lunch and, chagrined, I confessed my deception to my friend. He doubled up with laughter at my discomfiture, then pointed out that to err was human. Hopefully I demanded if he had similarly fallen from grace, and I think if he had done so, I would have been lost one more time, for misery dearly loves a friend also in distress. But not at all. No smoke had passed my colleague's lips, his resolve was still as high as the Eiffel Tower, and in that moment of utter disgrace, I knew that I had touched my last cigarette.

The chauffeurs waited in vain that night, and if they had kept their vigil for another quarter of a century it would still have been useless, for though there may have been other regrets since, not a single one has been concerned with tobacco dating from that memorable day in London.

And I went back to Nita a few weeks later feeling happier and healthier than I had in years. I had won the Battle of Nicotine and with it the marvelous prize of a love that I needn't justify to myself any more.

NITA was now a part of my revue. Singing and dancing in the first part of the show, she was young and appealing, and the audiences loved her as I did. Whether we were playing at the Casino de Paris or on tours of Europe or Egypt or Morocco or as far away as South Africa, life with this carefree darling was a new and delicious kind of harmony.

And the summers we spent at La Bocca together, contented seasons with the brilliant blue of the Mediterranean spread out far below our hilltop, were almost perfect. I say almost, because even here one couldn't ignore the rumblings of political strife in Europe. Nita seemed undisturbed by it all. Hitler's maniacal outbursts against the Jews, his avowed determination to stamp them out, might have been a million miles away for her. She was not uncaring, you understand, for her heart would be touched with the plight of a little injured sparrow, but rather it was a kind of refusal to recognize the evils that were springing up around us. Besides, it was hard for everyone to believe the hideous stories that filtered across the Rhine.

I had never been interested in politics, but now I was beginning to read the papers and listen to the radio in an effort to comprehend the confusion. Was Hitler bluffing? Would there be a war? *Anschluss.* Everyone talked about it, but what did it really portend? A thousand questions and no one knew the answers, unless it was Hitler himself.

It was Thursday, the 31st of August, in the climactic summer of 1939 when Charles Boyer, who had just arrived in Nice to make a picture, called me at the house. I was unable to meet him the next day because I had been invited for lunch at the villa of the Duke and Duchess of Windsor and a game of golf with the Duke afterwards.

Charles was concerned about the war rumors. "There won't be a war," I said firmly because I didn't want to believe there could be one. "Hitler knows we're calling his bluff from now on. He'll stop where he is."

My confidence seemed to calm my old friend. He trusted my logic and good sense, he told me. Good sense? Today I smile without humor when I think about how poor a prophet I proved to be.

Lunch with the Windsors had been set up in the garden, and though there was evident tension among us over the present troubles in Europe, all seemed to go smoothly enough. In the brief instants when conversation lulled, the day, I remember, was extraordinarily peaceful and still, with a kind of hush that often blankets the air along the Riviera. At such moments one sometimes feels that the single cry of a gull above the sea might carry for miles into the mountains that ring the coast. Suddenly one of these silences was broken by the distant, persistent ringing of the telephone, and at the same instant someone turned on the radio near the table.

A newscaster's voice, high-pitched and intense, was announcing that Germany had invaded Poland, that war appeared inevitable now since France and Britain were obligated to come to Poland's defense. We listened, so stunned with the impact of this news that we didn't notice a man whispering in the Duke's ear that George VI of England was on the phone from London to his brother, the former king.

When the Duke returned, his face was taut with strain, but he smiled gravely at me. "Monsieur Chevalier," he said, "I think golf is out of the question now. I'm sorry."

"I understand, Your Highness," I murmured. "Perhaps I should go now."

"Oh, no, please stay till lunch is over."

And so I stayed, and lunch went on politely and gently and very friendly. But it was only a surface reaction, for underneath we were shaken to the depths with the knowledge that in the middle of this innocent, pleasant meal the whole world had changed.

. . . *Trois*

Paris was black when Nita and I finally arrived from La Bocca. It had been a long, tiring drive, and doubly depressing because war had been declared while we were en route, and now to find our shining city of lights full of forlorn shadows and darkened street lamps was a saddening blow. We had stopped at a *charcuterie* to buy a little food for supper, and the proprietor had shrugged philosophically, even managed a smile and a joke because war was no stranger to him and he knew the uselessness of gloom. Nonetheless, we pulled up before my apartment with heavy hearts.

"Gas masks, monsieur," the concierge puffed as he mounted the stairs under a load of three large suitcases. "You must get them at once, it's urgent!"

"Well, it can probably wait till tomorrow," I answered, and he shook his head mournfully. "The German radio promised a hundred planes over Paris tonight," he said and dumped our bags in the foyer. "Suppose they keep their word?"

I felt Nita's fingers tighten against my arm. "Maurice, what do we do?"

"Do?" I said with a gaiety I didn't feel. "We find ourselves a pair of masks and get ready for the party."

And what weird contraptions they were! At the defense requisition center we watched a brief demonstration of their use, then located an air raid shelter near our building and returned home prepared for the worst.

Sometime in the middle of the night it came. We were wakened by the terrifying wail of a siren, and still a little drugged from sleep we dressed and seized our gas masks from a chair in the bedroom.

Nita looked unsurely at me for her next move. I hadn't remembered the instructions very well, but it seemed logical that one should protect himself against gas before venturing outside, so I helped Nita into her mask and nervously struggled into my own. Suddenly we looked like two ghostly creatures from another world. Or deep-sea divers.

I could see Nita's eyes appealing frantically to me and hear her muffled voice, but the words were lost. "What did you say?" I shouted above the scream of the siren.

"I can't breathe," she yelled back at me, and I nodded and loosened the strap around her head.

"Better now?"

She appeared to nod, and I led her from the apartment down the stairs toward the shelter. As we passed the concierge, still without his mask, he seemed to stare oddly at us. I read his expression as surprise that we had moved so quickly in this emergency, but when we arrived in the shelter to be greeted by similar looks from the other occupants who were carrying instead of wearing their masks, I began to wonder.

Finally when their astonishment turned to repressed laughter, I realized we had put on our masks too soon, but now I hated to appear more ridiculous by taking them off and admitting we were wrong. I determined we would suffer through this somehow. Still, it was getting more and more difficult to breathe in these monstrous appliances, and at last on the verge of suffocation I was about to signal Nita to give in when a warden burst into the cellar and shouted "Gas alert! Gas alert!"

Now everyone was donning his mask, but Nita and I who had been tortured in ours could breathe no longer and ripped them off. So once again we were out of step, and the others stared at us in disbelief.

"They think we're truly crazy now," Nita giggled.

"So do I," I said. "For coming down here in the first place." I took her hand and pulled her out into the fresh, sweet, welcome night air, and we walked happily back to our apartment, convinced that no gas could be any worse than the diabolical mask which protected you against it!

And as day followed day with no gas attacks or other bombardment from the *Luftwaffe*, the masks were shoved into a remote corner and life became almost normal in an oddly abnormal way. Shutters were closed and blackout blinds drawn, but behind them everyone ignored the shrilling sirens and settled down to a strange war that was not a war. "Phony," the newspapers and radio dubbed it, and even the soldiers in front-line outposts began to think of it that way as nothing really happened. Despite the tragedy of Poland, overrun by Nazi tanks, most Frenchmen felt that our strong defensive Maginot Line would simply deter the enemy till the conflict ended from pure lack of momentum.

We organized a troupe to entertain the soldiers in outfits facing the German borders. Josephine Baker and I were the stars, Nita had a featured role in the company, and on makeshift stages we sang and danced for one unit after another till the day we returned to Paris for the triumphal reopening of the Casino, closed since the onset of the war but now lit up again as another proof of public morale in the capital.

Gracie Fields came to Paris from London to play a public benefit. I flew to London in a military plane to do the same and returned that night in time for my regular stint at the Casino. And in December, at Lausanne in Switzerland, my path crossed one more time with Alphonso XIII, once King of Spain, but now since eight years an exiled monarch free to wander through every country but his own.

I had performed the evening before and seen Alphonso at the theatre. The next morning we encountered each other again outside our hotel. He excused himself to the very young and pretty girl at his side and crossed to throw his arm around my shoulder.

"Maurice, you were perfect last night, in wonderful form," he said with the open, engaging smile I had first seen so long ago when Mist and I had danced for him at the Ritz.

It was all I could do to refrain from saying, after glancing admiringly at his companion, "Alphonso, you're not doing so badly yourself."

Instead we talked in a more serious vein, and later I regretted all I had left unsaid, for it was to be our last meeting. A little more than a year later, in Rome, Alphonso died — and I had lost a good, good friend.

AND so the winter of 1939-40 passed, and the Casino was packed night after night, and from time to time one even forgot that Europe was at war. Denmark and Norway had been occupied by the Nazis in April, yet no one was prepared for the 10th of May and Hitler's lightning thrust into Holland and Belgium and Lux-

284

embourg and surely no one could imagine that a giant nightmare had begun. As Allied troops moved across Belgium to meet the invaders, little knots of Parisians clustered in the streets to reassure each other, to predict knowingly that the Germans would be stopped in their tracks.

But each day went by with Hitler's Panzer divisions knifing farther through our lines, and reassurance turned to silence. No one discussed the progress of the Nazis, for this was defeatist talk, but the enemy was pushing on inexorably and slow panic was building in the city. Railroad stations were jammed. An exodus was under way.

We had visited Nita's parents, and I saw the distress on the face of her father, a sweet, gentle old man who was dominated by his good-natured but courageous wife.

"I know a place near Bordeaux, called Arcachon," I told them. "I want to send you there, it's quiet and peaceful."

"We're not afraid," Nita's mother said. "You don't have to send us away."

"I'm not sending you away, it's just a vacation." I felt Nita squeezing my hand gratefully. "You'll come back in a few weeks."

When we left, Nita said simply, "Thank you, Maurice. I was worried about them."

"I know." I turned her to face me. "Are you afraid to stay on in Paris yourself, Nita?" She shook her head. "Then we'll wait and see."

That night we had less than a hundred people in the audience, and we played harder than we ever had before. It was almost as if we were determined to overwhelm with our performance all the fury of the thundering Nazi tanks. Joe Bridge, my old friend from Alten Grabow whom I had recently added to our company, stood in the wings when I finished my solo, his face heavy with weariness.

"God, will they get us again?" he said.

I laughed a little hollowly. "If they do, we can always pretend we're medical orderlies, Joe."

But the time for jokes was almost past. Nazi spearheads were aimed at Paris, and if we were to get out, it would have to be soon. Flight to La Bocca was impossible, for the French air corps had requisitioned my house there, disturbed by the menace of Mussolini's forces poised not seventy-five miles away in Italy. Desha, a dancer in our troupe, had a little house in Dordogne, also near Bordeaux, and I decided that if it became necessary to leave, I would organize a group to live there. But none of us would stop performing so long as an audience remained to see us, for this was our defiant gesture to prove that Paris was still unbroken.

One night at the end of May only ten people came to see our show. The Nazis were near. An odor of doom filled the city. The cast gathered on stage afterwards, sorrowfully waiting for the inevitable word. There were tears in many eyes, and my own were not dry.

"It's time to go," I said slowly. "I don't know when we'll meet again, but we will."

Nita and I left together. We would be up all night packing, making preparations, and at dawn we would be driving away in her tiny Fiat. The others were going to join us at Dordogne: Desha, Joe Bridge, Felix Paquet, a brilliant comedian in our revue, and his wife, Nita's parents whom we would bring over from nearby Arcachon, Desha's mother-in-law, and one servant who would help this strangely assorted household to survive.

At the apartment Nita and I went through crowded closets and packed drawers trying to decide what to take and what to leave. It seemed a hopeless task, for when one's life is falling apart, how does one choose the pieces to retain?

I gazed wistfully at my stage costumes — a dozen of them hanging in a colorful row — and I knew that something would have to be sacrificed. I would miss them, but after all we would surely drive the Nazis back from Paris and Nita and I would return soon and here would be my friendly costumes waiting, ready to be donned as I stepped out on stage again. On the other hand, suppose I didn't return so quickly? Could I work in the south without my familiar accoutrements?

"My hats," I said to Nita. "My hats and just the piano copies of my songs, it's enough to do a show."

Into a small black bag I jammed the boater, the fedora that was too big and the one that was too small, the comedy caps, the beret. Now at least I could make a living.

The sky was streaked with feathers of gray light when the little two-seater Fiat headed bravely toward the Porte d'Orléans, the southern city gate beyond which the road would lead us to Dordogne, more than three hundred miles away. Paris wore a bereaved, desolate face despite the surging green of the grass and trees and the riotous colors of flowers in public squares, planted in those happier days when the enemy was not at our throats. Somehow the contrast of beauty and despair made leaving doubly painful. Nita sat silently beside me, the *joie de vivre* that was always with her gone now. I had nothing to say myself.

It was worse on the road, for suddenly we began to see the thousands of refugees on foot who for days had been streaming out of Paris and the towns to the north which the Germans had overrun. Ruined people, desperate people, with their pathetic parcels of clothing or food, human beasts of burden trundling children's wagons loaded with a teakettle or a doll or a chicken coop. These hopeless columns of misery plodding on to nowhere made our fate seem infinitely more fortunate, but when the proud people of a proud country are running, solace is hard to find.

Steadily we drove to the southwest, and the countryside began to take on a peaceful, sleepy look as if war were a planet away. Tiny villages were shuttered for lunch as usual, youngsters

287

played in a schoolyard as they had done for generations, sheep grazed obliviously along the slope of a verdant field. And as night drew near, Nita and I felt this morning's sense of loss and abandonment dropping away, while in its place came a kind of numb acceptance of the inevitable. Events had suspended us in a vacuum. We must now adjust to living in it.

Ahead of us lay the little house our band was going to share, a simple, unprepossessing place with dun walls and a quiet, lived-in look. No coal, no gas, no electricity, no running water — it had no luxuries to offer but that of safe haven. And to Nita and me it was beautiful. The others would arrive, and we would hold our first meeting to set up places for sleeping and tasks for daily survival. Either on foot or bicycle, for there would be no gas from now on, some would go to the nearby village for supplies of food, others would be assigned to cooking or cleaning tasks. My own job was to be the woodsman, chopping and transporting the fuel for stove and fireplace.

Inside our bedroom I drew Nita close to me. "I don't know how long this will last, little one," I said, "but we'll go home one of these days."

"We are home," she said and began to unpack our bags and put things in order.

And for a few days life took on almost the feel of a holiday. Our house party had been born of necessity, but we determined to make the most of it, and we spent hours in lively, friendly discussions. There was a certain charm to being cut off from reality this way. Our only connection with the outside world was a battery-operated radio that sputtered and crackled most of the time or faded away altogether. But we heard enough to know that Mussolini had seized his opportunity to strike at our reeling country, and now the light moments were less frequent, for this meant that the enemy lay not only to the north but to the east as well. To the south lay the mountain wall of the Pyrenees and to the west the impassable Atlantic. Our refuge could one day become a trap with no avenue of escape.

Still, hope was very much alive. At this exact moment our army and the British might be blunting the German attack, even pushing the Nazis back, we told ourselves. Then four days later the insupportable blow was struck.

"Paris has fallen," the announcer said, and we huddled in stunned disbelief around the radio, certain there was some mistake soon to be rectified. "We have withdrawn and the Germans are moving in to take control of the city."

The "Marseillaise" was playing now, but its defiant, stirring strains were clashing in our minds with the sound of German boots striking harshly against the stones of Paris streets. Motionless we sat trying to grasp the horror of our Paris, our beautiful Paris under the fist of the invader. There was no mistake — our beloved city was lost.

I looked from one face to another, each a study in hopelessness. But my gaze stopped on Nita, for another horror had entered my mind. What if this massive thrust of the Nazis swept on past Paris, southward through the Loire Valley, and still south till it reached this remote haven? I knew that for all of us it would be difficult, but for Nita and her parents it could mean disaster. I had heard too much already of the fate of Jews who fell into Nazi hands.

They must never be allowed to reach this girl I loved, I was thinking. Or those she loved. Never.

. . . *Quatre*

THE NAZI tanks had moved south beyond Paris in the direction of Bordeaux, and that panicked city was teeming with political and religious refugees, each one filled with apprehension for the day the enemy's armored columns would penetrate and find them. I had formed a desperate plan with our little group, a story to be given the German soldiers should they follow the narrow, winding road to our house and suddenly hammer at the front door. Joe and Desha spoke a little German. They would explain that we were simply a troupe of performers come to this remote spot to work on new material. If, as I hoped, the enemy had seen my films in the past and recognized me now, they might believe us and let us alone.

But if they questioned us in our own tongue, Nita's parents, with their heavily accented French, could never pass. Nor did our house have a room which could be sealed off to hide them. I must find such a place in the village.

We cached them in a house where no ordinary search would ferret out their concealment, and Nita's mother stopped me anxiously at the door.

"Maurice?" Her eyes were heavy with pain. "What about Nita?"

"She'll be fine," I said with an assurance I didn't feel, and when I saw that she believed me, I left to walk back alone to Nita and the others.

The road was hushed, with only a bird calling without pattern from the distant, languid trees, then the silence was shattered by the sound of a truck behind me and I looked frantically for cover, certain that the Germans would be emerging from that bend in the road. But there was no place to run, and I took a deep breath and plodded on, steeling myself for what was next.

The truck was near now, and then it had gone by and I saw a load of soldiers in its open carriage. They were our own men in flight. Retreat. So it had reached us? Now it was only a matter of time till the pursuers were here as well.

The Nazis did not arrive. Instead, our radio which had grown steadily dimmer, almost as if it were ashamed to broadcast France's downfall, feebly announced that Marshal Pétain had asked for an armistice. Crowded around the set, straining to hear the words, we listened in despair tempered only by the dismal knowledge that at least we no longer need dread tomorrow, for it was upon us.

The radio spoke of two zones, one to be occupied by the Nazis, the other free. If there were a choice, I was thinking, where would we go? I looked questioningly from one face to another and felt the decision had already been made. Surely we would all choose to remain in the zone of freedom.

I wondered about my house in La Bocca. With the armistice, there would probably be no more French air force headquartered in it. "If we're lucky and the house hasn't been bombed, we'll go there," I said. "For the summer anyway."

"And the winter?" Joe asked, concerned.

"We live from one day to the next, Joe, there's no other way."

It was true. There was no longer any design to life, any future. One could deal only with the present. Two-thirds of our country had been amputated, yet in the one-third that remained we could learn to live again if we had courage and tenacity and hope.

But it was not so simple as that. Managing to scrape together just enough gas to make the trip, our group — minus Desha and her mother-in-law, who stayed behind in their own home — found my house untouched by the war, serene and peaceful on its hillside. But Cannes below was crowded with those who had fled Paris in the face of the conflict, and they were drifting aimlessly, uncertain as to what to do or how to live. Among the throngs were many of the capital's stars of the theatre, and a horde of actors, producers and directors from the film world. These people were lost without Paris. The amputation of our country had been no simple operation, not just the loss of a limb. France's heart had been cut away from the rest of her body.

Debates raged along the Croisette, that boulevard in Cannes lined with grand hotels on one side and the palm-edged sea on the other.

"It's over, we're defeated," some said. "So why not return to Paris and make the best of it?"

"At least we're free here," others retorted.

But even that freedom began to be doubted. Rumors were thick that the Gestapo had agents in every corner of the Riviera. The Germans knew every move we were making, every thought we were uttering aloud. Voices began to be lowered, but the arguments went on. To return to Paris or not?

Among those theatre people who were Jewish there was never any question. To enter the Nazi-occupied zone was an invitation to disaster. And for me there was none as well, for Nita and her parents were in my hands. So long as we were all together they were protected and safe. Moreover, with my Paris strangled by the Nazis, I wanted only to stay away.

Nita and I were on the terrace one afternoon when a black car entered the drive, and I sat up, startled. For weeks now we had been walking or bicycling because there was no more gasoline. The cars in use were driven by officials of the government or those suspected of involvement with the Germans. I wanted Nita in contact with neither.

"Hide, darling," I said and as she disappeared I moved to the front door to greet the two men who had dismounted from the car.

I recognized them, two important theatrical men from Paris, and as we sat in the cool shadows of the living room, I learned they had come to the Riviera to persuade top performers to return to the capital.

"The Germans admire you, Maurice," one of them said. "At least at the moment. But if you don't come back, they could get annoyed, even irritated, you know what I mean?"

"As a matter of fact, I don't," I said carefully. "Why should my staying here in my own house upset anybody?"

"Look, Maurice," the other said with a winning smile. "Paris has to start living again, we all know that."

"The war's over," the first put in.

"Exactly," the second agreed. "Now the public needs to see the performers it loves. Paris made you what you are, and people wouldn't understand it if you stayed away."

I rose to my feet. "I'm afraid they'll have to, gentlemen. I'm staying right where I am."

Their smiles faded, and moments later they left. I stood in the doorway as they whirled their car, tires screaming, into the road, and I was aware that the sun had dropped behind the hills to the west. At the same instant, a stray gust of wind sprang up from nowhere as if to augur a sudden summer rain, and I turned back inside with an odd sense of foreboding that wouldn't go away.

CABLE after cable was coming from America, propositions for Broadway and Hollywood, and I was pushing each one aside, for just as one does not desert one's mother when she is ill, so one remains with one's country when she is wounded. But I wanted to work, and benefits for patriotic causes were not frequent enough, so I decided to organize a show to tour the cities and towns of the free zone.

Without Nita, for I didn't dare subject her to the attention being on stage would bring, we survived impossible trips on trains behind schedule, filled with passengers fighting for places even to stand, their tempers rubbed raw by a steadily diminishing level of food rations and the trumpeting of the German-controlled radio and newspapers in Paris that France would be permanently under Nazi domination, that willing collaboration was the only recipe for endurable living. We recognized it for the evil propaganda that it was, yet still it added to the leaden weight of discouragement and desperation.

Nice, the center of the Riviera, became the hub of a frantic black market in gold and jewels and cigarettes and clothes and food, but this was a corruption to be expected and no one was surprised. What sickened me as the months passed was the surge of violent anti-Semitism that showed itself, demonstrations in theatres against Jewish performers by bands of hoodlums so that more and more of these entertainers who were my friends were being denied work. There was but one protest I could make: I could appear with them as often as possible in public places in an open display of friendship and warmth.

Nita greeted me unhappily one day and handed me a Paris

paper. It was folded to a story about me, a violent attack on my failure to return to Paris more than a year after the armistice.

"Nearly every important entertainer has come back," the account read, "but Chevalier stays on the Riviera with his Jews." I crumpled it angrily and threw it aside.

"Why do you waste your time reading that junk?" I said shortly, and I saw a look of pain cross Nita's face. "I'm sorry, darling," I murmured and took her in my arms. She was trembling, and I knew what this attack on me and others like it had cost her. She had said nothing all this time, but she had surely tortured herself with the belief that our love was to blame for what was happening to me, that I hadn't gone back to Paris because of her.

"We won't ever talk of this again," I said gently and kissed the frown from her forehead. "But once and for all let's get it straight. I love you. I stay with you because I want it that way, and no story or broadcast or threat is going to change it." I winked at her. "I'm a very stubborn man, you see?"

Slowly she began to smile, and we never spoke of it any more.

But others did. From every side I was told that life in Paris had become almost normal, that the way the war was going the Nazis would be in France for at least another twenty years, that the more I antagonized them, the shorter would grow their patience and one day the trap might well shut on me. I had heard all this before, but two new arguments were added, the first to the effect that whether it was occupied or not, Paris was still my town and thousands of my countrymen were there whose burdens would be lighter if I came to entertain them.

The second argument pointed out that our unoccupied zone was governed by men who were being forced to cooperate with the enemy. At the moment Nita was safe here, they said carefully, but no one was "entirely" safe with an arrogant conqueror calling the tune. It was a chilling implication, and it left me torn with indecision.

In September of 1941 I decided to go to Paris, but not for a whole season at the Casino, simply a few weeks to answer those who had demanded my presence.

I was saying good-by to Nita. "You're not to be afraid, you understand?" She nodded wanly, trying to be brave about it, but Joe Bridge and Felix and his wife had long ago returned to Paris and she would be here alone with her mother and father. It would be lonely for her. When I held her close in a last embrace, I wanted desperately to stay, but I pushed down the feeling. Paris was waiting. I had to go.

WORD was out that I was on my way. At the border of the occupation zone photographers and newsmen from Paris boarded the train, and at the Gare de Lyon, a Radio Paris reporter, microphone in hand, was waiting on the platform with a mob of people who cheered and laughed and called out as I appeared. I stood on the steps of the train with flashbulbs popping in my face, and I grinned and waved on command, but inside I was choking back tears, for there was no triumph in returning to my Paris when she was on her knees. I would do all I could to entertain, to lift morale, but with every song I sang I would also be praying for the day my beautiful city was free again.

The microphone was under my nose. Would I say a few words? What did I think of Paris today, didn't I feel that the city was really just as I had left it? I had steeled myself for these double-barreled questions which could have a political connotation, and I was determined to say nothing. What I had to offer would be sung and danced on the stage, for I was a performer come to entertain and that was all.

"I'm happy to be back with my people of Paris," I said slowly. "My emotions are touched, my heart is full."

The reporter was not content with my reply, I could see it in the narrowing of his eyes and his unwillingness to let me pass, but I had said all I intended to and somehow I pushed beyond him and through the crowd to the subway to become an ordinary Parisian on his way home. My apartment was still there, occupied as always by Mama Delpierre, my wonderful old housekeeper, and for a joyous hour everything seemed sane and normal and good again. I moved from room to room, touching almost wonderingly my paintings and books and furniture, blotting out the images of German soldiers I had seen patrolling the streets and the despair on the tired, hopeless faces of my countrymen.

But it was a brief joy. That same evening, sitting in my own familiar living room, I was brought back to the harsh, painful world outside by a bitter denunciation from Radio Paris. "Indecent," the announcer was saying, "to welcome back so noisily this infamous Chevalier who not so long ago was singing willingly and contentedly for the King and Queen of England!" I listened dumfounded. First they had attacked me for refusing to come to Paris, and now I was being hit for having finally given in and returned. It was crazy.

For one frantic instant I decided to go back that very night, to escape to Nita's arms and leave this insanity behind. Then I stopped short. No, if this Frenchman was using an attack on me to prove his loyalty to the Nazis and curry favor with them, then my fleeing would provide him with another weapon. I would stay.

The next day brought a new shock. At a press conference, in the midst of questioning about the show I was to put on at the Casino, a reporter suddenly demanded, "What do you think of Marshal Pétain?" It was a loaded question, I knew it, this query about the leader who had chosen to sue for an armistice with the enemy, yet I had to answer something, even though I had begged these newsmen to leave politics out of our conference.

"The Marshal?" I said, groping for a reply. "Well, I'm against war, as we all are," I stammered. "And I think it would be better if there were more understanding between people."

It was an innocuous answer, yet it seemed to satisfy my interrogator and I was relieved, in fact pleased, that I had dug myself out of a little hole. But afterwards on the front page of his newspaper I gazed aghast at an enormous photo of myself and a headline: "Maurice Chevalier preaches collaboration between the French and the Germans!"

Reading that monstrous lie over and over again, I felt a tight knot of anger and shock twisting in the pit of my stomach. The doorbell rang. Automatically I moved to answer, not even wondering who could be calling this late in the evening and for an instant I didn't recognize the man who stood in the doorway.

"Don't you remember me, Monsieur Chevalier?" he said finally.

Then it came to me. This was the journalist who had written the false story I held in my hand, and I looked coldly from the paper to him. "What do you want?"

His eyes were haggard, and I saw now that he was tense and strained. "I didn't write that," he managed to say. "Here's the piece I turned in." He held an envelope out to me. I ignored it. "Won't you read it?" he said pleadingly.

"Why?"

"So you can see what I really said. Please?"

I took the envelope and gestured him inside and quickly scanned the story. It was a simple account of my press conference with a direct quote of my reply concerning Pétain and no inferences drawn from it. "Then who wrote this thing in the paper?"

"The editor in chief. And a man from Nazi propaganda."

"And between them," I said, "they chose to try and crucify me." I was beginning to grasp the complexity of this giant trap, where whatever I said or did would be used to suit everyone's opportunistic purpose. I had been caught two times in two brief days. Was there any hope of escape?

"I'd like to keep your story for proof of what they did," I said and the man nodded, swallowing hard.

"If they find out about it, monsieur, I'll lose my job."

"Then I'll pay you till you find another," I replied grimly, and the instant he left I called an old and trusted newspaper friend to come over and told him everything.

"A denial, Maurice?" He threw up his hands in despair. "It's impossible. You couldn't get it past the Nazis. They're not idiots!"

"At least we could make an attempt."

"And lose our necks in the process?"

It ended with an article in the theater paper *Comoedia*, which simply commented on the exaggerations of the press concerning unnamed top stars who were playing in Paris and went on with a specific quote from me to the effect that I was just a singer who was uninvolved in politics and had nothing to say on the subject.

It was an empty vindication, I told myself, coming after the damaging injustice had been done, but at least I had put myself on record and it wouldn't happen again.

And from that moment I was a man walking on eggs, stepping gingerly from one day to the next. When Radio Paris officially invited me to do a group of broadcasts as I had done so often before the war, I dodged the issue on the pretext of my imminent departure from Paris. Even a simple invitation to lunch I suspected as a possible ambush, for there were Parisians whom one had always thought loyal and patriotic who now played games with the Germans, excusing themselves that there was no other reasonable course, and they sought to appear in public with well-known persons as a way to perfume the smell of their collaboration. And each evening as I performed at the Casino, I sang to the French people and ignored the scattered German officers in the audience who couldn't, of course, be kept away.

But the strain was beginning to tell. At night, when the show was over, I would come home to my apartment that was beginning to feel the chill of the oncoming winter and try to lose in sleep the heaviness of these dispiriting days. It was usually futile, for between the good dreams of Nita and La Bocca would come bad dreams of the unpleasant world surrounding me now. I was counting the days until my agreed six weeks would be over.

A few days before the end I had a visitor, a French government official with a request from the Nazi commander in Paris: Would I accept a singing engagement at the La Scala theatre in Berlin? I must have reacted in complete consternation, for he hastened to add, "You needn't worry; they guarantee you a great personal triumph."

"I'm sorry, monsieur," I said warily. "I'm forced to return to the south; I won't be able to do it."

"Maybe you should reconsider, Monsieur Chevalier. You see, while you're in Germany, our own government wants you to entertain at a few camps for voluntary French workers and prisoner-of-war camps as well."

"How can I?" I was trying to be reasonable, for I had no desire to antagonize this man. "I must go home."

"Paris is your home," he said flatly and glanced at the empty fireplace. "It's possible to get coal, Monsieur Chevalier, if one has the authorization. These Germans are no saints, but they repay favors."

"I'm not cold, thank you very much."

"And gasoline."

"I manage with my two feet and the subway."

He was obviously angry but he strove to keep his voice even. It was his eyes, steely blue beneath hooded lids, which gave him away. "You refuse then?" I nodded. "Even to sing for our prisoners? You, a prisoner once yourself?"

I hesitated. Flooding up within me were twenty-five-year-old memories, of month after despairing month when hope was dead and life had lost all meaning behind a grim barbed-wire barrier. And suddenly an idea sprang up within me.

"Alten Grabow," I said slowly. "Is it a prison camp today? With Frenchmen?"

He consulted a notebook. "Alten Grabow," he read with a nod. "What about it?"

"I'll play there."

"Good. And what others?"

I shook my head. "Alten Grabow, that's all," and before he could protest I went on, "and there's a price, monsieur. I'll go on one condition only: that the Nazis release ten prisoners from the part of Paris where I grew up."

"Release? Are you out of your mind?"

"Ten prisoners, released immediately and sent back to their families." Suddenly I was feeling exultant, in control of a situation for the first time since my return. I would go to Alten Grabow and perform for those French boys, bring a little light to the darkness of their days. And I could see by this man's face that I was going to win my point, that he would persuade the Nazis to release those ten prisoners.

"I'll have to let you know," he was saying at the door.

"One more thing, monsieur," I said, suddenly sobering and remembering. "No publicity. I go there, perform, the men are released, and not a word to the press. Is that agreed?"

"You'll hear from me." There was no pleasure in his face as he closed the door sharply behind him.

My phone rang early the next morning. My conditions had been accepted. The day after my closing at the Casino, I would leave incognito for Alten Grabow. I hung up, reflecting on the ironic twists life so often has in store for us, for here was I, returning willingly to the prison camp I had once risked death to leave.

WE ENTERED the gates of Alten Grabow, past the barbed wire and the forbidding watchtowers manned with Nazi soldiers and machine guns, and I felt my heart contract with the agony of remembering. I had long ago rejected from my mind the painful physical surroundings of this place, the drab barracks, the exercise yard, the infirmary, but now their pictures flashed vividly across my brain and I looked around me to find them again. They were gone. I could see nothing familiar.

Then the newly built barracks ahead of me began to disgorge their cargoes of human misery, and the past came back to life. Slowly the men moved out into the compound, marching toward the big hall where I would perform for them, and in the heavy, dispirited shamble of their steps I saw myself and all my fellow prisoners again, with resignation instead of hope in their faces. My eyes filled with tears. Could I simply with songs and sketches and pantomime lift that curtain of despair?

I stood on the makeshift stage before them and listened to their applause. It was loud enough. But the enthusiasm that only freedom can bring was missing. Then I gestured for silence, for suddenly I knew that I had more than entertainment to give these boys. I had hope. And I told them everything, how I had spent more months here than any of them, how I had almost lost my faith in eventual freedom and the world outside, how I had felt so many tortured times that love was gone and life, too. But I had survived, I went on, and a miracle had happened, for when I returned to life and love, they had finally become sweeter and warmer and richer than before.

"And so they will with you," I said. "I know, because once I stood right where you stand now, you see?"

There was not an answering sound as I finished, and then one boy began to clap and another and then they were all showing me they could hope again, and I grinned and signaled the pianist and began to sing. Song followed song until I could do no more and at last the yells and whistles and applause subsided and the stage swarmed with men who at least for the moment were smiling. For me, it had been a moving, rewarding afternoon.

Later, at the mess hall there was to be a dampening note. A Nazi lieutenant-colonel was waiting for me at the table. He rose as I neared and gestured amiably for me to sit opposite him. "I have made a special trip down from Berlin to see you, Monsieur Chevalier," he said. "With an invitation from important people, including, I understand, an old friend of yours." Puzzled, I said nothing and he went on. "Emil Jannings. You knew each other long ago in Hollywood, no?"

"Yes, very long ago," I said carefully, wondering what this was all about.

"Well, he is our biggest star in Germany, of course, and he will be there when the outstanding film people honor you with a big reception in Berlin."

A warning bell rang for me at this obvious attempt to keep me in Germany. "Thank you, Colonel," I said as politely as I could. "But I must hurry back to France; they're waiting for me there."

"One or two days, how much can it matter?"

"A great deal," I said firmly and the colonel's jovial mood was gone for an instant, then returned as quickly.

"Is this the way to treat an old friend?" he said expansively. "I promised Herr Jannings I would deliver you in Berlin."

"No. Thank you very much, but no."

The colonel regarded me with a hard level gaze, then abruptly pushed back from the table and rose. "So instead of the man," he said stiffly, "I am to bring back a refusal." He moved rapidly away. The door slammed behind him.

I was to leave by train early the following morning, and that night I slept little, magnifying every sound in the darkness to mean the arrival of someone to block my departure. And all the way back to Paris I waited tensely for the follow-up to my dispute with the colonel. When it didn't come, I was still uneasy.

"What about my ten prisoners?" I asked the French official who had arranged my trip to Alten Grabow. "I want to leave Paris, but I won't go till I know they've been released, and it's been two days already."

"The Germans gave their word," he said shortly. "What do you expect me to do?"

"See that they keep it," I said and hung up the phone.

On the third morning an announcement that ten prisoners were being repatriated was buried on the back page of one newspaper, but no details were given and I had no way of knowing if these were my men. But that afternoon Mama Delpierre opened the door of my apartment to tell me that a man was waiting in the living room. He had refused to give his name and he wouldn't leave without seeing me.

The instant I entered the room and saw the boy in the black sweater staring out the window I knew he had been a prisoner. There was something in the way he hunched his body as if to protect himself against expected disaster. I had known that posture myself, and when I emerged from Alten Grabow I had forced myself to throw my shoulders back almost defiantly to prove that I was free.

He turned toward me now, and his thin face lighted up. "I was at the camp, Monsieur Chevalier, I heard you sing, and they told us we were getting out because of you."

There was no need to ask this youngster if he were from Ménilmontant, for he spoke with the distinctive accent of my section of Paris. "You said 'us.' How many were you?"

"Nine others and myself, monsieur."

It was all I needed to know, and I felt my pulse quicken with happiness and the knowledge that my scheme had worked. At least this much of my Paris trip, I was thinking, had been a success, and now I could forget about the Jannings episode. I had won. There would be no further trouble.

I STEPPED from the train at Cannes and took deep breaths of free air and managed to find an old man with a horse and cart who would take my luggage and me up into the hills at La Bocca. He was a taciturn fellow and I was grateful for his silence, because it gave me a chance to imagine the feel of Nita against me, the softness of her, the warmth, the love. After my taut weeks in Paris I needed all of that more than ever, you understand, for when one is wounded and hurting inside, love has the power to soothe and finally to heal.

Her joyous cry reached me as we turned into the drive, and suddenly she was running from the house with that lilting, carefree step that had first won my heart. And then she was in my arms, making little sounds that were halfway between laughter and tears and even the sullen peasant was almost smiling and I could see Nita's parents in the doorway, holding back a little shyly as they always did but with a happy look of welcome on their faces. And everything was all right again.

How wrong I was!

Five days after my return I was walking in the streets of Cannes when I saw my name staring up at me from a newspaper stall, and stunned I looked at simultaneous editions of the Paris papers and those of the free zone, each with a long story of my visit to Alten Grabow. The Germans had not kept their word after all, I was thinking bitterly, but the bitterness became shocked anger as I read each report, for none of them pointed out what had really happened — that I had only visited one single camp, that this one had been the prison where I had spent more than two years in captivity myself, and that my price for this attempt to bring a message of hope to the men of Alten Grabow had been the release of ten prisoners.

Instead they strongly implied that I had visited many prison camps and then gone on to make a tour of many German cities. I shook my head in disbelief and I saw the woman inside the stall peering curiously at me above her spectacles.

"It's a lie," I said and she clucked sympathetically.

"If they would feed us as much food as they do lies," she said, "we wouldn't all be growing thin."

Yes, it was a lie, but where could I go to shout the truth, to right the wrong? Was there a newspaper in France that would listen, that would dare to print that the Nazis were lying? Which one of them would dare insult the conquerors, even in our so-called "free" zone, for here we only existed on the indulgence of the enemy.

The harsh reality had to be faced: My name was valuable to the Nazi propagandists, they would use it whenever they could, and they would twist whatever facts they needed to prove the point they desired. I was indeed caught in that trap I had feared — and my only hope lay in silence.

But it was no longer a hope for escape from the trap — only for survival.

. . . *Cinq*

Pearl harbor.

On the Croisette friends met and exchanged whispered words of hope. America was in the war now. It was far from over, but at last there seemed to be an eventual end to the avenue of despair. Here in our fragment of France that was free, yet not really free at all, one must live and work and pray — and ultimately perhaps fight as the moment of liberation neared. Bands of young, daring men were forming secret nests of resistance to the Nazis and calling themselves the *Maquis*.

And as the summer of 1942 came and rumors of this underground force grew stronger, so did the influx of Gestapo to the Riviera. They blended into the crowds of

307

Cannes, and suddenly one couldn't walk the length of a single block without the nagging urge to look back over the shoulder, because now there was always the nervous feeling that somehow somebody was watching.

For the first time I saw in Nita a new kind of tension that showed itself in an unexpected solemnity. When she was unaware of my covert glance, I would search her face that had always had a smile or a laugh poised ready to spring to life. Now often there was almost a shadow instead, and it saddened me to see my darling bird without song or soaring flight.

But there was nothing I could do to cheer her up. We were all paying the penalty of our cheerless times. I would console myself that at least we were sharing this trial except for brief days when my little troupe, performing in the region, took me away. And so long as I was near I felt that love would soften, even if it could not dispel, the gloom.

For a while one fear seldom left me: that more pressure would be put on me to perform again in Paris. This would mean another long painful separation from Nita and surely a repetition for me of that other difficult experience. But months came and went with no trouble, and I was beginning to forget the problem existed. Until a note arrived to set me quickly to remembering. It was a request to visit a government office in Cannes. The subject: Paris.

I sat before a round-faced man whose waspish attitude had begun to bite at my nerves. I struggled to hold on to my temper. "You have the record before you, monsieur," I explained for the third time. "It shows plainly that I performed for six full weeks in Paris."

"That was a year ago, Monsieur Chevalier. Do you normally work less than two months out of twelve?"

"I've toured dozens of towns in the free zone since then, and that's no vacation, believe me."

The other man, sitting slightly removed from the desk before me as if he were an audience rather than a part of this interview, shifted suddenly in his chair and I glanced his way. He was smiling thinly at me. "Then you've obviously no objection to performing, monsieur. It's only the locale that disturbs you?"

This was the first time he had spoken since my arrival, other than to acknowledge our introduction. He had a French name, and there was no trace of accent, yet I sensed something subtle in the pattern of his speech that set off a danger signal in my mind. Gestapo, I was thinking.

"Paris doesn't disturb me," I said, feeling my way with caution. "But I love this part of the country; my home's here now."

"Yes, it's very peaceful," he said sympathetically. "I dare say Mademoiselle Raya shares your affection for it."

Nita. Why had he brought her name into this? I felt a chill in my heart, and I summoned all my will to speak easily and naturally. "Over the years we've spent every free moment here that we could. She adores it."

"But you've also been together in Paris surely?"

"Yes."

"Then why not take her with you while you play there again?" His smile now was confident and knowing. "Arrangements can be made for you to fly there in the same plane, and that way she won't be lonely at all. How does that strike you?"

He was baiting me, I knew it instinctively. Somehow he had obtained information about Nita's religion, and knowing that I dared not risk disaster for her by taking her into the Nazi-occupied zone, he was using this to force me into a corner.

"Well, monsieur?" The smile was fading now, and he was regarding me with cold, steely challenge. "Or perhaps you'd prefer to be in Paris alone? You see, this, too, we understand."

"And as I pointed out," the first man was saying, "Parisians are clamoring to see you again, Monsieur Chevalier, so why not another engagement at the Casino?"

I looked from one of them to the other, and I was thinking:

309

Yes, they understand everything. Especially how to push a man back, back, back against the wall.

It was worse in Paris than before. Now "cooperation" with the Germans was more open and more widespread, and one had to be constantly on guard against inadvertent contact with those people who had begun by accepting what they called the "inevitable," then gone on to preach it and finally to profit from it. Four of my agreed six weeks still remained before me. In my melancholy, depressed mood it seemed a lifetime before I would finish this engagement and return to Nita, and the dismal thought kept repeating: how long before they would try and force me to do this again?

Then electrifying news swept along the boulevards that the Americans had landed in North Africa. Coupled with the Nazi reverse at El Alamein, could this be the turning point? Apparently the Germans feared so, because they ignored the armistice and swarmed across the border of the free zone in goose-stepping hordes and now all of France was occupied. But the day of liberation was surely coming, I told myself, and on my closing night at the Casino in December of 1942 I swore that I would neither sing on the radio nor play on a single Paris stage until that marvelous day arrived. Somehow I would find the way to keep that vow and still protect Nita and her parents.

Soon I was to be spending all of my time with them, for with the enemy now completely in our midst I quit the stage entirely, determined that the four of us would wait at La Bocca until all of France was free. The weeks passed — long, heavy, monotonous. Used to the feverish activity of my profession, I found this self-enforced idleness a difficult mouthful. For over thirty years singing and dancing and clowning before an audience had been as natural as breathing, and suddenly my work was gone and a kind of empty desolation had taken its place.

I remember wandering through the house so often feeling almost lost, as if my last friend had left me, and sometimes I would open up the case where I kept the hats I had brought down with me in that first flight from Paris. I would lift them out lovingly and look at them and sometimes put them on and hum the songs that each one represented. These were my memories, my souvenirs, but at the same time they were a way of touching the future, and as I carefully set them back into place I would feel the conviction returning in me that one day I would use them again in a theatre, not a room with only me to see and hear.

It was a comforting thought, and there was one other consolation. Here, at least, on our secluded hillside it appeared that my group was safe. Despite frightening reports from the German-occupied section beyond the mountains to the north, the Italian army, occupying the Riviera, seemed not to be bothering the Jews.

Overnight this changed, for the Italians moved out and Nazi soldiers and police arrived to replace them. Within hours a wave of Jewish arrests began. Many of them involved my friends — talented, quiet, gentle men and women who were caught and we never saw them again.

Now suddenly I was panicked. Black Gestapo cars were hurtling through the streets of Cannes, their hard-faced occupants staring stonily ahead until the carriages of death shrieked to a stop outside some apartment building and they moved rapidly inside. One never waited to see with whom they emerged later. It was wiser just to disappear. And as you moved away in sick horror, you wondered how these tyrants had found the way to their victims so swiftly and surely.

The answer became appallingly clear. Informers. In Cannes word began to spread of ordinary men and women, leading ordinary little lives, who had found it useful to spy on their neighbors. There seemed now to be no limit to degradation.

Ashen and trembling, Nita's father met me at the door of my house one night, Nita at his side. "Germans, Maurice, a whole truckload, I saw them this afternoon!"

I felt my entire body tense at his words. "Where?"

"On the road. I was in the garden."

"What in the world were you doing outside?" I said almost roughly and abruptly checked myself, upset that I had let the old man see my fear. I forced a calm smile. "Let's hope they didn't see you. Did they?" He shook his head. "Then it's all right, there's nothing to worry about, you understand?"

He was reassured and when he went to join his wife in their bedroom, I sank wearily into a chair. Nita had said not a word. It was obvious she was frightened.

"Is it true, Maurice? There's nothing to worry about?"

I pulled her down beside me with my arm around her, and for a long moment, trying to organize my thoughts, I said nothing. Only the sound of Nita's short, sharp breathing gave away the strain she was feeling.

"Darling," I said finally, "I have to find some place to hide them."

"But why? Papa won't go outside again, I promise you that, and if they stay in the house, how will the Germans know they're even here?"

"How?" I said sadly. "Cannes is swarming with Gestapo. One denunciation, one word from anybody who knows they've been living here all this time, and they'll be caught like all the others who're not in hiding."

"But where can they hide?"

"That's what I have to find out," I said grimly. "There must still be a few human beings left."

There were. In Nice, the prefect of the Alpes-Maritimes, the administrative head of this whole sector of the Riviera who had long been a friend of mine, proved that.

"This is a big city, Maurice, better than Cannes if one is just to be swallowed up," he said slowly. "I know a place in the old quarter of town behind the railway station. They'll be safe there." He looked at me with grave eyes. "What about their daughter?"

"We have to be together," I said simply. "Whatever happens."

He nodded. "Have the old people ready to move tonight at ten."

"But how? There's no train at that hour."

He grinned. "Surely the prefect is entitled to use his car on official business for the Germans, no?"

I left this man with renewed belief in honor and decency and humanity, but one fear rode with me on the trip back to Cannes and up into the hills of La Bocca. Nita. I had to protect her. Unlike the case of her parents, no one could really prove anything about Nita, but it would be safer if I could exchange this negative assurance for something positive. A startling thought crossed my mind: What if I went to Paris and somehow obtained a certificate which showed that Nita was not who she really was, but a French girl with an entirely different background?

The thought haunted me from that moment on. Could I get away with it? Could I risk bringing more attention to Nita and perhaps more danger?

We were alone in the house now, and we lived with an unspoken terror between us that each new day would bring disaster. I was being pressed with incessant demands to play benefits, to perform at government-sponsored galas, and to each request I gave the same answer — that I was too ill to work. Friends were warning me that one day I would go too far. Each time the phone rang, there was a moment of taut hesitation before the receiver came off the hook.

I never mentioned to Nita my fear that her parents might yet be denounced, though their whereabouts were secret to all but a few and they never emerged from their tiny apartment. Once we visited them in Nice, and it hurt to see them with the pallor that comes from confinement and the forced cheerfulness of the old lady, who was determined to keep up her husband's courage.

Our visit depressed Nita. Traveling back to La Bocca she was silent, but her face was drawn with worry she couldn't hide, and I noticed how thin she had become lately. I took her hand wordlessly, and it was cold, though the crowded train was oppressively warm. She answered my touch with a little pressure that was an unspoken appeal, almost that of a child who pleads for reassurance. I tried to offer it with a sure smile, but even as I did so I couldn't help wondering if I were as transparent as I felt.

We were opening the front door when the telephone rang, and for an instant we stood there transfixed. It rang again, sharp, demanding. Nita closed her eyes as if to shut out the sound of it. We both shared the same fear that somehow this call involved her parents.

"I have to answer," I said heavily and took the call, only to find a friendly stranger on the line from Antibes. He identified himself as René Laporte, a writer, and could I come to see him soon and meet someone who knew me very well? Hesitant at first, I let him persuade me, then hung up wondering if I had done the right thing.

But we went the next day, and as I shook hands with Laporte, a man emerged whom I had never expected to see again, a fine pianist and composer who had written many songs for my old friend Edith Piaf. He had disappeared when the first Gestapo roundup of Jews had begun.

"René's been hiding me ever since," he said. "He didn't dare mention my name on the phone."

I learned a great deal about Laporte that day, a sensitive, intelligent man with a deep, deep voice and probing eyes.

314

"1915 — after being wounded and captured by the Germans in World War I — entertaining my fellow prisoners in the camp."

"Twenty-four years and another war later:

At the front lines with Josephine Baker in World War II — again entertaining French soldiers."

"1947 — and I was facing an American audience for the first time in more than a decade. My old friend, Charles Boyer, and Ingrid Bergman came backstage when my one-man show was over."

"After my first live television spectacular Mary Martin said, 'You've won fifty million American hearts.' Maybe it was an exaggeration, but I loved it."

HARWYN CLUB

"There was a quiet and a sweetness about my mother and the beauty of simplicity, and her smile when it came was like a light. She seems always close to me now, just as she was alive."

"*My return to American films in* Love in the Afternoon *brought the double pleasure of working with fine actors, Gary Cooper and Audrey Hepburn, and marvelous director, Billy Wilder.*"

"*And then there was* Gigi. *Leslie Caron and Louis Jourdan — and myself as Uncle Honoré who sang 'I'm Glad I'm Not Young Any More.'*"

"With that adorable Audrey Hepburn on my 68th birthday. Am I truly 'glad I'm not young any more?' Of course not, but since you can do nothing about the march of years, you might as well not grieve about it."

"Myself — and many faces."

"Ten minutes beyond Paris in the little village of Marnes-la-Coquette is my home, surrounded by tall, stately trees and carpeted lawn and lavish gardens. It's a happy house."

Among the young intellectuals along the Riviera who had formed a Resistance group he was one of the heads, and when he spoke of our country's heritage and principles and the inevitable return of freedom I felt a new pride in being a Frenchman. Newspapers, books, poetry were being secretly printed, impassioned words to feed the spirit, exhorting our people to hold on to their faith and belief in the eventual overthrow of this tyranny that had swept over us.

"What can I do?" I asked him with a wry smile. "To write in secret is one thing, but singing's a little less practical."

"I'm afraid so," he agreed, then went on thoughtfully. "Would you consider being a letter box, Maurice?" He smiled at my puzzled frown. "Resistance men along the coast exchange messages and instructions by mail; it's safer than the phone. But it has to be indirect."

"Indirect?"

"Intermediaries — people not tied in by the Gestapo with the underground. Our letters come to these middlemen in double envelopes; they open the first, and deliver the second to the Resistance by hand. They have to be people like you, Maurice, who always get a lot of mail, so a few extra pieces won't be suspected." His smile had faded now. "Of course, there's always the chance of being discovered. I don't have to explain what happens then."

"Just being alive is a chance," I said. "When do I start?"

"Right away."

And so my friendship with René Laporte began that day. How little I realized in the dark months to follow how closely our lives would be linked.

My hands were shaking violently and I stared at them as if they belonged to someone else, but nothing could control the panic overwhelming me at the sight of this letter in my fingers. The single page bore a dreaded signature: Commissioner of Jewish

315

Questions. An investigation had been ordered, it informed me, into the subject of Nita Raya.

Proofs were wanted that Nita was "Aryan" enough for the Nazis — a birth certificate or a baptismal record or any document attesting to religion.

Over and over again I read the note for clues to its tone. It was not harsh, there were no threats or penalties implied, but why after all these months of ignoring Nita had this ominous inquiry arisen? Had someone denounced her in one of those anonymous missives that were rumored to be so frequent here now? I couldn't believe it, for no one had reason to wish Nita ill. Yet something had stirred up a malevolent interest in her case.

Almost without thinking I found myself in our bedroom pulling down a suitcase from a closet shelf, tossing it on the bed, starting to pack. It was as if I were impelled to move, to prepare for the trip to Paris that had lain in my mind as a desperation measure since the Germans had occupied the Riviera.

"Maurice, what is it?"

Nita had entered without my seeing her, and there was alarm in her eyes at the sight of the luggage.

"I have to go to Paris for a few days, Nita."

"But why? Has something happened?"

I put on a teasing smile. "Yes, you've driven me to it. Anything to get away from you, even Paris." In her fear she didn't seem even to have heard me, and I realized how little it took to frighten her these days. I took her in my arms. "I have to go, darling. It's not serious, but it's necessary. Now, cheer up."

"Why won't you tell me what it's about?"

"Because your pretty head is full of fancies and there's no room for more." I kissed her and I was thinking, Oh God, let this work, because if it doesn't, what can I do next?

And the thought was still with me as I waited in the drably furnished Paris office of a civil servant who would hear my request. It was February. The day was gray and damp and cold, and I felt sick inside, for I was about to tell a series of lies and this had never come easy to me.

The door opened and I rose, then stopped short as my eyes looked into a face I'd seen somewhere before. But this man was wearing the uniform of a German captain, and I knew no Nazi officers. He was smiling in a tight, humorless way, waiting for the recognition he knew would come.

"You don't quite remember, Monsieur Chevalier?" he said finally, and I shook my head. "Cannes, seventeen months ago, without the uniform?"

I was searching my memory, and then it came to me. This captain was the man in the government office whom I'd suspected as Gestapo, the one who casually and devastatingly brought Nita into the question of my performing in Paris. Terror struck me. Why was he handling Nita's case now?

"So you do recall?" He was shuffling papers on the desk and stopped with the letter I had brought with me. "And we come to the subject of your Mademoiselle Raya again, I see."

"It's a mistake, her name shouldn't be on that list."

"Then where is the birth certificate to prove she is not a Jewess?"

"It was lost when she left Romania with her parents. All the papers were lost."

He consulted the dossier again. "You say her father was French, and you want a certificate to that effect. Where is he?"

"Dead. And the mother, too." I wondered if he could read in my face that I was lying.

He was tapping a pencil slowly on an inkwell. It made a dry, metallic sound. "I suppose she told you she is a Catholic?"

"I've never asked."

"Then how do you know she's not Jewish?"

I felt the blood begin to pound at my temples. "Because she said so when all this started."

"And you believed her?"

"Completely."

I forced myself to breathe slowly and deeply to still the turmoil within me as the captain's eyes never left my face. Finally he dropped his level gaze. "We will study the case."

"That letter," I said feeling my way, "what do I do about it?"

"You do nothing till we study the case." He began collecting the papers as if this interview was over and I thought, I've failed but at least I've won a respite. Then he straightened up to face me pointedly again. "We get reports you are a sick man, Monsieur Chevalier, too sick to perform." I nodded. "Perhaps one of our German doctors could miraculously restore you to health."

Suddenly in my mind I could see myself being summoned before a commission of doctors and given tests which would show that my physical condition was good, and I decided instantly that I would claim vertigo and loss of memory and fainting spells. These no medical examination could disprove, and I could point to having suffered similarly twenty years ago before my breakdown. All of this raced through my brain, just as the last thoughts of a drowning man.

And then abruptly the captain turned away and only stopped long enough at the door to say with his same smile that went no farther than his lips, "Your memory will undoubtedly be better the next time, monsieur."

He was gone and I was alone, my heart hammering wildly, and the next thing I was aware of clearly was the chill winter wind outside and the stark limbs of trees above me as I walked quickly away with fear as my companion.

"ARE YOU sure nothing bad happened in Paris, Maurice?" Nita was looking strangely at me, just as she had done all day since my return. I had told her nothing, but evidently my face or my mood was giving me away.

"Nothing, believe me. Now, you mustn't talk, Nita."

We were sitting by the radio as I tried to tune in London and the Free French voices we secretly listened to each night for news and messages of hope for better days to come. The volume was muted to a whisper, for monitoring Radio London was forbidden by Nazi edict. On this night, too, there was a little static, and we strained to hear. A French song writer who had recently escaped and made his way to England was lashing out as he did each evening at Nazi chiefs and those Frenchmen who had collaborated with them.

Tonight he was citing those of his own métier, men and women of the theatre, who had found it expedient to cooperate with the Germans. I heard the names sadly, for most of these people in my profession I had known at one time or another and the course they had taken was a depressing one to me.

"Maurice Chevalier!"

The first instant I heard my name spoken I thought I'd understood wrongly, but Nita had sat up in sudden shock and I knew in one stunned realization that this man had indeed accused me with those others of collaboration with the enemy and gone on to say in a cavernous voice that everyone listed should be punished to the ratio of his wrongs.

"My God!" It was the first thing I could utter above the pain that seared through my heart, and then almost stupefied, over and over again: "It's awful, it's awful!" Nita's fingers were digging into my arm, but overcome with the enormity of this lie I barely felt the pressure. I could only think that millions of my countrymen had probably heard this shameful, unwarranted attack.

A sleepless night passed before my friends in the Resistance, equally staggered by the accusation against me, came to the house to discuss what could be done to set it right.

René Laporte was saying reassuringly, "Around here, they all know it's a lie, Maurice."

"There's more to France than the Riviera," I said. "Do they all know it, too?"

One of the Resistance heads was writing a message to be slipped through immediately to London. "Mistake on Maurice Chevalier," it read. "He has given proof of his loyalty and will give more."

"Your name won't be mentioned again," he said. "I'm sure of it."

"But that's not enough," I protested. "The only way to remedy the damage is to broadcast a retraction, let the whole country know the truth!"

René nodded unhappily. "Including the Nazis, Maurice? Do you realize what could happen then?" He glanced meaningfully toward the next room where Nita was waiting for me.

His implication was achingly clear. If Radio London came on to retract its statement about me or even merely to deny it, the Nazis, who of course monitored these broadcasts, would assume the Resistance had come to my defense. To the Germans this would mean only one thing — that my "inactivity" was a pose, that I was in reality actively working against them. Surely they would seize me, and then how long would it be before they seized Nita?

"Will it be all right, Maurice?" she said in a frightened voice when my friends had gone.

I held her close to me. "Completely," I said and tried to keep the anguish from my voice.

. . . *Six*

THE RESISTANCE message concerning me reached London, and my name was never mentioned again on those condemning broadcasts. But as I walked through Cannes where people smiled and called out to show they hadn't believed the accusation in the first place, I could only think of the myriad towns which knew nothing of me but what they had read or heard. I realized what many there must be feeling about me now, and the unfairness of it chained my spirit. If ever the invasion came — there were rumors it would happen this spring — and France were free again, I was determined the truth would be known.

Three weeks had gone by when I thought I saw the Nazi captain and all else left my mind.

I had bicycled into Cannes for the papers, and a funeral cortege had blocked the street where I was waiting to cross. The entire procession was on foot, even the bearers of the casket with their grim load on six shoulders, and all traffic had halted until they would pass. Suddenly around a curve in the narrow street where I stood, two cars emerged with blaring horns, slowing down only long enough for the mourners to break ranks and permit the vehicles to plunge through.

In that instant's pause I glanced at the first car. Three German officers sat deep in the back seat and argued with violent gestures. One turned abruptly toward the street as the car moved forward and in one chilling second of dread the face I saw was his. Then it was gone, and I was only half sure, and I tried to dismiss my worry, but it refused to go away. Climbing the hill to La Bocca I felt panic growing in me, and before I reached the house my imagination had painted a canvas of horror in which Nita was being dragged away and forced into that car to disappear forever.

But she was standing at the front door, and I must have shown my giant relief for she looked at me concerned. "What is it, Maurice?"

"Nothing. I'm just glad to be out of that madhouse in town."

"Well, someone's waiting here for you. He's on the terrace."

"Who?" I said in sudden alarm. "Who is it?"

She smiled with the weariness I saw more and more often on her face. "For once it's not bad news," she said wryly.

It was a young man whose brother I knew, a friend of Desha with word from her in Dordogne that her husband's mother and father were living now in a large farmhouse remote from any town. "Safety," she wrote, "away from the Riviera and its beehives of Gestapo." There was room for Nita's parents and us as well if we wanted to leave Cannes.

Leave Cannes? From now on each time I looked down at the town gleaming in the sun below I would see that face in the car and feel the imminence of disaster. It was surely time to run. But moving these two old people from Nice was a fear, for should they be singled out for questioning by the Germans they were lost. They could obviously not travel alone, yet to journey with Nita and me would surely draw attention to them. I needed some way to make them inconspicuous, simply a part of the crowd.

"They could be my parents," my visitor was saying. "No one would suspect an old man and woman traveling with their son." He grinned. "I know how to talk to Nazis."

I looked at him uncertainly. He had the face of a boy, but his eyes were a man's. One grows up swiftly in these times, I was thinking.

And so it was arranged. Quickly we moved, the boy to Nice with instructions and Nita and I to pack a single suitcase and jam ourselves into the one crowded compartment reserved for civilians on a military train to Dordogne. We walked through shadowed, almost deserted back streets to the station. Yet each car that passed found me averting my face and praying.

It was a fearful trip, two people fleeing the Nazis surrounded by an entire trainload of their soldiers, but it was over at last and we entered a simple home in open country four miles from the nearest village. The first spring buds were swelling on the trees, and regarding them in the midst of this incredible tranquillity I felt an emotion burgeoning in me that had long been buried. Hope. Reunited now with Nita's mother and father, safe from the Gestapo who restricted themselves to the larger towns, we could wait for liberation with hope.

"Come here and our former little family group will be almost complete," I wrote Felix Paquet and his wife in Paris. "Relax with long walks in the woods and learn to sleep dreamlessly again."

It was not to last very long. The peaceful, deserted forests around us, where I had walked so many quiet hours, were rumored to be filling up with strangers — young, hard-eyed patriots who moved stealthily in the night to sabotage trains and blow up German supply dumps. A Maquis group had chosen this wooded fastness as a kind of headquarters. Quickly the Germans answered with reprisal raids, and Gestapo cars began to roam the roads. A kind of guerrilla war had sprung up almost on our doorstep.

Now the Maquis were striking doubly. Peasants accused of collaboration with the Nazis were snatched from their farms and summarily executed, and I couldn't push down the thought that some of these desperate freedom fighters might have heard that single broadcast against me from London. And not knowing me, as the Resistance people along the Riviera did, they might have believed what they heard.

It was a dispiriting thought. At Cannes the only danger for me and mine had been the Gestapo. Here I now had that danger and an added one — the risk of destruction by a revenging underground which didn't know the true story.

I curtailed my walks to move in smaller, safer circles in the fields around the house, and I returned one day to find Nita in our room. The door was open and as I approached she was standing oddly silent, staring into the armoire at her clothes hanging inside. She didn't hear me, and I watched the look of infinite sadness on her face without speaking until suddenly she turned, startled to see me.

"What were you thinking, Nita?" I asked with a kind of apprehension I couldn't explain.

"Nothing important, Maurice," she said with a shrug and closed the armoire door as if to dismiss this moment.

But I was impelled to go on with it, for something told me that an instant ago I had seen a veil stripped from Nita's face, that there was deep meaning in the unhappiness I had seen in her eyes. I took her shoulders and turned her gently toward me.

Finally she sighed and said a little tensely, "All right, I'll tell you. I was looking at those few pitiful clothes and thinking how nice it would be to wear beautiful dresses and drink champagne and dance and be alive instead of just existing." Tears sprang into her eyes. "Does that shock you, Maurice? To know that after four long years of running and hiding I want to stop and live for a minute?"

She turned abruptly and ran from the room and I made no move to follow, for though I wanted to give it, there was no comfort I could offer Nita. She was suffering as all the young people in our country were suffering. This war had stolen her youth. All this time she had been helplessly watching the marvelous young days drop away one by one without knowing the ecstatic abandon that only comes in those extravagant years. In its own insidious way life itself had robbed her.

And there was nothing I could do to help.

THE morning began like any other. We rose early, resigned to another endless day, and then the young man and his wife from the neighboring farm were running across the fields shouting garbled cries that all seemed to end in one hysterical word, "Invasion!"

It was June 6, 1944, and this day was going to be different.

They had heard the news at the village post office on the one radio in the community. The Allies had landed in Normandy, and though here we were still in the grip of the Germans, liberation was surely on the way. I remember we laughed and pounded each other on the shoulders and opened a bottle of wine and Nita's mother was crying openly the tears she had held back so long.

Felix, who was with us now, said over and over again, "I knew it would happen when we came back with you, Maurice, because I believed in your star. It's lucky, you know that?"

I was too happy at that moment to put in a wry challenge.

And he was still saying it days later when the two of us hurried to the village to hear the latest news. On the road one could hear sporadic gunfire, for this entire vicinity, inspired by the invasion, was in revolt against the Nazis. The Maquis had been joined by peasants, prison guards, policemen, hordes of men who had hidden weapons during the years of occupation.

The announcer was reporting a new German reverse in Normandy, and a cheer rose from the old villagers in the room. It was interrupted by a frantic voice at the edge of the crowd. "Monsieur Chevalier, Monsieur Chevalier!"

Forcing their way through were our young neighbors, their faces frantic. "Don't go back home," the man was stammering. "They're looking for you!"

"Who?"

"Men from the Maquis, I never saw them before, two cars full. They said they'd come to kill you."

"Run away and hide, monsieur," his wife said. "You mustn't go back there or your friend, either. They want him, too."

I turned to Felix. He had blanched, and I couldn't help thinking bitterly: Poor Felix, he followed my lucky star and look where it led him. Because he was with me, they wanted him also. I stood there for a moment, afraid, of course, and yet resigned to this reprisal from men, inflamed with the fever of war, who didn't know the truth and wouldn't wait to find out.

And now that it had come, suddenly I was tired — tired of these accusing lies, tired of being unable to fight back. If those men were determined to kill me, they'd find me sooner or later, for there was no disguise which could change my face. And dying had become an academic matter; it was inevitable in the end, so why not just settle for bullets today instead of a natural death on some future tomorrow?

"Maurice, what are we going to do?" Felix said in a quavering voice. "Where can we go, what can we do?"

326

His fear brought me sharply back to reality. This was no time for giving up. If they were going to kill me, they would at least have to work for it.

"Friends of Desha," I whispered to Felix. "Delemarre, you know them?" He nodded and I turned to the two friends who at least for the moment had saved our lives. "Delemarre," I said tautly. "Tell Nita we won't be back. She'll know what to do."

With that we walked quickly out of the post office onto a road which led to the village of Cadouin, five miles away. It was a flight where each sound of an approaching car or motorcycle sent us darting into the woods for cover. But finally I recognized the house through the trees and we raced the last hundred yards to safety.

Delemarre, a performer himself who played the small towns in this region, was incredulous that the Maquis would want to harm me.

"They want to kill me," I said grimly. "It's much more permanent."

That night, hidden in a back room on the second floor where a few months before Delemarre had sheltered a group of Resistance men, I heard a threat in each snapping twig and rustling leaf outside my window, and I was wondering if I would ever see Nita again. The thought that she might never call my name again and come running with that marvelous grace to meet me and press her warm body so close that I could feel the fervent beat of her heart, the thought that I would never again know that delighted sound of her old-time joyous laughter brought me sharply awake, and I sat up in the darkness till the first light of dawn crossed the sky.

But the next day Nita was there, leaving her parents behind, come to share the hiding place I dared not leave. For weeks we were to secrete ourselves in this house, caught between the menace of the Maquis who were undoubtedly still seeking me

327

and bands of Germans who were still entrenched in pockets nearby and who sallied out to burn and pillage and kill. It was a terrifying vigil. One day we watched in horror as a Nazi bombardment virtually wiped out a village only a mile and a half away and asked ourselves if our turn were next.

Then suddenly the Germans, threatened with being squeezed into a trap by the Allied advance from the west and a new invasion from the south, were retreating. As our group hid in the protective covering of a little grove of trees we could see truckloads of them pulling out for the north. And now the Resistance were in complete control in the area.

"I have friends in the Maquis," Delemarre was saying. "I'll tell them the whole story, Maurice."

"Yes, but will they take your word for it?" I asked despondently. "Up to now, it seems they've accepted that story from London."

"They'll believe me."

But there was no chance to find out, for the German radio, using me for their propaganda to the last, signed my death certificate with a single incredible broadcast. "The voice of Germany in Paris," the loudspeaker crackled. "Details are coming in little by little on the murder of the popular Maurice Chevalier. Recognized on the street by a band of patriots, he was seized and beaten to death. And his only crime was to sing in France during the Occupation and bring comfort to prisoners in Germany."

I heard this news appalled. The Germans weren't reporting my death, rather they were condemning me to it with half-truths and implications. For would the Maquis, not being told the reasons for my one trip to Alten Grabow or my two brief, forced appearances in Paris or the fact that I hadn't sung there in eighteen months, believe me or Delemarre now?

The days ran together in a kind of hopeless waiting. Paris was liberated, and the realization that I might never look at the

Seine again or walk those streets where beauty lived was a taunting anguish, for surely, I would tell myself over and over again, it was not meant to end this way for me.

Delemarre was tuning in the Liberation Radio from Toulouse, the largest city in this section, more than a hundred miles away. It, too, was now in the hands of the Resistance. I was only half listening, when slowly I became aware of the announcer's deep, rich voice. "It's René Laporte, it must be," I said and called Nita.

She heard and nodded excitedly. "Of course it's René. Is he in Toulouse now?"

The thought came to both of us at the same moment. If I could get to Laporte, who was speaking as the Voice of the Resistance, I could be cleared and safe. But there were no phones in operation now, and it was suicide to risk the journey.

"Not for me, Maurice," Nita said. "I'll go to him." I shook my head, and she went on. "There's no danger for me, darling, the Germans are gone. I'm free now."

Free. It was true. Nita was free now and secure. And it was I whose death was so near, and ironically, at the hands of my own countrymen.

NITA had been gone less than two hours, and I was sitting alone in the living room trying to chart the course René Laporte could take when she reached him. Would a broadcast in my behalf be sufficient? Stories had circulated of these tough young men who shot first and sought details later. I was a man marked for execution, and how was the mark to be erased?

Suddenly the scream of brakes sounded from the road, and a car pulled up in front of the house. Three men with tommy guns emerged, and for an instant I sat frozen before I could dart upstairs to hide in my back room. They were hammering at the door. With my own door opened a crack I heard Delemarre answering.

"Chevalier? There's no one here by that name."

"He's here, so let's not play any games, monsieur." The voice was hard and assured. "We've come to arrest him, where is he?"

"All right, he was here," my friend was saying. "But he's gone now, I don't know where — Toulouse, maybe."

"He's lying." This was a thin wire-spring of a voice.

"I know he is." It was the first one again. "Delemarre, we're going to search the house, and after we find him, we'll decide what to do to you."

There was no choice left for me. I descended the stairs as steadily as I could and confronted them. "What do you want?" I said slowly.

The one with the hard voice stepped a pace forward. "You're wanted for questioning in Périgueux."

Questioning, I was thinking. It's probably their polite term for execution, but why drive me thirty miles to do the job?

"Let's go, monsieur." He gestured the other two to the car and motioned me toward the door with his gun.

The thought flashed across my mind that at this very moment Nita was en route toward the man who might be able to save me, but hours would surely pass before she was at his side, and even then they wouldn't know what was happening to me. No, by the time they finally did know, it was going to be an eternity too late.

... *Sept*

WOULD YOU like a cigarette, monsieur?"
I shook my head and the leader of the three men turned back to stare at the road ahead, his gun cradled in his arms. I was in the rear seat with the youngest of the three, a boy with a shock of reddish hair and an open, innocent face. He had said nothing since I entered the car, but now he leaned forward to catch my eye. "Are you scared?"

It was such a ridiculous question, with me riding at breakneck speed on a possible road to my own execution, that I couldn't help a humorless smile. "What do you think?"

"I think yes," the driver said, the boy with the wire-spring of a voice. "We do this all the time, you know that?" He glanced quickly back at me in a kind of pleased way. "Delivery boys, that's our job. Only sometimes we don't quite make it."

"Shut up," the leader muttered.

The boy seemed not to have heard him. "We get to a certain point along the way, then we stop and invite our clients to take a little walk. You like to walk?"

"Not particularly," I said as casually as I could, for I knew what was coming next, it was so predictable the way a bad film is.

"We're not walking anywhere," the man beside him said firmly. "So forget it, huh?"

"Two of us go for a walk, only one comes back; it's pretty simple," the driver went on determinedly.

The youngest boy looked as if he might be sick. "He's only joking, monsieur, he wouldn't do anything like that."

You're wrong, boy, I was thinking. If there were just the two of us now in this car, he'd do it in a minute.

The driver turned to grin at me. "That's because you're special. Double Mètre said so."

"Who is Double Mètre?" I asked.

"He's the captain," the boy beside me answered. "That's where we're taking you."

Double Mètre. These men in the Maquis assumed names to hide their identity from the enemy, and I had heard many of them — The Sun, The Arrow, others as unrevealing — but somehow this particular name had for me the sound of threat in it. And logically so, I told myself, this is to be your interrogator, and he *is* a threat.

We were in Périgueux. The car threaded its way through milling hordes and drew up outside a house from whose windows men and women were peering as if our arrival had been awaited with eagerness, and I heard my name called from one

332

to the other as I descended from the car. An enormous feeling of depression swept over me, for it was as if I were some bizarre animal on display in a zoo; yet the eyes that stared down at me were not all hostile. More of them, in fact, were friendly, and a man came up to me as we approached the building to say, "It hurts me to see you in this situation, monsieur."

I wasn't ready for words of sympathy, and I blinked to force back tears, and then suddenly a kind of anger pushed aside all other emotions, anger that I was being paraded this way for a baseless, unjust reason. When the guard at the door said in a low, surly voice as I approached, "I'd like to take care of this guy myself, I'd fix him," I stared at him coldly till he moved aside and I mounted the stairs to the third-floor interrogation room. I was resigned to what destiny had waiting for me, but it was an angry resignation.

An army major confronted me with the charge of collaboration. I explained quickly and succinctly how it had all come about. Slowly his severe expression softened. "This will all have to be verified by the Resistance committee in Paris, monsieur," he said finally. "We'll need a signed statement, then you can go back to your house and wait."

"Just a minute," a voice said, and I heard murmurs of "Double Mètre" around the room. I turned to confront a giant of a man, whose body seemed completely out of proportion. He was too tall and too fat, and his skin had an oily, unhealthy pallor that seemed to accentuate the menace emanating from him. He was smiling a strangely unpleasant smile at me while he spoke to the major.

"I'll take his statement," he said, relishing it. "We have to treat this man with the respect due his position, every respect."

The words were genial but the sarcasm in his tone was deadly, and the same old helpless resentment I'd always felt at this kind of cruelty welled up in me. I was still trembling with it

333

when the room was cleared and I was left alone with Double Mètre. He was smiling no longer. Now he was gazing at me with undisguised hate and little beads of sweat began to pop out along his forehead and upper lip. Finally he motioned me to sit down and summoning a stenographer to a typewriter on the desk beside him, he said his first direct words to me.

"You were condemned to death by the Resistance, Monsieur Maurice Chevalier, when they were sitting in Algiers." He was speaking with such repressed fury that each word was difficult. "And two months ago we would have had the delight of carrying out their sentence ourselves right here and now. But unfortunately today we have to wait for a decision from the new headquarters in Paris, especially in the case of celebrated traitors like you."

The venom in him was so intense that I could only stare at him in horror, seeing suddenly in his eyes the viciousness and cruelty I'd seen in those of a Gestapo agent arresting an old Jewish man last winter in the railroad station in Cannes. I tried not to betray what I was feeling.

"I don't understand why you're speaking so harshly to me, monsieur," I managed to say.

His complexion grew even paler, and he took a long difficult breath. "Not 'monsieur,' " he said hoarsely and pointed to the stripes on the shoulder of his uniform. "Captain!" Then he began the same interrogation I had gone through half an hour before. As I repeated my story, he frowned throughout and seemed not to hear, but at the end he started to dictate the deposition I would have to sign. I listened with intent concentration, determined this evil man would not have a chance to twist my testimony as he would obviously have wanted it.

"Périgueux, September 14, 1944," he dictated. "Before us, Captain Double Mètre, chief of the Department of Exoneration for the region of Dordogne, has appeared Chevalier, Mau-

334

rice, music hall entertainer, arrested on evidence broadcast by Radio London and sentenced to death by the Tribunal of Free France.

"I, the undersigned, Chevalier, Maurice, certify that I quickly realized when the government asked me to sing for French prisoners in Germany, in December, 1941, that they were seeking to compromise me. For this performance, instead of a fee, I demanded that ten prisoners be freed and this was promised. I certify, and it can be proved, that this was my only trip to Germany. German and French propaganda seized on this single performance and turned it into a 'tour.' I protest, for I did not make a tour in Germany. And since that time, I have never sung at any affair connected with politics. For four years I have refused to make a film.

"The proof that I was not favored by the German authorities is that I have not had my share of gasoline," Double Mètre went on to the typist.

"Wait a minute," I interrupted, shaken. "I said that I've never had a car or gas and never asked for either, that I've been happy to use the subway in Paris and a bicycle in Cannes."

Double Mètre regarded me coldly, then ignoring my protest, continued to dictate. "During the entire German occupation I sang only twelve weeks in Paris, and from the end of 1942 have never reappeared on the Parisian stage. In April, 1943, I completely retired from the stage and remained on my property above Cannes.

"I put myself and all proof at the disposition of the Resistance. Signed, Maurice Chevalier." As the typist struck the last key, Double Mètre ripped the paper from the machine, looked it over and thrust it at me. "Sign."

I scanned the words trying to focus on the phrase about gasoline.

"Come on, sign it," he said harshly and I put my signature

to the page, suddenly so weak from the ordeal of these past hours that I was afraid I might collapse. When I stood up, I held my shoulders straight and stiff to sustain myself.

Double Mètre had opened the door and the room was swarming with men and women who wanted my autograph. What grand irony, I was thinking, that I should be accused on the one hand and applauded on the other. "No demonstrations," Double Mètre shouted.

"How do I get back to Cadouin?" I asked him.

"Any way you can," he snapped back.

I could only wait uncertainly, for I knew what could happen if I returned alone on the road or even on the train. The death sentence was still hanging over me. Any overzealous patriot who recognized me might decide to carry it out himself. I knew I would never arrive at Delemarre's house.

The man who had spoken kindly to me when we arrived was beside me now. "I have a friend with a car downstairs, monsieur. I'll see you get back."

"Hold on, Barrière," Double Mètre said heavily. "Let him find his own way home."

"You're only the interrogator, Double Mètre," the man said quietly. "That's all. I take my orders from Paris the same as you."

He took my arm and started down the stairs with me. As we entered the waiting car, I heard Double Mètre crying out to the crowd of people who had surrounded me with silent sympathy, "Shut up, down there, no demonstrations!"

It was not until we had driven away from Périgueux that I could shake off the pursuing, vengeful shadow of Double Mètre.

"In a way it's a kind of revolution, monsieur," Barrière was saying a little sadly, "this Resistance of ours. And we search so violently for the guilty that sometimes we strike down the innocent."

336

It was morning again, and the sound of a car reached my room. I was lying there exhausted and dulled from a sleepless night spent in going back and forth over my narrow escape from death and my continuing imprisonment in this house.

A knock sounded at the door and I stiffened. Then slowly it opened and Nita was there, and we were embracing and her words were coming to me from some faraway planet to say that she had seen Laporte and a Resistance colonel and a car was waiting to take me to Toulouse.

"But it's no use," I was saying. "They'll recognize me on the way; I'll never make it."

She held out a piece of paper. It was a pass from the Resistance to be presented at all barricades along the road, authorizing the transport of an "unidentified" passenger.

"They sent two men with machine guns to protect you," Nita said, but I must have still seemed unconvinced, for she insisted, "It's true, darling, it's all over. By this afternoon you'll be with René."

The pass was for a single passenger. "Aren't you coming with me, Nita?"

"I'll be there tomorrow on the train. I want to see Mama and Papa and let them know you're safe."

At the door Delemarre shook my hand. "Good luck, Maurice, you're safe now."

Was I? Somehow I found it hard to believe that each turn of the wheels was taking me farther from Double Mètre and his sadistic desire to see me dead. I shrank back into the cushions of the rear seat, grimacing strenuously at each roadblock in an effort to avoid recognition, but that pass and my armed escort worked miracles, for not once were we stopped for longer than a moment before being waved on toward Toulouse and freedom.

René Laporte was a wonderful friend. As he brought me to his mother's house where Nita and I would stay, I poured out the

337

story of my nightmare months since we had said good-by in Cannes. "There were moments when I never thought I'd be safe again, you know?"

"Maurice," he said slowly, "you're not — not yet. You have to hide here. You can't go out of the house till this whole thing is cleared up." I looked at him in consternation. "The streets are full of trigger-happy men, and you're a good target."

"You're the head of the radio here. How much time does it take to go on the air and broadcast the truth that it's all been a hideous mistake? Surely it could be repeated till everyone in the city hears it."

"It's not so simple as that, I'm afraid." He motioned me to sit down but I was too tense and I paced as he spoke. "The report from Double Mètre has gone to Resistance headquarters in Paris. They're the ones who condemned you, they're the ones with the authority to clear you, don't you see?"

I saw too well. I was still caught in my weird, unreal trap. "How long will it take to set them straight?" I said wearily.

"Days, weeks maybe." He smiled wryly. "There's a little matter of a war we haven't won yet, so they're pretty busy." A tight band of pain was constricting my brain, the knowledge that I had simply found refuge here, not freedom. "I'll do everything I can, Maurice," René was saying, "just be patient," and I nodded to express my thanks. At that moment I could say nothing. I could only think over and over again, I've come so far and there's still so far to go.

THE days in hiding seemed endless now. At least in the country I had been able to walk around the house and in the fields, but here I dared not venture from the apartment. By the hour I sat at the radio and listened to the names of those arrested by the Resistance for collaboration. Nearly all the top stars of the theatre seemed to be suspected. Sometimes it was true, sometimes not, but I noticed that only the accusations, never the

338

retractions, were trumpeted, for, sadly, a man being charged with a crime is bigger news than the same man being cleared.

Nita was leaving for the afternoon to pick up her parents whom she had brought to Toulouse and who were walking the streets now with broad smiles at every passer-by because they were so happy to be free again. They had been caged in fear for so long. It was the one good note for me in this disconsolate time.

"See you in a while," Nita said airily and was gone. Oddly I felt a tiny touch of annoyance. Now that our positions were reversed and I was the prisoner, Nita had become almost too buoyant in spirit for me. I hadn't really expected her to suffer with me the pain I was experiencing, this eternal waiting for something good and right to happen, but I needed her understanding and support and somehow it just wasn't there.

I peered through the curtains and saw her on the sidewalk below walking with a light, bouncing step, and then I rebuked myself a little. The bird is loosed at last and wants to fly, I was thinking, so give her a chance, and once she's used to it she'll be your wonderful companion again.

A car drew up in front of the building as Nita disappeared, and instinctively I pulled back from the window, for the men who were emerging were strangers in uniform. Whatever their mission was here, I didn't want to be seen.

But their mission concerned me. They were a group of British aviators and a war correspondent who had learned of my hiding place and flown down from Paris to see me. The journalist was with the great London newspaper, the *Daily Express*, and he wanted to help me by telling my true story on page one. I remember looking at their sympathetic faces, realizing that finally I would be able to reply publicly to my accusers, and I was so moved that for a moment I couldn't speak.

Then the whole story poured out of me in a torrent of words, and when the interview was done I signed the reporter's notes to guarantee their authenticity. Suddenly a light had entered my darkness, and I could hardly wait for Nita's return to give her this first good news in so long a time.

She burst into the room and pirouetted around the chair in glee. "Darling, I've made a tremendous decision. The minute we return to Paris I'm going back to work."

"Good." I was smiling at her excitement. "Now let me tell you something." I recounted my afternoon's experience with the newspaperman and watched her face expectantly.

"Then we'll be leaving any day now," she said eagerly. "That's wonderful!" And she began to list all her plans, the producers she would see, the kind of act she would plan, the new songs she would learn. She was babbling away about these unimportant things, and suddenly it stung me.

"Nita, maybe you didn't hear what I said. Do you realize my whole life may be about to open up once more?"

She was taken aback, and faced me with wide, startled eyes. "Of course, Maurice. But it was bound to happen eventually, we both knew that."

As I looked at her and saw she really didn't understand or even care maybe, the annoyance I had felt this afternoon rose up in me again. And this time I could make no effort to dismiss it.

But too much was beginning to happen to dwell too long on these unexpected and disappointing reactions from Nita. I was being asked to meet my accuser face to face, the song writer who had begun this whole horror with his broadcast from London.

"He's on his way to Paris," René was saying. "He wants to talk to you, to try and straighten this out, Maurice."

"What's there to straighten out?" I said angrily. "He was wrong. Why isn't he man enough to stand up and say so?"

"Because it takes a very big man simply to admit he's made a mistake, Maurice," René said quietly, "without trying to rationalize his way out. Perhaps that's why he wants to see you."

Still I hesitated, sickened at the thought that I should shake hands with a man who had done me so much harm. "If he'll go on the air and acknowledge openly that he erred," René said, "then you'll be cleared that much faster, don't you see?"

"I'll meet him," I said at last.

An hour later the man stood before me, a lieutenant in uniform, small, compactly built, eyes steely and hard. We shook hands, and all that I could think was that this human being had tried to destroy me in the eyes and hearts of my countrymen. With no attempt at verifying the smear he was to hurl over a microphone, he had almost cost me my life and, truly more important, my name. I was choked with emotion. Part of it was a giant anger at this slanderer. The other part was misery that this shame had ever come to rest on me.

Struggling to control my feelings, I went point by point over my story. At no point did he express his regrets or offer an explanation for his reckless error. Instead, he questioned me like a judge and finally asked for a statement of all I had told him which he would present before the Committee of Exoneration set up by the Resistance in Paris.

"I'll plead your case," he said. "I like you, Chevalier."

He was gone, and I stood at the door shaking in helpless rage. Plead my case? If it hadn't been so vital for me, I would surely have burst out in embittered laughter before him. I was being forced by destiny to accept my accuser as defender.

Yet René was right. Whatever rationalization this man succeeded in devising for himself, his appearance before the committee in my behalf would hasten my clearance. I could only pray that it would come quickly.

But other events were to come first. Three days later another British military plane landed in Toulouse, this time with a newsreel cameraman to record my story. The *Daily Express* article had appeared and parts of it had been broadcast in many countries. Now Paramount News wanted shots of me in my present hideout and then a statement to be filmed in my Paris apartment to be shown around the entire world.

"Paris?" It seemed almost a dream to me, too much joy.

"You'll fly back with us," the cameraman was saying. "And Miss Raya."

I looked at Nita and there was surely pure radiance in my eyes. Paris. Finally to come home among the people who had known me and taken me to their hearts so many times before. Finally a chance to speak the truth and be heard and seen as well. Finally to lift the curtain of despair.

Nita was warm in the circle of my arm, and the doubts and the fears were gone. Life was waiting for me. And love. Everything would be right again, for we were going back to Paris.

. . . Huit

To MY RIGHT was the laced-steel finger of the Eiffel Tower and below was the familiar pattern of Paris streets emanating from a hundred circles like the spokes of wheels and then the plane was on the landing strip at Le Bourget. The day glistened with autumn sunlight and men in American and British and French uniforms milled around the airport. A few civilian faces were among them, and some recognized me in surprise.

"So you're not dead, Maurice?" a workman in grimy coveralls shouted with a grin and I grinned back because there was warmth in that voice and welcome. To me it was a sign that I had come home again.

Climbing in the car the Paramount man had arranged,

I was recalling so many other grave moments in my life when Paris had been waiting for me, each one the end of a chapter of living: My return from prison, the end of the years with Mist when memories had haunted rather than helped me that day, the fearful road back from Saujon, the farewell to Hollywood. Each time Paris had marked a beginning, a turn into a new road. Not so now, at least not yet, for the future couldn't begin until the present had ended. But riding along these familiar boulevards, I told myself, I was surely heading for the finale of that grim present, and once it had played out its role, the bright new days would start.

How beautiful the avenues were! The trees wore their first hint of yellow, and the houses seemed to smile, even those whose façades wore bullet holes and shattered cornices from the fighting on the eve of the city's liberation when Resistance men battled to dislodge the last Germans and their sympathizers. And how different the streets were from those dismal days of occupation when Nazi soldiers moved stiffly along them! Now a host of friendly fighting men were casually strolling the boulevards and appreciatively eying the pretty French girls as they raced by on their bicycles, skirts ballooning in the wind. Yes, it was so beautiful that my heart hurt with the joy of it.

When we reached my little apartment we made the newsreel for Paramount in which I gave the factual story of my visit to Alten Grabow and why it had never been possible up to now to establish the truth. I finished by singing one of my old American songs, "Up on Top of a Rainbow," and I truly believed the words I sang.

That same evening Louis Aragon, the editor of a leading Paris paper, *Ce Soir*, came unbidden to see me with several other newspapermen who wanted to set straight the lies that had been told about me. He informed me that he was publishing my story on the front page tomorrow. Moreover, as one of the Resistance chiefs along the Riviera, he and the men from his underground group would be in the front ranks of a great liberation parade through the city on Sunday morning, and he wanted me at his side.

"Let the people see you, Maurice," Aragon said. "Show them you've nothing to fear."

When they had left, I fell wearily but happily into a chair. This had been a long and trying but enormously fruitful day. There was still the question of clearance by the Committee of Exoneration ahead of me, but I was confident that my erstwhile accuser had already set those wheels in motion. It would surely be only a formality.

Once cleared, I was thinking, I must appear on the stage as quickly as possible. There was a driving need in me now to return to the theatre, to re-establish contact with my public, to feel the surge of life within me that my work had always brought. There would be plans to be made and people to be seen, new numbers to be developed and rehearsed. I felt my pulse quicken at the prospect.

Nita had entered the room wearing a little frown, and in my sudden optimistic turn of mind I teased her. Paris was free now, I said, and alive with hope and the war had moved far beyond us and final victory was not too impossible to foresee. "So what's worrying you, Nita?"

She was looking around her. "Four years away, I'd forgotten how small this place is, Maurice. There's hardly a corner to rehearse in."

"Don't you worry about it, I'll manage somehow."

"I was talking about myself," she said. "How can I learn new songs with no room to work on them?" She kissed me lightly. "I'll be under foot, darling, and please don't hate me for it."

Blithely she wandered away, and as I sat there I began to

think of this new fever to work which had sprung up in Nita, this urge which seemed to be making her career the focus of her life. It was of course her right, but once our love had been that most important focus and now a subtle gap was appearing between us. It could widen. At that instant, I knew it could.

I had hoped for a letter the next morning from the Committee of Exoneration, for there had been time enough since the song writer had seen me in Toulouse. If he had done as he promised, there should have been no delay. But the mail arrived and with it no notification. What had gone wrong? This was a routine clearance, a matter of paperwork by a committee set up specifically for this purpose, so why shouldn't it be here?

I ran through the letters again to be sure, and suddenly I realized that my hands were trembling violently. It was more than tension, more than nerves protesting from the racking months I had undergone. This was a kind of anger at the failure of an expectation, the disappointment of hope. It robbed me of the glow of yesterday's optimism.

"It'll be along, Maurice," Nita said gaily on her way out. "You worry too much."

It was a flighty thing to say and a little unthinking, but she meant no harm and I knew it. Still it was a tiny grating fingernail drawn against my skin, another scratch of resentment. At this moment when I needed a woman with deep comprehension and sympathy and feeling, I was getting a child.

"But you loved her for that very reason, remember?" I said aloud to myself. "You knew she was a child."

It was true, I had to face it. But ten years had passed since that first night I had watched Nita on the stage with her marvelous youth and grace. Now I had seen and felt and lived too much, and love must be more than just a light, gay heart.

I did not need love to lean on. I never had, I never would. But if it were in my life now, it should be there beside me for comfort and for warmth. One must always find his strength within himself, but love can often help him find it, and at this moment of my life I had more than ever to be strong.

A knock at the door broke into my reverie and I moved to answer. I was hardly prepared for the woman who faced me in the doorway. She was in uniform, and no female had ever looked more beautiful in one, for Marlene Dietrich was as lovely that day as the first time I'd seen her a dozen years before.

Affectionately we embraced each other, and I was too stunned at the unexpected sight of her to do more than stammer questions. "How did you know I was here, how did you find me?"

"This." She held a copy of *Ce Soir* in her hand. "And it wasn't hard to get your address." Her eyes were reading my face compassionately as we moved into the room. "You look tired, Maurice."

"I am. But you look marvelous, and what are you doing in Paris?"

"Performing, entertaining the troops." She laughed that wonderful sudden laugh I remembered. "The Yanks have landed, have you noticed?" Then she sobered. "I'll only say this once, Maurice, because it's certainly no surprise, but you should know that your friends in Hollywood and New York never believed those stories, not the people who really knew you." Abruptly her mood changed again and now she was brisk and purposeful, and I had to smile, remembering those lightning plays of her personality. "Noel Coward and I are going to sing at the Paris Stage Door Canteen, and it's time for you to go to work, so will you make it three?"

I hesitated. "You read the article, Marlene. I'm waiting for my official exoneration," I said ruefully. "Which should have been here this morning and wasn't."

"But it will be, we know it will. So is it agreed? You, Noel and I?"

She was beautiful and persuasive and I was suddenly sure that she was right. There would of course be word from the committee at any moment now, and I would be working again and the vistas were indeed sparklingly bright.

THE parade was to begin at historic Père Lachaise Cemetery, a landmark of Paris since the days of bloody civil war that raged in the city after the Franco-Prussian War. Louis Aragon met me at the entrance to conduct me himself to his group. I was to march at the head with him, flanked and followed by important leaders of the Resistance, moving proof from these men that I was beyond reproach.

I was hopeful the same acceptance would come from the people massed along the boulevard leading from the cemetery to the heart of Paris, the route of the parade. I had had moments of doubt as to the wisdom of what I was doing now, exposing myself openly to the public when my official clearance had not yet come through, for there was still the danger of attack from some misguided zealot. But, as Aragon had said, I had nothing to fear and I must show it.

Assembling within the cemetery, we marched among the tombs to the reviewing stand, then moved into the street and the long parade began with flowers thrown from the spectators and cheers rising every hundred yards. Slowly we marched, and I held my head high to remind myself that only a little more than two weeks separated me in this proud moment from the depths I had fallen to that day with Double Mètre.

Suddenly from the crowd someone shouted, "Bravo, Maurice!" And then as if it had been the signal for all of them to respond, voices cried approval from all sides. Men and women, old people, kids, each vied with the other in affectionate calls: "Sing for us, Maurice." "He's one of us." "Vive Maurice!" "Bless you!"

348

"Now we know how the people feel, Maurice," Aragon said and turned to me with a broad smile. "They adore you."

I couldn't answer. My heart and throat were both too filled with a very big happiness.

BUT I was far from happiness the following morning when a letter, forwarded from Toulouse, was delivered at my door. It had been written from Paris by my accuser, the song writer, before I had been flown here by Paramount News.

Tensely I ripped it open. It was brief. He had read my deposition to his comrades on the Committee of Exoneration, and they had nothing against me. But he personally had felt it was necessary to consider public opinion, and therefore if I would make a statement to the press saying that I had been deceived into doing certain wrongs but I regretted them, then he would countersign it, read it on the radio and I would be cleared once and for all.

I felt the hot sting of blood in my face. Was this to be a further rationalization for the man who had caused all of this? Well, I had made my statement and made it truly. I intended to make no other. I moved quickly to the telephone, and a moment later his voice came over the wire. His greeting was friendly enough until I began to point out my position. Then he quickly cooled.

"You got my story in Toulouse," I said firmly. "Since that time it's been on the front page of Ce Soir. And I've marched in the liberation parade with heads of the Resistance to the cheers of the public. I've made my explanations to the people, and you know there is nothing more to add."

There was complete silence at the other end. I thought he had hung up in my face, but a repeated hello finally brought a chilly "Yes, yes," in reply. And when I politely and pointedly

349

thanked him in advance for what I was still counting on him to do, there was a remote-voiced good-by and the wire was dead. I slammed down the receiver and turned away, driving my fist into my palm in impotent anger.

I don't know how long I sat there in my living room hearing and hardly reacting to the noisy jeeps and command cars rushing through the streets that were almost free of civilian traffic. Somewhere in the distance a sidewalk vendor was hawking freshly picked cherries, and his cries were triumphant, for Paris had been starved of fruit during all the weeks when fighting was near. But these sounds of the city were almost beyond my notice because of the turmoil raging within me. If my accuser continued to evade his responsibility, I was thinking, if he didn't openly admit his mistake without the self-justification that my new statement would have given him, would the committee grant my immediate clearance? And if not, which way could I turn to force their hand?

I knew the answer to that: there was no way. I would be at a painful, insoluble impasse.

The key turned in the lock and Nita entered, her cheeks glowing and her hair wind-swept. She was carrying a parcel.

"Hello, darling," she said with breathless excitement and threw her coat across a chair. "Wait till you see what I've got. Close your eyes."

I was in no mood for games, but I complied. Papers rattled and then she commanded me to look. She was holding a silk evening gown against her body in a kind of mannequin pose.

"Well, what do you think of it?" she asked. "It should be perfect for an opening number, it has a wonderful color and it's chic and easy to move in." She stopped with an expectant look. "Well?"

My mind was many miles away, but I managed a reply. "It's very nice, Nita. It's a good choice."

350

It was obvious she was hurt. "You're not very enthusiastic, are you, Maurice? But then you seldom are these days."

"Look, I have a million problems today, Nita, I'm sorry." I told her of the letter and the phone call.

"He'll come around eventually, Maurice," she said and busied herself with the gown. "After all, you can't undo in days what's been going on for months and months. And besides, darling, I have problems, too, and clothes are one of them."

"Then settle it for yourself," I said sharply and felt no regret for my anger.

"All right, I will. But while we're at it, there's one I can't settle: that appointment you said you'd arrange for me and haven't."

I had promised to speak for Nita to the producer of an important music hall, and she was right, I hadn't done it yet. Without a word I moved to the phone and set up a meeting between them, turning back to Nita at the end of the conversation. "He thinks there'll be something for you in the show. You're to see him tomorrow at noon."

Suddenly she was contrite and moved to kiss me. "I know it's silly of me, darling, to be this eager, but you've been a star so long you can't understand what it's like almost to be starting a career."

She was folding the dress, humming a few happy notes, and I was no longer upset with her, but rather a little disappointed. And as I watched her I found myself proposing that I take an apartment for her parents who were returning from Toulouse and that Nita move in with them. She turned to face me surprised. "You mean not live with you any more?"

"I think it would be better, Nita. That way we could see each other as often as we wanted, yet I wouldn't have to burden you with all these weights I seem to be carrying nowadays." I heard my voice saying this as though it were someone else speaking, for I knew that at this moment I was beginning to push

351

Nita from my life, yet I could do nothing to stop it. It was almost as if my old tired nerves were forbidding any more demands upon them such as Nita seemed to be putting every day.

"All right, Maurice," she said gravely, and then she nodded. "You know, darling, I think you're right. I'll be working desperately hard, and we wouldn't be together all that time, would we?"

I agreed a bit sadly, for though this separation plan had been mine, I suppose I would have been a little happier if she had accepted it not quite so readily.

THE days dragged into weeks. It was not easy to find apartments with so much of Paris requisitioned by the military, but somehow Nita managed. It was so warming to see her old mother and father happy again and secure, and Nita and I were continuing to spend a lot of time with each other. But still no official clearance from the Committee of Exoneration, and the delay was grinding at my nerves.

Then one morning I was finally summoned before them, not for interrogation but simply to be told that they would be satisfied when the song writer and I were in complete agreement. What a vicious circle it seemed to me, but I contacted him anyway, only to be informed icily that he was too busy with his work to appear before the committee. But one day he did go to them and the committee wrote an official letter to the Ministry of Beaux-Arts saying they had nothing against me and I could go back to work again.

René Laporte was leaving my apartment when I was notified, and he listened with a wry smile. "So it comes to pass," he said. "Does it strike you as a miracle, Maurice, that through the twists and turns of men and government, the lies and excuses and questionable motives one so often encounters, that the good and the just usually manage to emerge?"

"I'm still waiting, René. Simply the privilege of working again isn't enough. I want a paper that says 'complete, unqualified clearance.' "

"You'll get it, my friend." He turned at the door. "A few more convolutions, perhaps, until all the red tape is unwound. But the good is emerging, Maurice."

He shook my hand and left, and I moved back into my living room. In the mirror above the mantel I caught sight of my face and I looked at my image appraisingly. I would be bringing an older Chevalier back to work, I was thinking, with little lines that were not there five years before, and new gray hairs.

I gazed at my reflection as if to unearth marks of regret there for having remained in my country for those five rigorous years when I could have been safely sitting out the war across the sea. There were none. Because whatever had happened, however harshly those years had treated me, I could honestly meet my own eyes and say that I would have done it all again the same way. My convictions and my principles were unchanged by the severity of circumstances.

Suddenly I grinned at myself. An enormous step had been taken today. I was going back to work. And René Laporte was right. The good was emerging.

He was right, too, about the clearance, for ultimately the committee was to announce my absolute exoneration with no blame of any kind attached to me, and all the French papers trumpeted the news. At last the real story of my visit to Alten Grabow was "officially" accepted, although the people had long since known its truth. And while I'd waited, my phone had rung with calls from those boys who had been rescued from the hell of prison camp by my appearance there. It was a kind of consolation for what that appearance had cost me.

WORK.

How marvelous it was to be singing and dancing and pantomiming again before an audience! It began with a regiment of Maquis stationed at my old camp in Melun where thirty years before I had marched off to war. And then the Stage Door Canteen with Marlene and Noel and one benefit after another and finally a big music hall opening in Paris. No matter what stage I stepped on, applause rolled up to welcome me back and I stood there wanting to laugh and trying not to cry. God, how wonderful life had become again!

But it was only on stage that it was wonderful, for a strange thing had arrived with me. People were saying that I had never been stronger or more enthusiastic in my work, and true, I had never felt more alive in the theatre. Yet when the curtain would fall, an odd lassitude, a heaviness of spirit would descend, as if I had spent all my forces out there and had none left for the other hours of each day of living. In order to work at night I had to husband all my energy and resources for the big effort.

Looking back today I can see that much of it was a kind of weariness of body that came with too much war and a deep exhaustion of the spirit that was born of enduring so long the bitter trial of being mistrusted without reason. As for the rest, I think it was the crumbling of love that was tearing at me. I was watching the bits of it drop away, helpless to stop the disintegration.

Nita and I were pulling apart from each other, there was no deluding myself. In a way I still loved her, had a great tenderness for her like a child that you have saved from death. But in these past months we had become two different people. Making up for the years she'd lost, Nita was thinking of nothing but her parties and clothes and dreams of stardom. And I for the first time was finding myself unable to contend with the demands of both love and profession. Yet if I were forced to give up one, I knew it could never be my work.

354

So we were sharing a kind of half-love, and this was a mistake, for to me love is truly good only when it is a complete emotion. I don't say, you understand, that everyone must love with all his heart or not at all. I only say that for me it must be that way to be a fine and happy love.

Nita and I had known this kind of love, and perhaps one day we might again. But now each time we met we gave off tiny sparks of dissension which I knew would inevitably burst into flame and consume everything if we stayed together. It would be better to part before that unhappy moment.

Yet it is not easy to sever a relationship between a man and woman that has been so strong and is still not entirely weak. With Mist and me it had all been over for so long and we knew it, and Yvonne and I had been separated by impossible conflict long before we parted. But Nita and I had gone through so much together, and though there had never been an explosive physical passion between us, we had shared an enormous affection of which there was still so much left. The morning we said good-by, I could hardly force the words from my throat.

I was still in bed. She was wandering around the room, humming softly as she so often did, occupying herself with those mysterious feminine details of the morning — worrying over clothes or make-up or jewelry for the day.

"Nita," I said, "would you sit down here for a minute, I want to talk with you."

She turned toward me and broke off her song as she met my eyes. A serious look came into her face, and she sat beside me, silently attentive, almost as if she had sensed this moment and was prepared for it.

Painfully I went over all that I had been feeling these past months, the toll my performances were taking of me, the belief that she should be free to devote all her time and thought and love to the career she obviously wanted. "And I need to be free for mine, Nita," I said unhappily. "With every bit of energy and effort and concentration, darling, just to break even. Do you understand what I mean?"

She nodded, still without a word, but her eyes were beginning to fill with tears.

"You're young, and life is opening up in front of you, and each time you want my help you'll have it. But I think when you go your way and I go mine, it will surely be better for both of us. Surely."

In the table drawer I found a handkerchief and gave it to her. She dried her eyes with a little sniffle and then she managed a wan smile, and looking at her, so appealing and desirable, I was torn with the knowledge that I was ending something that had once been beautiful.

But when I've coped with my work, I thought suddenly, and this draining away of my resources, maybe it could be beautiful again. And I found myself halfway hoping at that instant that Nita would say, All right, Maurice, I understand you need to be alone now for some time, but I love you and couldn't be happy with any other man so I'll wait for you and when you're freer then we'll live again the way we have been.

But she didn't.

Instead she said in a little voice, "So long as we part friends, Maurice."

It was over. Perhaps I was wrong, but I thought I read a kind of relieved acceptance in her face as if already she were formulating the road ahead to that stardom she craved so eagerly now. In that final moment there was a lingering sadness inside me for what might have been. I was thinking that this might never have come to pass if years ago, when I had first loved Nita, I had not chosen to instill in her my adoration for the theatre. It was I who had made her a partner on the stage, given her an enthusiasm for work she had never had before. In a way I had planted the seed of love's destruction.

356

Still the ultimate choice had been mine, and it was done. I had been compelled to choose between my profession and my love — and love had lost. There was no time now for tears. There was too much work to be done on a whole new career at fifty-seven.

The door closed softly behind Nita. I was alone.

She gave me eyes, she gave me ears;
And humble cares, and delicate fears;
A heart, the fountain of sweet tears;
And love, and thought, and joy.

— WILLIAM WORDSWORTH

IV

Love
and
Thought
and
Joy

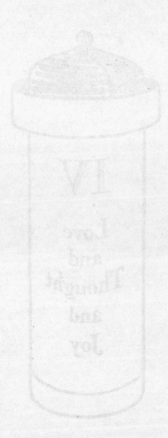

. . . Un

MY HOUSE at La Bocca was full of memories as I wandered from one silent room to the next on this summer afternoon with the war just four months over. Windows and chairs and shadowed corners summoned up images of the past, for Nita was still a part of this place, and time was needed to erase her presence. There was no bitterness in these memories, only a kind of regret that after so long a time love's fulfillment had not lived up to its promise.

Nita had come to see me in Paris just before I left on this first trip to the Riviera since we had fled the menace of the Gestapo together more than a year ago. I had opened my door one morning to find her standing there with a tremulous smile.

"Should I have called first, Maurice?" she asked uncertainly. "It all happened so quickly. I was only walking by and suddenly I wanted to see you and talk and I just rang your bell without even thinking."

"I'm glad you did," I said and led her inside the apartment where we had said good-by so recently. Looking at her now, her eyes so serious and her lovely body a little ill at ease, I felt my heart move toward her in that old protective way and I kissed her lightly and gently. "Now, what's the problem? Is it work?"

She shook her head. "Everything's fine. I've been talking with the Folies Bergère. There could be a spot for me soon."

"Good."

"It's something else, Maurice." She hesitated, then took a deep breath and the words rushed out. "There's a man, he's very rich and I think he's in love with me. I've been seeing a great deal of him and I thought you should know."

I looked at her with surprise. "Well, Nita, I'm pleased and I'm happy for you."

"You don't object?"

"But how can I? You're completely free, my dear, and so am I. We owe each other nothing, and certainly not allegiance."

"I think he might want to marry me," she said with almost a kind of defiance.

"If he's a good man, Nita, and you love him, then you should surely consider it. Do you love him?"

She said nothing, but her gaze met mine in a way that said only a part of her heart could be given to this other man, for a part still belonged to me. And recognizing this was poignant for me, because in a way I had missed her. Since our parting I had encountered transient amorous adventures, but how unimportant they were and remote from love!

Still what had once burned between Nita and me was a waning flame, and we were beyond fanning it to brilliance again.

"Marry him, Nita," I said. "And I wish you well."

In a moment she had gone, and I had thought that was the end of it, but returning here to La Bocca with its remembrances had brought Nita back into my mind again.

"It's the right way and all for the best," I told myself and thought of the marvelous work that lay ahead. Cannes and Nice had become a vacation center for the American army, and I had been asked to sing for the thousands of soldiers who were on leave here before their ultimate shipment home.

On the Croisette this afternoon I had passed dozens of them who smiled in warm recognition and groups had stopped me to say they had seen my last films ten years ago. They had been mere children then, these young men who had come to fight and win a war, and it was heartening to be remembered.

Two nights later seven thousand of them remembered when I went to Nice to see Bob Hope perform and was called up from the audience to be introduced on stage. I hadn't expected this, and I remember standing there blinking back tears as they applauded and whistled and cheered. I sang "Louise" and "Mimi" that night, and a random thought crossed my mind, the tiny beginning of an idea: Why not return to America?

I was intrigued by the idea. Not Hollywood. I had no regrets for having left it when I did or why, but I also had no illusions. I was aware that Hollywood was a town with a short memory. My personal friends there had not forgotten me, but the producers? I was sure that I had been dismissed from most of their minds half an hour after my train pulled out of town. Still it was nothing to feel bitter about. I had chosen to abandon Hollywood, so I could surely not blame it for probably having abandoned me.

But the stage? Ah, there was my métier, I was thinking, and I should use the theatre as my way to get acquainted with America again. Of course, if I were to go back after all these years, it would have to be something new and different, a unique kind of performance. I finally fell asleep without the answer.

Then slowly it came. Not a new answer, for I had dreamed of it more than a decade before when I'd seen the marvelous American monologist, Ruth Draper, do her one-woman dramatic show in London. At the time I had thought vaguely of a one-man musical show — no other acts, no dancing girls or acrobats or comedians but an entire evening built of my songs and sketches, a performance completely on my own. It meant freedom and challenge and excitement.

The war had come and I had put the plan aside, but why not take it out again and give it a try in Europe? And if it worked, why not dare it in New York for a start and then travel with it from one American city to the next? I was sure it would work.

My friends Marlene Dietrich and Charles Boyer, whom I saw later in Paris, were sure it wouldn't. "Ninety minutes on stage with only a piano to help you? You'll kill yourself," one of them warned. And afterwards the other said with a dubious shake of the head, "American audiences won't pay musical comedy prices to see a one-man show, Maurice. You could fall flat on your face."

I had proved them wrong when I tried out the idea recently on tour in Belgium, but America was different. Unlike the countries of Europe, who had seen me up to the beginning of the war, the United States had heard little from me since I had sailed away almost a dozen years ago. That Charles and Marlene could be right was a dampening thought and an irritating one.

In my Paris dressing room just before curtain time I was going over their arguments for the thousandth time with almost a kind of annoyance when a page poked his head in the doorway. "Telephone, Monsieur Chevalier. He says it's the Duke of Windsor."

It was obvious the Duke of Windsor wouldn't call me at the theatre, and I was in no mood for guess-who jokes on the phone, whoever it might be at the other end of the wire.

"Hello?" I said belligerently.

364

"Monsieur Chevalier?"

The voice of the man on the phone rang no bells in my mind. "He just left to have supper with Napoleon," I answered shortly and hung up.

The next morning my phone rang at home. "Maurice, I tried to reach you at the theatre last night." Now I recognized at once the friendly voice of a man I hadn't seen for years. "No luck, though. This is the Duke of Windsor."

I was caught between embarrassment and laughter. Yes, I reflected wryly after accepting an invitation to sing at a big party in the Duke's Paris home, my head is so full of America it's affecting my hearing!

But my return to New York was put aside for the moment when René Clair, the French director who had won renown both at home and in Hollywood, asked me to work with him in Paris. The film was to be called *Silence est d'Or*, and my starring role would be that of an older man who falls in love with a young girl, only to be later tormented when he loses her to a boy of her own age.

For the first time in my movie career, I wouldn't end up with the girl. But the man I played would finish with something else — a kind of wisdom and experience and understanding. And the idea was suddenly appealing. The years had not stood still, I was fifty-eight now, and wasn't this a chance to do a type of role which could open up marvelous new avenues for me? Even the thought of Hollywood crossed my mind. If this picture were a success, I might be called for something there again in a different genre from the old musical comedy, "cute" days.

"When do we start?" I said happily and the deal was made.

THE film was done. And in my pocket was a contract for my one-man show in New York with a producer who had come to La Bocca especially to convince me the time was right. He had done a good job of it. I was fired with a great ambition to keep

365

rolling now. René Clair was editing *Silence est d'Or*, to be released about the time of my return to Paris, and my career was in a good high gear.

"HOLD it, Maurice!"
"Let's have the straw hat bit again!"
"And the smile. Come on, smile!"

The photographers who came out to meet the ship in New York Harbor before it docked could have been carbon copies of those I'd encountered two decades ago on my way to Hollywood, the same shouted instructions and genial, breezy insistence, the same fast exit once their photographs were done in order to seek out their next target. But it was good to be remembered, and I looked up at Manhattan's skyline and felt almost as if I were coming home again.

My American pianist was waiting for me at the hotel to talk of songs, rehearsals, routines. Now I was truly caught up in the fever, for I was here at last and in four days I would know the New York verdict.

"I need a haircut," I said distractedly and caught a glimpse of his face in the mirror. He looked shocked.

"Not till after the opening," he said. "It's bad luck, didn't you know that?"

I laughed. "For you, maybe. It's not one of my superstitions."

I had others to be sure. In my more than sixty years in the theatre I have yet to put a hat on a bed or go under a ladder or whistle in a dressing room or open an umbrella on the stage. And when I was only twenty-two I gave La Louque a little ring with tiny diamonds which I've carried with me always since her death and kissed before every performance to bring me luck.

But no haircut? It seemed ridiculous.

Or was it? That night I lay awake and listened to the muted sounds of New York from the street below, the rumble of traffic, the ambulance siren, the growl of Fifth Avenue buses as they picked up their passengers and rushed away. This was the pulse of a colossus I was hearing, and two miles away in Henry Miller's Theatre a stage was waiting for me. I was going to walk out alone on that stage to face an audience accustomed to the finest theatrical fare in the world. My heart was unafraid, but my body trembled at the prospect.

I slept little, but I arose with a firm decision: I would need all the luck I could gather for the trial ahead, so there would definitely be no appointment at the barbershop until opening night was behind me!

It arrived so soon. On the way down from my room, I felt a tight knot of nerves inside me, the way a diver must feel when he prepares to take one of those daredevil plunges from a hundred-foot ladder into a tiny tank of water. There was a cable waiting for me at the desk, and when I opened it I saw that my hands were shaking.

"New York is a lucky town to have you tonight," it said, and it was signed simply, "Nita."

It was a nice thought to carry with me to the theatre. Henry Miller's is a jewel box of a house. The stage is small and intimate, the orchestra and two balconies seem almost in your lap, the audience is at your fingertips. It was perfect for this one-man show, I said to myself moments before I walked out to face the people, for close contact with an audience is doubly important when there is only one of you and so many of them. I was telling myself this because I was frightened. So much depended on me tonight, and I needed reassurance.

And happily it came. From the instant I stood in the spotlight and began to talk and sing, those wonderful people were with me, and they never changed. If it is possible to applaud with the heart, that is surely the sound I heard that night. And there was unanimous praise the next day from the critics and a rueful admission backstage from Charles Boyer, who had traveled five days by train just to be with me at the opening.

"Shall I eat my words now or later?" he said. "And when are you coming out to Hollywood with this tour de force?"

Hollywood? I had scheduled Boston and Philadelphia and four cities in Canada for this tour but I hadn't considered Hollywood, because I was building a new career in America on the stage, not in films. Yet the thought was pleasurable. Irving Thalberg had predicted I would return one day. This was surely not what he had in mind, but I rather liked the idea of making my appearance before Hollywood with a solid success under my belt.

I left the theatre in a marvelous glow that night and later bought the morning papers to read the reviews and still later returned to my hotel riding the same wonderful wave of excitement. Nita's cable was in my pocket. I read it again.

It made me smile a little sadly to think how nice it would have been had the Nita I used to know and love been here to share tonight's miracle with me. All my life I had felt that happiness holds an extra savor and delight when there is someone to enjoy it with you, someone who really cares. Once there was La Louque whose eyes would sparkle for me with each touch of good fortune, and Mist when our love was high and strong, and Yvonne in those early days when her strength was my bulwark. And Nita, until time had run out for us.

Nita. Two years had gone by since we parted, yet often the thought of her had crossed my mind in the solitary hours. I was not lonely, not in the least; this I could truly believe, for with a simple phone call I could be surrounded with people. And my work was going marvelously now. The only missing ingredient of the recipe to make life perfect was that special someone who cares, who loves.

I was ready for love, I told myself.

It was the last thing I remembered before I fell asleep on that wonderful night in New York.

I FELT almost like the motorman of the trolley who reaches the end of the line, only to turn right around and make the whole trip again. I had returned to Paris from America just a few weeks ago, and here I was on the verge of leaving a second time, this to be a tour of my one-man show that would start in Washington and play city after city all the way across the country to Hollywood and back once more to New York.

In the house at 9 Rue de Beaujolais, I was seated at the bedside of the *grande dame* of today's French novelists who, ill and infirm and approaching seventy-five, was still writing books to captivate the world. Her full name was Sidonie Gabrielle Claudine Colette, but it was simply by her last name that she was known to millions of devotees.

I had known Colette for over four decades. We had met in Lyons, the French city which is famed for its sleek, lustrous velvets, when we appeared on the same music hall bill. A handsome young woman with large shoulders and the beautifully curved figure that was the mode in 1906, she appeared in a sketch which was startling to say the least. In a fight scene with the man she loved he would rip her gown in a strategic place and bare to the audience her nude breast. It was shocking and fascinating, even to her fellow performers who saw this denouement each night. And I was among them, a mesmerized eighteen-year-old.

But though I was enormously attracted by the physical beauty of Colette, we remained only casual acquaintances in those days backstage. I was overawed by her, for it was obvious this was no ordinary woman. Recently divorced, she had gone on the stage to earn needed money, but her great talent — so her partner assured me quickly — was as a writer. He predicted that Colette would one day become a brilliant author, and I asked myself how I, with my simple background, could hope to know better a woman who was not only lovely but endowed with a deep perceptive mind.

So I said nothing, convinced I had no chance with Colette. Years later, when we had become good friends, I laughingly confessed the yen I had had for her that time in Lyons.

She looked at me with a mournful smile. "How silly, my dear Maurice," she said. "You should have told me then. What a pity I'm a fat old lady now and it's too late!"

Now much later on this rainy afternoon in 1947 we were talking of a shared feeling — the pleasure that one must find in his work to be truly happy. "It's such pain to write," she said, "such anguish to fill each page." Then she sighed. "But such joy, too, so I can't stop. You can't either, Maurice."

"Not so long as I can stand up," I said.

"Will it last many months, this tour?"

"More than six."

"And then what?"

I shrugged. "The world is so wide, Colette, and the future so inviting." I could see that she was becoming tired and I rose to go. "I'll have the answer for you when I return."

As I started to go, a book on a table nearby caught my eye and I picked it up. "Have you read that one, Maurice?" Colette said. "I wrote it during the war."

I shook my head and put it down again, little realizing that I had just touched a story that was to play an important part in my life one day.

The name of the book was *Gigi*.

THE future looked bright for *Silence est d'Or*. It had already won first prize at the International Film Festival in Brussels, and today's announcement from the Locarno Festival had put all of us, gathered in a little club near the Arc de Triomphe, in a gay, celebrating mood. The picture had won top award, René Clair had been named best director, and I had been given the first prize for male performance. It was quite an accolade.

An actor I had known for years was shaking his head in broad resignation. "We all have to grow old, but Maurice does it and wins an award." He threw up his hands. "There's no justice."

I laughed at his mock dolor, but the very pretty girl sitting next to him said sharply, "What prizes have you won — young, old or in-between?"

It was a surprising response, but somebody changed the subject and everyone forgot her reaction. Except me. I was aware of her gray, candid eyes on me across the table. It was almost an appraising gaze, and afterwards when we were dancing together it was still there.

I couldn't resist an attempt to tease a smile to her serious, intense young face. "Thank you for coming to my defense, Françoise, especially since we've only met tonight for the first time."

"I wasn't defending you."

"What then?"

She looked at me with that odd, penetrating expression. "Let him speak for himself about growing old. You only acted the part; he lives it."

I was amused at her implied compliment and taken with it at the same moment. And when she moved closer into my arms without another word, it was a kind of flirtation I honestly enjoyed. It went no further than that, you understand, for the dance ended and soon afterwards the evening itself was over. I would probably never see Françoise again, and it really didn't matter one way or the other.

...Deux

I HADN'T seen Sunset Boulevard in almost fifteen years. Hollywood was different now. Gone was the small-town feeling I had known, and in its stead had come a sense of urgency and growth and speed. No longer did one drive past acres of woodland or fields to reach those studios that once sat on the edge of town. Today there were houses and shops and buildings and people and thousands of cars rushing, rushing, rushing. Unlike Paris, whose face never really changed over the centuries, Hollywood and all the sprawling new towns that had mushroomed together to make Los Angeles surely the widest and longest city in the world had been transformed in less than a short decade and a half.

I felt a little lost as I made my way toward Beverly Hills

and my meeting with Charles Boyer. It was not a sense of let-down or disappointment, for truly in the seven years I worked in Hollywood I had not considered it my home and this was therefore no homecoming; yet I would have felt more comfortable on my first day back with old and familiar surroundings.

Then I turned into the quiet, palm-lined, gently curving streets of Beverly Hills and suddenly everything was the same again. The green lawns and tranquil homes were still an oasis of luxury and I found myself driving up one road and down another wondering who lived where now. Some of the houses I passed evoked memories best forgotten, for Yvonne and I had lived there with the wreckage of love.

Charles was waiting for me at his door. "So you finally came back," he said. "And after tonight's opening, what?"

"Many more nights of the same. It's a long engagement."

"What about films? You're here, you should do something about it."

I shook my head. I was here because Los Angeles was a great city and a logical part of my one-man tour. I'd heard the house would be filled tonight with important Hollywood people, and I was not ashamed of the satisfaction I felt to be showing I was independent of them. I had already decided in my heart that I would take no step their way. If they wanted me back for films, the gesture must come from them.

From the moment I stepped onto the stage that evening there were cries of welcome from those who hadn't seen me in these many years. To my pleased astonishment Hollywood had seemingly not forgotten. And when the final curtain fell, a swarm of visitors came to my dressing room. I remember Bob Hope and Red Skelton and Gene Kelly and Gregory Peck. L. B. Mayer was there and Jesse Lasky, the man who had brought me to America so long ago.

Marlene was smiling at me and telling Billy Wilder, a great director, that she had rashly predicted I would fall on my face and how wrong she had been. I saw a thoughtful look come into his eyes, and the next day Marlene was to tell me how enthusiastic he had been after he left my dressing room and talked of wanting to do a film with me. To which I replied thank you and chose promptly to forget because talk costs nothing and often means less.

But it was a marvelous evening, and I was happy that I had returned to Hollywood. As the days went by, however, I honestly didn't think I would be coming here again, at least not to make a picture, for no producer had been sufficiently impressed by the critics' praise and nightly lines at the box office to try luring me back.

Christmas passed and the whole week was a blaze of sunlight and warm days and I recalled how unreal this season of the year had always seemed in Hollywood. For those who have grown up in hot-in-summer-cold-in-winter places there is a kind of comfort and security to snow and biting winds for the holidays.

But it was good being among old friends, and a New Year's party at Ronald Colman's house brought sentiment and conviviality and gentle midnight kisses to welcome in 1948 from Benita Colman and Pat Boyer and the other lovely ladies. It brought reflective moments of accounting, too, of weighing how far I had come with this new one-man career of mine and where it might lead me yet.

THE Lido night club in Paris on the Champs Elysées is enormous and famous for its shows and a mecca for tourists. But Parisians gather there, too, and I was at a big table with a dozen friends and bottles of champagne and in the center a huge birthday cake with sixty candles flaming. I drew a ten-gallon breath and blew them out while everyone clapped and cheered in that pleasantly silly way that makes a birthday party what it is.

374

Sixty candles, six decades of living, I was asking myself, aren't you a little bit depressed that so much life has already gone by? To which I could honestly reply no, for what I cannot change never makes me unhappy, never has. If I do my best and I cannot change it, then I have to accept it and not get crazy because it's stronger than I. So I was accepting sixty and thankful that I had made it.

Despite my success with my one-man show, time and again I had found myself thinking of retirement from the stage after almost fifty years of performing. Friends with whom I discussed it refused to believe me when I described my dream of seven months each year lazing on the Riviera and the other five spent in making an occasional film in France, infrequent radio performances and perhaps an essay into that new medium of television.

Still I had done nothing about it. I had signed to do three weeks of shows in Paris and then four more in London, and this was surely no way to sample the pleasures of retirement. Pretty soon, however, I was telling myself, pretty soon.

"Excuse me, monsieur." The waiter was tendering me a note on which was written simply, "Françoise. Remember?"

"Who gave you this?" I asked, and he glanced toward a table in the corner. A girl was sitting with a group of people, and she was looking my way with a kind of half-smile that said "Surely you haven't forgotten?" But I had. I hadn't the least idea in the world who this pretty young woman could be, so I smiled politely and vaguely and turned back to my friends.

"Perhaps if I had really been defending you," a voice whispered in my ear a few moments later, "you might have remembered."

And of course I did then, the girl who had thought I only acted the part of an older man. Well, that cake on the table with its sea of candles would surely give her the truth now. When I gestured toward it, she said, "If you'll dance with me, I'll tell you how little I think of birthdays."

She was so solemn and big-eyed and grave that it would have been cruel to say no. And I found myself dancing another time with this child I had thought I would never see again. She danced marvelously, with a lithe grace and a kind of yielding to the rhythm that I had not encountered since Mist. She was very young, but at that moment I felt very young myself.

"With a different make-up I could look ten years older," Françoise said unexpectedly.

"No female in her right mind would ever do such a thing," I smiled.

"She would if it mattered." She was silent for a moment as we danced and then she said quietly, "It matters to me. Because you talk to me like a child, and I'm far from that. I'm twenty-two and I can look thirty-two and perhaps then you'd think of me as a woman."

She was an adorable woman, in fact, but to a man celebrating his sixtieth birthday twenty-two can seem many miles away. When the dance was over, I led her back toward her table. Halfway there she stopped me.

"Is this the way it's going to end, just as it did before with your thanking me for a dance and it's over?"

She was so naïvely honest that I was taken aback for an instant. "It's the usual way."

"I'm not the usual girl, Maurice." She was regarding me with that level, candid gaze from our first meeting, and almost without thinking I found myself agreeing to an afternoon rendezvous with this extraordinarily direct youngster outside this night club tomorrow where she would join me in the long walk I took each day along the boulevards. At her table we shook hands formally and said good night.

Oddly, I found myself thinking of Françoise when the evening was through, but I insisted on looking at it all with a kind of paternal tolerance. A stroll, an *apéritif* at a sidewalk café — it was a harmless amusement which would finish with a friendly *au revoir*. Yet even as I sat alone in my apartment and told myself this aloud, a tiny doubt was there. Today I had become sixty but I was nonetheless very much alive and certainly not her father, so why not admit the truth — that I was anticipating tomorrow's appointment because I found Françoise both interesting and provocative?

As I approached the Lido the next day she was already there waiting. "After I talked you into this last night," she said, "I was afraid you would change your mind. I didn't really expect to see you." She extended a book to me. "But I brought this for you anyway, and I'm glad now I did."

It was a volume of poems by Baudelaire, such a logical gift from a child trying to appear a woman, and she was regarding me expectantly. I repressed a smile.

"Thank you, Françoise. I like Baudelaire."

We walked a long while, much of it in silence. Almost at once she had taken my arm in a pleasingly intimate way and walked with her body close against mine. From time to time I would glance down at her and wonder what she was thinking, for her lovely face was unsmiling and intense. At last when we stopped along the Seine to peer over the bridge into the swirling, dark water, she turned to me suddenly.

"The man I was with the first night we met, did you know I was living with him?"

From someone else it would have been a startling question. Somehow it seemed completely natural coming from Françoise. I nodded.

"I thought there was a chance of it, yes. You were angry with him in a kind of too personal way."

"It was over soon. I didn't like him." She straightened

377

abruptly. "I live a block away from here. Will you walk me home?"

At her door I started to say good-by, but she shook her head. "Please have a drink with me," she said slowly. "I live alone."

It was not such an unusual story with such an unexpected ending, because these things happen. And later, emerging from Françoise's apartment, I might have been saying to myself that this was a little amorous adventure which had come to pass and was now over and should be forgotten. But I was not able to dismiss it so lightly, because this had been no ordinary encounter in the afternoon. Françoise was a disturbing experience. There was a smoldering fire in her that had awakened a similar fire in me, and I was shaken with what it might portend.

In the weeks before I left for London I was to see Françoise constantly. It was a kind of physical attraction that frightened me, because I didn't want it to stop and my reason told me that it should. The protestations of this alluring girl could never change the fact that I was old enough to be her father. Perhaps I was not yet December romantically involved with May, but I was surely at the November of my life and this was a danger.

"I love you, Maurice." She said it over and over again. "I've never been in love in my life before, and I love you now."

It was such tempting music. It tempted me to believe that I loved her as well, that years mean nothing in the calendar of love, that this magic which had come to me at a time when love had seemingly gone forever could be a lasting magic.

But still a little pocket of resistance remained. The heart insisted yes while the head replied no. The heart said happiness is worth all risk. The head pointed out that I had joked in many of my songs about the miseries of age in love with youth, and I had done a film about that very problem, so why should I now become a victim of the very plot I knew so well?

The head was winning. As the days drew near for my departure for England I began to count on those four weeks away from Paris as my opportunity to end it. I would write Françoise from London to prepare her, and then on my return I would take the final step.

This was not all I would end in England, I told myself. After my four weeks there, I could tighten the reins and pull my stage career to a close. In a way I would be retiring from two love affairs at the same time. Sixty was a good round number — the perfect age to slow the race and exchange tumult for tranquillity.

MY SHOW at the Hippodrome was a hit. The London papers were unanimous in calling it that, and I set the reviews aside in my hotel room on a lazy Sunday afternoon with a glow of gratification. I was ending my years in the theatre with the biggest performance of a long career, this one-man show that had won plaudits in America, my own country and now England. It seemed the ideal moment to quit.

Leaving to stroll through the darkening city streets, I wandered across town toward the royal palace where pretty young Princess Elizabeth was at that very moment awaiting the birth of her first child. London's face, except for a few bomb scars from the war, looked just as indomitable and permanent and proud as it had that year I had come here with Mist so long ago.

But the palace looming ahead of me in the twilight was different, for today an enormous crowd had gathered outside the gates, their eyes fixed on the three lighted windows of the room where an eventual heir to the throne was to be born during this night. Quiet, orderly, patient, these men and women and children were waiting for history to happen.

"Look, there's Chevalier," a voice said behind me. "Hello, Maurice."

I turned to see a stout man and woman grinning and waving at me. I'd never seen them before, but I waved back. And then the word swept from one bystander to the next until a throng was milling and pushing around me. Slips of paper for autographs were being shoved at me, hands were shaking mine, my back was being clapped by well-wishers who were glad to see me here again, and I was undergoing an affectionate but nonetheless painful buffeting.

Two bobbies beat their way through to rescue me. Clearing a path ahead of them, they guided me to the edge of the mob where I stood panting for a moment. "Thanks for saving my life," I managed to say.

The taller policeman chuckled. "We've only been seeing you here for thirty years, Mr. Chevalier. Have to keep you fit for thirty more." He saluted and with his partner moved back into the crowd.

Thirty more years, I was thinking as I walked away. Why, three weeks from now I might be announcing my retirement.

"RETIREMENT, that's for me, Maurice. It's due soon, and I'm champing at the bit." My old friend from Alten Grabow, Ronald Kennedy, the man who had taught me English, sat across the lunch table from me.

"It sounds good to me, Ken," I said. "How do you plan to fill your days after you give up teaching? A business perhaps?"

He smiled and shook his head. "My garden and my house. I'm tired of working, old boy, aren't you?"

For an instant the question caught me off balance. Was I tired? Was this my reason for wanting to leave the stage? Or had I simply drawn an arbitrary line of demarcation across my life at the age of sixty? Was I on the verge of abandoning the profession I adored to give myself months of leisure to be spent only in regretting what I had done?

The thought stayed with me when lunch was over, and we left

the restaurant to face the dreadful fog which had enveloped London for days now. The world was a murky wall through which one stumbled to the nearest subway, for most of the surface transportation had stopped. Coughing and gasping we made our way underground and parted, Ronald to head for his home in the country which would occupy all his days soon, I for the Hippodrome and a matinee performance.

Wisps of fog invaded the theatre and hung across the stage, phantom shapes trapped in the glare of the spotlight. It attacked my throat. I felt the way a dancer does, performing on an injured leg. But I managed, and the theatregoers who had jammed the house despite the weather were with me all the way. It was a performance that left me exhausted but happy, and afterwards I had a conference with myself as I so often do in my dressing room mirror.

Retirement? Impossible. Would the tranquillity of a house and garden fill my days, or did I need the excitement and the challenge and the reward of my métier to keep me alive, competely alive? I knew the answer. So long as I was physically able to walk out on stage and sing and dance and clown I must do it. Sixty, seventy, whatever the number of years allotted me, I now had the answer.

And Françoise, the other part of my life I had thought to renounce in London? I had a letter from her in my pocket. "Do you walk and sleep and live with me beside you as I do you?" it asked.

In a way I did and more. I had argued interminably with myself about her. There was a hazard in our affair, I had agreed, but every day is a risk of some kind from birth to death. Now I was looking into my own eyes and finding a vigor and vitality there which had only returned since Françoise. Surely it was better to live dangerously perhaps and be truly alive than oh so prudently and only half exist?

Yes, exactly as I could not justify retirement from the stage, so I couldn't vindicate a kind of retiring from life. I had not written Françoise that it must be finished between us, I knew it now, because I hadn't honestly wanted it that way. I would not write. For whatever pain it would bring, the affair was not ended.

It had only begun.

. . . Trois

IN PARIS the piercing wind blew off the river in icy
gusts and found its way through every street to make
whirlpools of leaves and scraps of paper. It spent itself in
sibilant, mournful dirges and then sprang to life again. This
repeating pattern beneath a sky that was heavy and low and
wintry turned the world outside to gloom.

But inside, for Françoise and me, the world was a warm
and glowing and contented place. There was something so
remote and secluded about our affair, as if we were two
people in a cocoon withdrawn from the cares and fears of
the millions around us. Glancing up from my book in the
evening to see her curled up on the couch opposite, her
deep, grave eyes belying the hint of a smile at her lips as

she watched me, I would be filled with delight and comfort at the same time. We were two alone and enormously happy.

Françoise seemed to want nothing more than our being together. And I was the same. When I could see her near, I felt a surge of joy in me, but in those hours we were apart it was a kind of emptiness and longing that sent me hurrying back to her. Those separated hours I made as few as possible.

An offer came to do a weekly radio series for a network of hundreds of stations in the United States, to be recorded soon on the Riviera with well-known Americans who were visiting there. Eddie Cantor and Elsa Maxwell and dozens of others would be arriving with spring. Cannes would be headquarters, my house was so near — it's perfect, I told myself, except for Françoise because I think I've fallen in love, and this miracle I can't leave.

"I'll go with you, Maurice," she said simply, and it was like a weight dropping from me. "Without you, Paris holds nothing for me."

Now with winter left behind in Paris we had everything on our side. Not only could we share the solitude of my house at La Bocca when the cool evening settled in from the hills, but there were beautiful days with the marvelous southern sun to warm us as we took long walks through Cannes or picnicked alone on the deserted beach beyond the city or simply relaxed on the terrace and savored the view of sea and land spread out before us.

I was going over the lyrics of a new song for my broadcast, and Françoise sat on a cushion beside my chair, her head resting lightly against my knee. Her eyes were closed. I set down the paper and leaned over to kiss her, and she smiled without opening them. "Are you bored with this one-man existence?" I said, surprised to hear myself saying aloud something I had thought of before but always dismissed.

Her smile faded and she sat up to look at me. "Have I said so? Or even implied it?"

"No, of course not."

"You should know me well enough by now. I say what I think."

She was very serious and intense, and it gave me a sense of pleasure to realize that this adorable girl was obviously content with our life together. And relief as well, for though we had never spoken of the span of years that divided us, ignoring them couldn't obliterate them for me. I was living the love affair of a young man, but I was sixty years old.

Later, walking in town with Françoise, I had forgotten those momentary misgivings. This girl on my arm was a girl in love. It was wonderful with us, and if time was running out, there was surely no indication of it. I found myself grinning at youngsters playing tag along the sidewalk and feeling as lighthearted as they.

A red motor scooter was clattering toward us, its exhaust echoing off the buildings on either side of the narrow street. As it passed, I noted that incongruously a guitar case was strapped across the seat behind the young, dark-haired driver. An instant afterwards, we heard the shriek of tires and turned to see the scooter whirling around. It drew to a stop beside us.

"Françoise?" The driver had leaped off and come toward us.

I glanced at Françoise. Her faced lighted up in recognition. "André!" She threw her arms around him in a delighted embrace and they held each other till she broke off suddenly, remembering me. "Maurice, this is an old friend of mine. We haven't seen each other for ages."

She introduced us. He was about twenty-five years old, handsome in a kind of sullen way, and they talked excitedly for a moment of the paths they had followed since their last meeting. When they laughed together over a shared incident in the past

385

when he had played in the orchestra of a club where she had danced, I found myself reacting with an odd feeling of exclusion. It hurt me, and at the same time I resented it. Then abruptly he said good-by, kissed Françoise amiably on the cheek and was gone.

She continued to wave after him.

"Isn't that enough?" I said. "How far can he see you?"

Something must have been in my voice, for she turned to me with a startled look, searching my face. "Did I do anything to annoy you, Maurice? Are you angry?"

"No, no," I said shortly. "Let's go on walking."

As Françoise walked silently beside me I kept thinking of the unreserved joy of those two at their chance encounter and that casual farewell kiss. A persistent thought intruded that my odd feeling was more than a sense of being left out, that it almost had the stamp of jealousy. I refused to believe it. It made no sense. Yet somehow the edge had been taken off the day for me.

I LEFT the hotel whose ballroom was being used as the studio for our broadcasts and strolled along the Croisette toward my little car. At the edge of the gardened park beyond which lay the sea was a pretty young woman I had seen before. Wearing slacks and an old sweater, her dark hair pulled back in disarray from her fine-featured face, she had an appealingly Bohemian look as she sat before an easel and brought the street alive on canvas.

I had watched her get this painting under way as I emerged from last week's broadcast. Today it seemed almost done, and I thought it was good. I told her so, and she glanced up with a gamin smile. "I hope the critics think so."

There was a haunting quality to her work that I liked. I was surely no expert on art, but for ten years I had been interested in paintings and had begun a collection that I hoped would grow to something fine. I'd started with two works of Vlaminck whose work had always moved me but especially so after I had grown to know him personally with his sudden resounding laughter and powerful gestures and forceful, explosive words. His overwhelming character was reflected in the violence of his paintings. And Utrillo. I had led him to my old neighborhood in Ménilmontant and he had painted for me the peaceful church square that held so many memories. Now I had dreams of owning a Cézanne and a Bonnard and a Renoir.

"And my teacher," the girl was saying. "It would be nice if he approved, too."

"Who is he?" It seemed the polite thing to say, so I asked it, little thinking that this young woman's professor of art could have been the great Henri Matisse. But it was the master, himself, who lived not far away in the mountains above Nice. I told her of my admiration for Matisse.

"Would you like to meet him with me sometime, Monsieur Chevalier?" she said suddenly and then laughed in embarrassment. "If I remember my manners long enough to tell you my name? It's Nicole Delande."

She was charming and enthusiastic and bright, this Nicole Delande, and though I doubted if she really meant it about our visit to Matisse, we shook hands on it and I drove away reflecting that the world is full of genuinely nice people and I had just met one of them.

"Françoise?" I called when I entered the house. She was not around and I felt a stab of alarm. An unreasonable fear had entered my mind that she had simply gone away without a word, and I moved quickly to our room. Her clothes were there, and I went searching for her outside. On my way to the terrace the cook called out that Françoise had gone into town, and I realized how ridiculous my panic had been. You're obsessed with her, I was thinking, so much that even a tiny separation can frighten you.

Moments later a familiar sound from the drive brought me

around the house, and I heard Françoise's voice before I saw her. "You're a darling, André," she was saying. "Thank you for everything."

I quickened my step but the motor scooter had already descended to the road before I reached the front door, and I stood there listening to its receding din with a kind of sick, suffocated feeling as if I had been hit in the pit of the stomach. So this was where Françoise had been?

Seeing me enter the house she ran to kiss me with a secret smile that did nothing to soften my upset. "I have a surprise for you, Maurice," she said. "Would you like to see it?"

I hardly heard her. "Have you been with him all afternoon?"

"Who?" Then she understood. "Oh, André? No, I just ran into him outside the store and he gave me a lift home." Her smile became a puzzled frown. "Why on earth would I be with him?"

With an immense relief I saw how wrong I had been, and I felt a marvelous lightness bubbling up in me. "I was just wondering where you were," I said. "Now, what's this about a surprise?"

She left the room and returned a moment later. "Look."

I was staring at two bizarre masks, one a devil's head, the other a skeleton. "What's this?"

"For Mardi Gras night at the carnival in Nice. We can go, can't we, Maurice? Please?"

I knew what it would be like at the carnival — thousands of revelers crammed into the streets, jostling each other in a determined effort to have fun, being hit in the head with confetti and flowers and often more painful missiles, shouting oneself hoarse to be heard above the roar. I knew this shambles from long experience, and I was about to protest that it was an evening only for the young, but the words stopped in my throat.

I couldn't say such a thing. I would be there, I had to be.

388

THE carnival was noisier even than I remembered, and Place Masséna, that immense square in Nice, was a mass of bodies fighting for room to gape at grotesque papier-mâché figures towering two stories high and teetering through the streets in a weird, spectacular parade.

Swept up in the brash gaiety of the moment, Françoise was exhilarated and sparkling and stripped of the child-woman pose she wore with me. Now she was really an exuberant kid again and surrounded by a gleeful group of young people singing and laughing and dancing. Youth is a magnet for youth, I thought a little sadly, and tried to respond more eagerly to this festival of confusion.

It was not easy, however, because the novelty had worn off for me long ago, and when Françoise proposed that we go to a club a block away I readily agreed. But the moment we stepped inside, a kind of slow anger began to build inside me, for André, the guitarist, sat on the platform with the orchestra and I could see this came as no surprise to her. She waved as we were led to our table, and at the song's end he came over.

"They'll play without me. May I dance with Françoise, monsieur?" His eyes were impassive but they seemed to mock me nonetheless. When I nodded, he led her away, and I watched with torment, for now I knew that it really had been jealousy I felt the first day I had seen them together. The thought revolted me. Jealousy is an unworthy, destructive emotion, I told myself, and tried to push it away and failed, for my gaze wandered to them dancing the slow, sensuous rhythm and I fancied a kind of intimacy in their embrace.

Half an hour later we were in the car driving toward La Bocca. "But why did we have to leave?" Françoise wailed.

"Let's not play games any longer," I exploded. "You knew he was in Nice, you planned it perfectly. What was the next move, Françoise? To leave me at the table while the two of you disappeared for more of those casual kisses?" I heard myself saying the words and I wanted to stop because they were demeaning, but I was helpless to control my temper. "I'm sorry I spoiled your fun, my dear."

There was a long silence before she spoke. "Is that honestly what you believe?" she said sadly.

"When you're so flagrant with this thing? Don't tell me I'm confused, Françoise."

"I shan't tell you anything, Maurice."

She said nothing for the rest of the trip, and my emotions simmered as the miles went by, but slowly their intensity dropped away while a kind of regret and shame took over. A scene like this was so foreign to me and I could only remember with sickening clarity Yvonne's unreasoning jealousy and my horror of it. In reality, hadn't I done the same injustice to Françoise, jumped to the same unfair conclusions?

She entered the house, shoulders rigid and her gaze resolutely ahead, refusing to meet mine. I watched her move in stiff silence toward the stairs, and suddenly I could stand it no longer.

"Françoise?" She stopped without turning around. "We all make mistakes. Please forgive me."

For an instant she stood there, then she wheeled and ran straight to my arms, and she clung to me intensely as if our closeness must wipe out this hour that had pulled us apart. And holding her so near I thought that surely this boy could be no true rival for Françoise's love, because it was completely and joyously mine.

A week later Charles Boyer telephoned from Paris on his arrival, and I invited him down to spend a few days in the sun. How good it was to hear my old friend's voice, and I hung up happily anticipating the hours of good conversation we would have. Charles would like Françoise. Her seriousness would match his own.

As I turned away, the phone rang again. A man's voice asked

for Françoise. "She's not here at the moment," I said. "Is there a message? Who is this?"

"Never mind, I'll call her again." The phone clicked off and I held the receiver, puzzled for a minute because I had heard that voice before. When I remembered, that same sensation of being smothered overwhelmed me. I was choking on the realization that although no mention of André's name had occurred between Françoise and me since that night in Nice, he was still a shadow across our lives, for that was of course André who had called and I could only wonder what other times he had telephoned when I was not around.

This time, however, I was determined I would not give in to the pangs of jealousy assailing me. I would say nothing of this to Françoise unless he should call again when we both were here. And as I sternly read myself this edict, a dissident voice was asking: What if he phones when you're away, how will you ever know? How will you ever know if they're planning to meet? If there's nothing between them, why did he refuse to give you his name?

I found myself watching Françoise all evening for some sign of uneasiness on her part, and when there was none, when she seemed exactly as she always was, irrationally it made me surer than ever that she was hiding something from me. And all the time the intelligent and reasonable half of me was struggling in vain to turn back these new suspicions. I slept badly that night, and the next day my nerves felt raw and worn. Day after day it was to go on this way until I felt haggard with the strain, drained with the insidious torment of doubt.

I had to be honest, to face the unpleasant truth that the difference in years between Françoise and me was demanding the recognition I had rationalized away in London. This boy André was young. Françoise was young. Wasn't I competing on an impossible battlefield, and wouldn't I spare myself ultimate heartbreak if I retired now from the fight?

391

But as I asked myself the question, I rejected it, for I was too consumed with this turbulent affair, too torn with longing for this girl to walk away. I might admit that the time for renunciation was nearing, but I was not prepared to take that step. Not yet.

The day before Charles was to arrive, Nicole Delande was waiting outside the studio after my broadcast. "Are you up to that visit tomorrow?" she asked brightly.

I had forgotten all about Matisse and I was on the verge of saying no when I decided impulsively that we would make it a sort of holiday, this sparkling young artist, Françoise and I. We would pick up Nicole in the morning, lunch on the way, meet the venerable Matisse and spend a day entirely without care. I need this, I was thinking, I need it badly.

"Aren't you ready yet?" I called up to Françoise the next morning.

She appeared on the stairs frowning, her fingers pressed against her forehead. "I feel dreadful, Maurice, do you mind if I don't go?"

"Then I won't either. I'll phone that girl and tell her we can't make it."

"No, please," she said quickly. "You go without me." She came downstairs to kiss me. "Matisse means more to you, anyway, than he does to me." I hesitated. "Please go, Maurice."

"All right," I said finally. "Charles won't be here until seven. I'll get back by six at the latest."

As I entered the car, she stood in the doorway to wave good-by, and dressed in a pair of fisherman's pants and a shirt knotted at the waist she seemed younger to me than I had ever seen her before. It was disturbing, for it made me somehow feel even older.

MATISSE lived in a grand apartment within an ancient palace atop the mountains. Nicole and I entered the great hall with its white marble floors and gleaming staircase and imposing statues, ascended to the second floor which was a vast library and finally sat beside the eighty-year-old painter who, though confined to his bed, worked every day from a rolling table covered with the materials of his craft.

Allowed to work only two hours a day, he had covered the walls of his room with sketches drawn with the aid of charcoal attached to long poles. Ill health had forced his body into this restricted life, but he met us with eyes that were clear and strong and his hands still moved with confidence.

"A man's work," he said and gestured to the table, "is worth loving above everything. If he's faithful to it, it's still there when all else is gone." He turned to Nicole with a gentle, paternal air. "And you, little one, are you trying every day to paint better?"

Her face shone with obvious adoration as they talked. Nicole had a moving and refreshing grace, no quality at all of the coquette but a kind of marvelous warmth. When she spoke of painting, however, this deepened to an intensity, an inordinate concentration. It was apparent that Matisse's philosophy had won her completely. I found this astonishing in one so young.

Driving home a little later I told her so. "It's true," she said. "My life is painting, that's all. But at least it's never disappointed me." She smiled sadly. "As love did."

It was the first time she had mentioned her personal life, except to say casually that she was divorced and the mother of a five-year-old daughter.

"Love often disappoints," I said. "But it rewards, too, you know."

She shook her head. "I can't be true to both. Not passionately. If a woman loves a man that way it possesses her. There's no force left in her for another consuming devotion."

She was very wise for her years, this girl, I was thinking, and strong. Whether from Matisse or from the depths of her own spirit, she had evolved her *raison d'être*, and now she was living it with satisfaction. And for me there was a kind of comfortable contentment in her company, a quiet sense of ease. I wondered if my knowing her feelings about love had done this. Normally when a man is thrown together with a pretty girl and he likes her, instinctively he tries to make an impression. There is a flirtation perhaps, the thrust and parry of provocative phrases and glances to create interest, the male and female egos at work.

But with this intelligent and practical and at the same time charming Nicole there would be no such motive. We would be friends. It was a pleasant idea. When I dropped her at her home in a village near La Bocca, I was still smiling at the thought.

The smile faded abruptly as my little car drew near my house. Around a curve I heard an imperious horn and as I hugged my side of the road a flash of red whirled by. In our split second of encounter I recognized the motor scooter and its driver. André had surely been with Françoise. A picture of them together seared across my mind and left me shaking, for it was so plain to me now why she had pleaded illness this morning and stayed at home. Suddenly all the tortures of these past weeks were crystallizing into one giant pain.

I pulled into the driveway. When Françoise ran to greet me, I met her with cold anger, and she stood there as if I had struck her.

"I saw your friend on his way home," I said flatly. "I trust you two enjoyed your day."

I was walking almost blindly to the stairs when her voice stopped me. "Maurice?" I turned. "Please look at me." Her eyes were bright with tears, but there was a kind of dignity about her that confused me as I met her gaze. "André called me this afternoon from Nice," she said quietly and levelly. "He was in trouble, he wanted to borrow some money, and I told him to come here for it. He was in this house about five minutes altogether." Her shoulders sagged wearily and she moved past me, stopping only long enough to say, "I didn't enjoy my day at all." Then she walked from the room.

I could only watch her numbly as she left, for I was sure that I had just been told the truth and I was stunned with the enormity of what had happened between us. Yet I knew it would happen again. I knew with a terrible certainty that it was only a single scene and there would be others, different perhaps, but still the same, because I would be jealous of every young fellow who looked at her. I would be helpless to fight it, and the knowledge of my weakness filled me with an awful terror.

It had not disappeared by the time Charles arrived from Paris, and when we were alone I told him the whole painful story. He listened with the gravity that was so typical of him while I paced up and down the room pouring out my fears. "I can't see the end of it, Charles," I said finally.

"The way you tell it, Maurice," he frowned, "how can it ever finish happily?"

"It won't, that much I know."

"Well, be careful, or this might turn into a sort of senile jealousy," he said slowly. "Do you realize that?"

Senile! The word was a knife slash within me. I had never been afraid of growing old and I was not now, but this conjured up a distasteful picture of infirmity and feebleness, of judgment and balance destroyed, a fate I prayed would never come to me. Yet Charles could be right, for hadn't my nagging suspicions already caused me much mental disquietude and physical anguish? Surely if I went on this way, it would only become worse with each tormented day until this love affair, instead of bringing me happiness, would ultimately bring complete misery.

Charles was regarding me with concern. "I didn't mean to disturb you, Maurice. Perhaps I exaggerated this thing a little."

"Perhaps you didn't," I said slowly.

We talked no more of it, but after Charles went to bed, I

stayed behind in the night-silent living room to sort the demanding thoughts in my mind. A single lamp threw deep shadows across the room. I sat, head buried in my hands, and tried to reason with the present and prepare myself for the future. It was so clear to me now that there was but one way out: I must end it with Françoise at once.

I had been wrong about May and December, or even November, at least for me. For a few ecstatic months it had been perfect while we secluded ourselves from the world around us, but in time it would have failed, for we were hiding from reality and sooner or later it would have found us. No, the moment to renounce had come, and if I didn't break this off immediately, today's pain would only be greater tomorrow.

But once that was done, I was asking myself, what then? Would love repeat its hurtful pattern of enticement first and disillusion later as it had done to me before? I knew myself well enough to realize that it could happen again, for I was human and a passionate man who could one day be attracted by a beautiful woman and find himself once more in a tempestuous love affair. Yet if I came to no decision now, if I said, Well, this one is over and we'll simply wait till the next one occurs, then I had learned nothing from this whole bittersweet experience.

I must forbid love from my life. There could be no more serious passions, no more involvements. From this hour on I would find my total happiness in my work and old friends and paintings and books and the myriad wonders each day of living could offer. My last years could be full and rich and rewarding without love. It was the right way. It must be.

The whisper of a sound turned me in my chair. Françoise stood in the doorway, and as she moved nearer I saw that her eyes wore the bruised look of many tears. She sat on the stool before me, still without a word, and my heart ached with what lay ahead for me to say.

396

"It's late, Maurice," she said. "Are you feeling all right?"

I nodded. And then slowly I told her everything. Her eyes widened as I spoke, but she said nothing, made no move to protest or stop me. When I had finished, we sat there for a long moment, two images frozen in place.

"Oh, God," she said finally, "it's so wrong. It's so foolish and useless and wrong."

The temptation to agree, to take her in my arms and start the whole despairing cycle again was almost unbearable, but it couldn't be. It was the end.

Tonight was the end of love.

. . . Quatre

"IT'S A TAKE," the director called, and I breathed a sigh of fatigue. "That's it for today, everybody."

We had been shooting exteriors all day for a film called *Ma Pomme*, in a vast square in Paris not more than two miles from the street where I was born. Now the last tiring scene was done, and I moved past the camera and mike boom and sound equipment toward my car.

"Monsieur Maurice?" A group of cameramen and grips and technicians was blocking my way. "Would you sign this with us?"

One of them handed me a list filled with signatures, and I glanced at the text above them. It appeared to be a petition to outlaw the atomic bomb as a weapon in war, and I hesitated.

"Is there anything political in this?" I asked. "If so, I want nothing to do with it."

They laughed. "Absolutely not. It's just whether you like the atom bomb or you don't, and if you feel as the rest of us do, you sign to say that you don't."

It seemed reasonable to me. I surely had no affection for bombs. I added my name to the list and hurried away. It was the last time in my life, however, that I would put my signature to other than my own personal documents, for the repercussions of that apparently trivial incident were to prove enormous for me and filled with pain.

That seemingly innocent list, I was to learn later, was the Stockholm Peace Petition, a Communist-inspired propaganda appeal which was signed by millions of Europeans before the truth was revealed. And ironically enough, I had put my pen to it in a Parisian square called Place Stalingrad.

THE months after Françoise had not been easy. I had thrown myself into work, playing my one-man show through France and Switzerland and Belgium, doing a command performance for Queen Elizabeth in London, returning from a tour of Italy to do *Ma Pomme*, but no day had passed without a memory of that last night with her at La Bocca. For the step I had taken then was so grave that I had not been able simply to accept it without subsequent thought or question.

Time and again, sitting alone and pensive in a hotel room I might never see again, too keyed up from my evening's performance to seek sleep, I would be assailed by doubts of the wisdom of my course. Love had been an immense force in my life, a deep part of my being. To exclude it arbitrarily, to bar it forever, I would say aloud, was to rob myself of the glory and the summit of living. Wasn't I allowing the fear of pain to cost me the chance of joy?

But that experience with Françoise had projected too frightening a picture to be dimmed with arguments. Though I had often remained awake until the first light of morning reached my room, I had always fallen asleep with my conviction unchanged, until at last I acknowledged the necessity that love must truly be over.

The day that *Ma Pomme* opened in Paris a cable was delivered to my door which taught me that talk is never cheap with men of sincerity. It was from Billy Wilder, who had seen and liked me in Hollywood and told Marlene of his hope to do a film with me. At the time I had chosen to call it idle words. He had not. Instead he had persuaded Paramount to produce a lavish musical in color, starring me in a story that revolved around my own career. If I agreed, the deal was set.

I read Billy's enthusiastic message with the kind of nervous exhilaration which always comes to me with a new challenge in my work. Despite my having made no effort for a comeback in Hollywood, in my heart I had wanted it, and now I was returning as a star, just as I had left. But it was surely a challenge, for many years had gone by and I must prove this didn't matter. I had to be good.

This film would take me away from France for two-thirds of a year, because I had signed for a tour of my show in Canada to precede the stint in Hollywood. The day I sailed on the *Empress of Canada* bound for Montreal I watched the summer-green shore recede, a little disturbed by this long absence from home and asking myself if I hadn't accepted one offer too many. Surely the movie would have been enough for this trip, I was thinking, yet something within me had insisted that I work, work, work to the limit of my endurance.

Had this preoccupation with career become even stronger with the renunciation of love, as it was with Nicole Delande? I was remembering her now, for in my pocket was a letter forwarded to my apartment two days before from the Paris theatre where I'd been playing.

"Dear Monsieur Chevalier," it said. "How long it has been since that day we visited Matisse together! As you can see from the enclosed brochure, I'm having a show in Paris, and it would be wonderful to see you there. Warmly, Nicole Delande."

I would be missing the opening by a week, and I was sorry. She was a talented girl. There were almost fifty paintings listed for this show, I noticed, which surely indicated that work was still the focus of her life. In that we were alike now. As I turned away from the rail to walk along the deck and meet the fresh, sweet breeze of the sea ahead, I wondered if she, too, had occasional misgivings.

We were almost at Montreal when the captain asked to see me privately in his cabin. His usually jovial face was furrowed with a frown when I entered. "We've just monitored an American newscast." He gave me a sheet of typewritten paper. "I thought you'd better see it before we landed." He shook his head sympathetically as I started to read.

For an instant the shocking words before me took my breath away. The State Department was announcing from Washington that because of a new law concerning political suspects Maurice Chevalier would be denied an entry visa into the United States. I read it again, certain there was some mistake, but this new nightmare in which I was unjustly accused of political involvement was real enough. But why? The question raced through my mind, and then suddenly a memory of that day at the Place Stalingrad flashed through my mind.

Oh, God, I was thinking, now am I considered a Communist? It was too much.

"Thank you, Captain," I managed to say evenly, but when I turned away toward my stateroom, a wave of sick disbelief came over me that this fantastic misunderstanding could befall me from a country I had always loved next to my own and whose public had shown me so much affection for so many years.

A few hours later we docked at Montreal, and a battery of newspapermen surrounded me for a statement. I told the simple truth. "I'm a performer," I said. "I've never belonged to any political sect, and I never will. The only dictates I can follow are those of my own heart." Then I explained my signature on that petition and ended with a declaration that I had no bitterness for this incredible disgrace. I did not explain that I had learned from the grave trial I had suffered once before over unjust charges that neither bitterness nor hatred could change such events, they could only add an extra burden of sadness.

"Aren't you going to file a protest?" someone demanded.

I shook my head firmly. This interview was to be my last word.

From my hotel I sent a telegram to Paramount asking that my contract be abrogated, for I had no way to comply with it, and the next day I was to receive a regretful wire that they were acceding to my request. I felt almost like a sleepwalker as I moved through the hours that followed. I was stunned and dispirited and afraid that my shows in Canada would draw unfriendly audiences and this added blow might be the one to make me consider permanent retirement.

But the complete reverse happened. The theatre in Montreal thundered with applause. No one took the visa refusal seriously, and afterwards the professional society of Canadian journalists in an unusual meeting made me an honorary member to show their faith. It was good to have friends.

When I reached Toronto the phone rang in my room and a crisp voice said, "Maurice? Jack Dempsey. I'm refereeing a fight here, and I read you were in town. Maybe I can do you some good."

Though I had known Jack Dempsey slightly three decades ago in Paris, we hadn't seen each other in years. Yet here he was to say that he knew scores of people in Washington and wanted to help me. I was tremendously touched, for apparently

I had friends I'd never imagined. I thanked him and asked him to do nothing.

"One of these days they'll admit their mistake, Jack," I said. "But I won't ask for it. I'll have to wait till they do."

Less than a month later an unofficial telegram reached me on my last day in Canada that the State Department had changed its mind, that if I were to request a new visa, this time it would be granted. But I was leaving the next morning for an extended tour of South America — engagements I had accepted after my contract with Paramount was broken.

The plane took off from Montreal for Caracas, and soon after we were aloft the lakes and forests and mountains of New England appeared below, and as we winged ever southward I tried to push the past weeks from my mind. I would be returning to these United States one day, I was sure of that now.

It was a happy thought.

WHEN I saw Paris again, it was spring, and there is nothing anywhere in the world like an April afternoon in Paris when the sun is shining and the flower stalls are crammed with color and young lovers are holding hands as they stroll along the Seine. All of this I was absorbing as I walked along the boulevards thinking how lucky a fellow I was to have lived in this marvelous city and been a part of it for so long.

There are so many picture galleries in Paris. You find them in the expected places and the unexpected as well, because art is in the air everywhere. Today I was entering a gallery I had never even seen before. Through its window I had spied a Renoir on the wall and I still was looking for one. In a way selecting a painting is for me like choosing a song to perform. It must have more than the proper form and substance; it must have a personal message for me, and when it's there I know it almost at once.

This Renoir was beautiful, but there was no message, and

apparently I was shaking my head, for a voice behind me said teasingly, "Perhaps you'd prefer a Matisse, monsieur." I turned to face Nicole Delande, dressed in the same unconventional manner as those times I'd seen her on the Riviera, but her warm smile was still very attractive and appealing.

"How was your show?" I asked. "And I'm sorry I had to miss it."

"Good, but so long ago I'm ready for another."

"Why don't you tell me about it over an *apéritif?*"

She nodded and we went in search of a sidewalk café, which, too, is not hard to find in Paris. And as we drank a glass of white wine, I studied her face and realized how interesting it was and how vital were her eyes. She had been working hard, she was thinking of moving to Paris, and work was still the grand passion of her life. Suddenly she stopped answering my questions.

"I don't want to talk of me any more," she said seriously. "I've followed you in the papers. South America, Africa, Spain, Portugal — don't you ever stop?"

"Not often," I said wryly.

"Well, you should. At least, rest occasionally," she went on half scoldingly, "because you look weary." I found myself smiling a little at her almost maternal intentness, but at the same time in an odd fashion it pleased me that she was concerned. "Why don't you go down to La Bocca and relax?"

"I wish I could, but I'm going into rehearsal for a big production at the Empire," I replied, and then surprisingly I began to tell this girl whom I had seen so few times before all the details of the spectacle I had agreed to star in and of my worries in having accepted the task of carrying a whole show on my shoulders as in the old days instead of just continuing with my one-man performances.

Somehow it seemed so comfortable to be confiding in her, for she was a marvelous listener in the way that certain people are who act as a kind of sympathetic sounding board. They can't really advise you, but you feel so strongly their intelligent understanding that often your tension disappears and afterwards there is the wonderful sense of everything looking brighter.

She was leaving soon for the south and I wouldn't be seeing her again perhaps for months, but the hour I spent at that sidewalk café with Nicole was a warming thought that stayed with me long after we parted that afternoon. And truly I felt a little wistful as I reflected how good it would be if we were friends who could talk with each other more often than an occasional encounter.

We would surely not be meeting on the Riviera very frequently, for soon after that day at the gallery I made arrangements to give my house at La Bocca to a society of composers and lyricists, who would use it as a charity home for their members who had come upon bad times. It saddened me to think that my mother, not strong enough to make the long, tiring journey, had never seen that lovely retreat on the Mediterranean hillside which I had named for her.

Now there was to be a new "La Louque." Ten minutes beyond Paris in the little village of Marnes-la-Coquette I had bought a house surrounded by tall, stately trees and carpeted lawn and lavish gardens, presently in disarray, but soon to be restored to even greater beauty. A few hundred yards away a distinguished American general stationed in Paris was my neighbor, but he was to return to his country eight weeks before I moved into my new home, and we were not to meet until much later when I would be presented to him at the White House in Washington. His name, of course, was Eisenhower.

Soon after "La Louque" was ready, our show at the Empire closed and in rapid succession, touring my one-man show, I lost my voice and had to cancel a performance for the first time in my life, found a fraction of it three days later, thanks to penicillin, but was forced to use a microphone for the first time in my life, and still struggling with laryngitis weeks later met the one and only Louis Armstrong, also for the first time.

Since we were both playing in the same city, the newspapers brought us together for pictures, and I told Louis that I was managing to sing just on the edge of my voice and I was getting frightened, so much so that I was afraid I might have to give up.

"Don't you worry, man," he said with that wonderful Armstrong grin. "I'm going to send you my recipe. It ain't never failed yet."

The throat medicine, half glycerine, half honey, which arrived at my hotel that afternoon worked a miracle for me by nightfall, and I've carried a bottle of Louis' magic elixir with me ever since, taking a swallow before every performance. And each time I do, I laugh as I recall that marvelous scratchy Armstrong voice and wonder what it would be like without glycerine and honey to soften it.

It WAS my fifty-fifth year in show business, and at the elegant Théâtre des Champs Elysées I had just played the last of fifty-five commemorative evenings of song. From my dressing room I could hear backstage those sounds that have always brought me a little bit of sadness — the distinctive bustle of props being removed, a set being struck, lights taken down — that come with the end of a run. It's a reflective time for remembering the peaks and the lows, that night when everything was absolutely perfect and the one when a buzzing fly persisted in circling your face caught in the glare of the spotlight at a critically poignant moment in your song.

But the time for recollection is brief, for soon there comes a knock on the door and friends are there to say farewell for this season and to query you about the next. And the past is set aside to make way for the crowding future. Even after more than half a century of it, I was thinking, you can't simply stand still. You either quit entirely, or you must keep going forward.

The knock sounded and the door opened and there stood Mist, a little in shadow. She was more than eighty now, but the smile that lighted her face was still provocative. Her voice had grown paler, but she had never forgotten how to use it for just that right effect.

"Cio?" she said and she laughed. "I have no photographers up my sleeve. May I come in?"

She moved into the light as we embraced and suddenly I saw that the years had done their inexorable work. In those which had gone by since I had last seen her, Mist had begun to look really old as if she, too, had almost reached the end of a run, but of life itself. She had a fragile, drawn, too-thin look, and as we talked I saw that the smile which once was so daring now wore the strain of effort.

"Are you well, Mist?" I asked, concerned.

"I was watching you tonight, wasn't I?" she replied and even at this moment when life had stolen so much from her, she summoned the determined pride that had always been her mark. "And I'll be out there the next time, too."

She didn't stay long. She was obviously tired, and as she turned at the door she didn't know that I saw her holding to it for support. "Au 'voir, Cio," she said and moved away, and I greeted other friends who had come up, but a nagging edge of worry about Mist had crept in which wouldn't go away.

NICOLE had moved to Paris. She had a studio crowded with paintings, and I was there to buy one. I had made my choice and I was pleased and buoyed as I always am when I add a new picture to my collection, but she seemed a little less than overjoyed.

"For a girl who's just sold her work, you're pretty downhearted," I teased her.

She managed a smile. "You know I'm delighted. I don't hang

beside Utrillo that often." She crossed to the huge window to stare out into the brooding afternoon and spoke without turning. "Would I be imposing on a fairly new friendship if I asked for help, Maurice?"

"Of course not. What's wrong?"

She faced me with deep seriousness. "I'm selling canvases all the time. I guess in a way I'm a success at all this, but it's not enough because I'm not going anywhere, do you know what I mean?" I nodded. "I'm on a lucrative treadmill, and I want to step off and experiment with a whole new approach." She smiled miserably. "But I'm frightened, because it might not work and then where would I be?"

"Happy, I think," I said, "at least for having tried."

I told her how so long ago I had learned the danger of complacency, that no matter what his profession one should never be satisfied with his efforts or the world would eventually pass him by.

"Do you know something?" she said at last. "I needed you to tell me this, because there was no one else I could trust. Thank you, Maurice."

I was touched that she would want my advice and I said so. "And when I return from America," I grinned, "perhaps you'll show me what I've wrought."

"America?" A frown crossed her face. "When?"

"Right away. I've signed to do my show on Broadway for six weeks."

"Then you're coming back?"

I shook my head. "Probably not for a while. One thing there usually leads to another."

"Oh, I see." She smiled a little unhappily. "I don't see you very often as it is. I'm going to miss you."

"I'll miss you, Nicole."

I could see it approaching at that moment, a kind of marvelous, friendly affection between us. It was pleasing, this unde-

408

manding sentiment we were beginning to share. It seemed to offer the promise of more than an ordinary friendship, I was thinking, though I couldn't say the difference. No, I could only feel it, because it wasn't clear yet. But somehow, in a way I didn't quite understand, Nicole Delande and I were surely drawing closer each time we met.

LIKE Nicole, I was trying something new, and the experience was overwhelming. My first live television show. And of all the cities in the world in which to undertake an exciting and at the same time awesome ninety-minute spectacular in a studio crowded with cameras, each with its own crew, banks of blinding lights with their operators crawling on narrow catwalks above you, dancers and singers and musicians in the bedlam of final arrangements before dress rehearsal, New York was surely the town. For New York itself with its rushing throngs and subways and skyscrapers and vitality is surely the greatest spectacular of them all.

It was marvelous to be working again in America. The weeks on Broadway had sped by and then more as I sang in a beautiful room at the Waldorf-Astoria and finally this "Maurice Chevalier Show" with a talented, sensitive producer named Max Liebman, who was a kind of father of these long, lavish shows done live on television.

And as this last rehearsal ended and all the cast were giving him a big hand, I said a little tentatively because I was not at all completely confident, "I hope you're satisfied with me."

He gave me a wonderful smile that was so warm and sincere. "It's more than that. I'm enthused."

The cast who had been grouped around us echoed his words, and suddenly I had the feeling that it was all going to be all right. I had not been so sure before. I was not playing now in a theatre or a grand hotel room in front of people who had prob-

409

ably come to see me because they remembered me from the Hollywood days or my brief tours here after the war. No, with this fantastic new medium of television in a way I was opening cold, making my debut before an entire new generation of Americans, and I could cut my throat in a single hour and a half.

The warning cue came from the assistant director, the red light of Camera One flicked on, and the show had begun. It was long, and in a way it was devastating because so much was hanging on every line and expression and bit of business that must be exactly correct lest the show falter and the camera glaringly reveal your mistake. But it was done at last, and for the first time in two decades I had met America from coast to coast. As I moved past the young performers who were grinning and patting me on the back, I knew that I would have my answer tomorrow whether the judgment from America would again be favorable. If I had flopped tonight at sixty-seven, it was all over.

Before I reached my dressing room, a stagehand called me to the phone, and standing there in the hallway speaking on the wall telephone to Mary Martin and Helen Hayes calling together, I got my first response.

"Maurice," one said, "you've won the heart of America once more."

"Fifty million hearts," the other put in.

And I stood there beaming, even though I was sure it was an exaggeration of the moment. They were good critics, and I felt there was a chance that others would agree.

They did. Telegrams, newspaper reviews from every corner of the country bore unanimous congratulations. In one show I had begun to march on a new road in America.

I didn't know then that the road was leading toward Hollywood, for the first result of television was an engagement at the Dunes Hotel in Las Vegas. Danny Kaye was there to introduce me on opening night and the audience was amiable but not too enthusiastic. It seemed to me that they listened with only one ear while the other was straining to hear the sounds of slot machines and roulette wheels from the rooms beyond.

Marlene, who was there for the show, hoped I would change my orchestrations, she found them a little "thin," and Danny thought I should wear a little make-up, while Sophie Tucker spoke of working nearer the music. Obviously I hadn't exactly dazzled them at Las Vegas in my debut.

But the audiences who followed, though not exalted, were pleased enough, and I settled into that strange life of this Nevada oasis where one stays up most of the night and sleeps till the late afternoon, then goes to the pool to soak up sun and energy to repeat the pattern once more. I didn't gamble. I never have, because I know myself. I have in me that excessive streak which can be like an army of demons, and if I let myself go with gambling, I fear it could be almost a disease.

I walked past the dice tables and the others and went up to my room. Rather absently I switched on the radio. The news was on, but I only half listened, because my mind was on a slight change I might make in one song tonight. I was debating the idea when the newscaster's voice said "Mistinguett." I whirled to hear, and with each word of that broadcast the chill in me grew greater. Mist had suffered a stroke this morning in Paris. Her chances for survival were not good.

The voice went on to another story, but I heard no more, for I was too heartsick with this news of Mist. I had seen she was not well that night in the theatre and been concerned, but one seldom thinks truly of the worst till it's happening. Now she was lying still and helpless in a hospital bed, her life ebbing away, and I was sitting in a strange hotel room in a desert town — remembering.

So many memories were crowding each other: Our first kiss, wrapped together in that extraordinary rug; the fight with that other man when Mist became mine completely; those days when prison camp was at last behind me and Mist brought joy into my life again; and finally the ending of the rich, full years of the greatest love I would ever know.

Almost mechanically I moved to the phone to cable her that in three weeks I would be back in Paris, that I would come to see her at once, that I sent my love and friendship and support. But even as I sent the words, I wondered if she could even hear or comprehend them now and if she would still be there when I arrived.

IT WAS very early in the morning and I was asleep when the phone rang. It had a shrill, stark, demanding sound as I groped for the lamp in the darkness. Somehow I knew the message before the newspaper in New York gave it to me.

Mist was dead.

. . . Cinq

A GAIN AND AGAIN the phone rang in the early hours of
that fateful morning. I spoke to every caller in a voice
a little dazed. Mostly they were radio and press people
seeking the reactions of the man who had been most closely
linked with Mist in life, but it is not easy to sort one's
deepest emotions when the blow of death has numbed
them. Finally to the representative of the French radio
I promised a cable which would express my feeling, and
in a pool of lamplight that made the blackness outside my
window seem even more opaque, I sat alone with my
thoughts and wrote.

413

Tu ne pars pas.

Tu ne disparais pas.

Tu te transformes, voilà tout.

Tu seras toujours là où la vie me conduira.

*Ton visage, ton regard, ton rire, traverseront les ombres
bruyantes des endroits où l'agitation tente de remplacer
l'amour.*

Tu as été ma femme, ma maîtresse, ma plus grande amie.

Tu as aimé ma mère.

*Par toi, j'ai compris beaucoup de ce que la chance et le
travail m'ont permis de compléter par la suite.*

Notre métier nous a un jour séparés. C'est à notre honneur.

*Mais rien n'a pu faire que dans ton coeur et dans le mien,
nos places n'aient été cimentées par nos enthousiasmes,
nos victoires, et nos erreurs.*

Tu peux te reposer, Mist.

*Tu as représenté la Parisienne mieux que personne avant
toi, aussi bien que quiconque pourra le faire dans l'avenir,
si un astre se lève.*

*Tu as été le physique, l'esprit, la gouaille, le chic de la
Ville de la Femme.*

*Tu as été adorée de la galerie comme des fauteuils et des
loges.*

*Tu resteras pour tous une lumière entre les lumières de la
Ville Lumière.*

Éternellement.

MAURICE

It's not so easy to say it exactly in English because certain
words in every language defy translation. But the meaning and
the sentiment are surely there, no matter what tongue you put
them in, for they are phrases of the heart, and that I think is
an international language.

You are not leaving.
You are not disappearing.
You are changing — that's all.
You will always be where life will lead me.
Your face, your look, your laugh, crossing the noisy shadows
    where turmoil attempts to replace love.
You have been my wife, my mistress, my greatest friend.
You loved my mother.
Through you, I've understood so much of what luck and
    work have allowed me to accomplish afterwards.
Our profession separated us one day. We can take pride
    in this.
For nothing could change in your heart or mine.
What we meant to each other had been cemented by our
    enthusiasms, our victories and our mistakes.
You can rest now, Mist.
You have represented "La Parisienne" better than anyone
    before you, as well as anyone ever can in the future, if
    another star should rise.
You have been the beauty, the spirit, the magic, the sym-
    bol of the city of women.
You have been adored from the balcony as well as the
    orchestra.
You will remain for all a light among the lights of the
    City of Lights.
Eternally.

MAURICE

I sent the cable, and life went on as it must, but Mist's death
left me desolate. I told myself over and over that she was
very old, that in a way she had been freed from days without
serenity, that it was best for her and those who cherished her.
But the words all seemed a little hollow, for you think of some
beings as immortal. Then one morning you learn, stunned, that

they are gone, and you follow your own road troubled, dispirited and with a coldness in the blood.

My television show apparently had impressed the movie people in Hollywood, for an invitation had come to participate in my first Academy Awards celebration, when Ernest Borgnine was to win an Oscar for *Marty* and Anna Magnani that wonderful award for *The Rose Tattoo*. My part in the evening's entertainment had begun with a singing scene from a film I had made here almost thirty years ago, projected onto a screen in the theatre where the Oscars were being presented. From the wings with a microphone I had finished the song and moved out on stage to do another.

And afterwards I had been seated at the Academy dinner next to a storybook princess who was leaving the next day to marry her real-life prince. Grace Kelly was a Dresden doll, I thought, with a kind of platinum beneath the delicate porcelain, a beautiful girl who I felt was always in control of her world. When I asked her to dance, she replied with quiet dignity that much as she would like to do so, she had decided to dance with no one until she danced again with Rainier in faraway Monte Carlo. I had to admit it was admirable.

It had been a memorable night for me, but how very much so I didn't realize till the next day when Billy Wilder telephoned.

"Maurice," he said briskly, "seeing you last night has given me an idea. Can we meet and talk about it?"

Sitting across from him that afternoon as he spoke with quick, concise gestures, I was thinking how marvelously tenacious was Billy's loyalty and affection. He had never abandoned his idea of seeing me in a Hollywood production again, and now he was offering me a part in a picture he was shooting in Paris with Gary Cooper and Audrey Hepburn to be called *Love in the Afternoon*.

"You won't sing or dance in this one, Maurice," he was saying. "You'll just be the kind of good dramatic actor I know you can be."

I couldn't help a wry grin. "You mean not cute?" He looked at me quizzically. "I'll explain it sometime, Billy. But I'm interested, and what's the part?"

"Audrey's father. You'll be perfect for it."

So I was to be the father of that adorable Audrey Hepburn whom I had met at a Sam Goldwyn party in New York a few months before. Well, I was saying to myself, you're too old to play the lover, so why not settle happily for what you really are and be glad they didn't make you the grandfather? We would be filming in Paris, and I would be doing in an American picture what I had wanted to do two decades ago — be more than cute. It was a chance to jump at, and I jumped.

But on the day that shooting began, I was wondering what I had taken on for myself. As Audrey and Gary and I listened to Billy's concept of the film that first day on the set, I suddenly began to worry about my English. Because the way I speak this language is surely a part of my personality. Yet in this role I was to put that old Chevalier aside and be someone else, a private detective who was the father of a charming, incurably romantic young girl, and if the accent were the same, could I be anything but my old self?

The combination of a marvelous dialogue coach and Billy Wilder, a great director with whom I found myself working as easily as I had once done with Ernst Lubitsch, dissolved my worries in a single day. Billy came up to me when shooting was over and put his arm around my shoulder.

"I was right, Maurice," he said excitedly, and there was another echo of Lubitsch. "You *are* the father!"

Coming from the man who really had taken a chance on me, it was delicious praise. And from that day forward *Love in the Afternoon* became work that was truly a pleasure. When it

417

ended and Billy said we had a good movie and we shook hands on it, I knew I had been lucky to have been involved with such a talented man.

IT WAS the time of the Suez crisis, and a mood of gloom and pessimism had settled over Paris. With little gas and oil now coming into the country, rationing had been resumed, bringing with it unpleasant memories of similar days during the war. It was winter and cold and depressing.

In my heart this morning was an added chill, for I had come down the Rue Royale past the famed restaurant, Maxim's, to the beautiful church of the Madeleine at the foot of the street to attend a memorial mass for Mistinguett. A year had passed since Mist's death, but today was bringing it near again.

Inside the shadowed sanctuary the solemn Latin chant echoed off the stone walls. It was a heavy, somber sound. Only Mist's family and those who had known her closely had been told of the ceremony, and for an instant time went backward and one could almost feel Mist herself a part of this intimate group. Then the liturgy was over, and one spoke subdued good-bys and emerged again into the street and life returned to the present.

I moved slowly down the steps, weighted with the sadness that occasions like this must bring, feeling just a little lost.

"Maurice?" A figure had risen from a bench on the sidewalk to move toward me. Surprised, I recognized Nicole. She read my expression. "You mentioned you were coming here, and I decided it was a good day not to paint but wait for you instead."

"You've just been sitting out in the cold?"

"It's a warm coat." Her eyes were questioning mine intently. "I know there are times when one prefers to be alone with his memories," she said gently. "But days like today can be difficult, and I thought if you came out and you happened to want company, I'd be here."

It was such a tender gesture, reaching my heart so strongly, that for the first time I saw what my friendship with Nicole had become. Ours was a bond of more than ordinary friendship. It was a drawing together of two people with more than ordinary warmth and affection and admiration and concern for each other. It was a loving friendship.

A *loving friendship*. The words were being written across my mind, and I could see how far we two had come since the day we had visited Matisse together. Returning that afternoon I had thought of Nicole as a future friend, for I had known many women in my life that way with a rapport which was pleasant and congenial and impersonal. But in none of those relationships was there the great gift of tenderness, that compassionate response in the heart. And here it was now, so plain to see, between this pretty girl and me.

She was pretty. Her cheeks flushed with the cold, her eyes glowing with youth and intelligence and vitality, she was very pretty, and I had to admit I was aware of that in her. But even as I admitted it, I knew I would make no move to endanger this loving friendship which so slowly and gently and sensitively had come alive. Each of us had renounced love, so physically there must be nothing between us, but spiritually and emotionally we could share all the richness that life holds when you care deeply about another human being.

"I think you'd rather be alone, Maurice," Nicole was saying. "I understand." She smiled quietly and started for the subway entrance a few yards away.

"Nicole, wait," I called and she turned back. I moved to her and took her hand. We looked at each other with a kind of silent understanding and then walked away together.

LOVE IN THE AFTERNOON had clicked, not with a smashing, record-breaking success but with a solid, comfortable reception. People had liked it. They had emerged from theatres around the country wearing pleased smiles, and I wore one, too, for it looked as if Hollywood and I were going to get together again.

In the entertainment world one is always juggling offers and plans, weighing this one, rejecting that, postponing consideration of the next, accepting finally the one that seems right. A cable from my agent in Hollywood intrigued me. "M. G. M. wants you for musical version Colette's *Gigi*. Fine part, fine songs for you. Advise."

I was remembering my visit with brilliant, enchanting Colette, dead almost three years now, and the book on the table which I had later read. Gigi — the engagingly piquant young girl who is tutored to be a courtesan only to end up by marrying the rich young man. And I would be the worldly uncle of the young man, a kind of charming, rakish old fellow, wise in the ways of life and love. It was a role with zest. It was surely the one to accept.

And soon I was meeting, first in Belgium, then Paris, with Alan Jay Lerner and Frederick Loewe, authors of the fabulous *My Fair Lady*, who would be writing the book and lyrics and music of *Gigi*. They came over just to meet me, to talk, to get the flavor of my work. In Ostend they saw my one-man show, and in Paris an idea for a winsome song was born as we exchanged feelings and reactions.

It was to Alan Lerner that I told my philosophy of love, how in these later years I had abandoned any tempestuous romantic involvement, how I was not any more the man to play that game, and how I had no deep regrets about it.

A thoughtful expression crossed his face. "You mean you're glad it's all behind you?"

I shook my head a little unhappily. "You're never glad of it, but you can be satisfied if you have had that side of living in a beautiful way."

He said no more at the time, but later they gave me a nice tune to sing, inspired by our conversation — "I'm Glad I'm Not

Young Any More." And since you can do nothing about the march of years, you might as well not grieve about it, you see?

Much of *Gigi* was shot that fall in Paris with all its color and charm, but for a scene with Hermione Gingold that was supposed to be Deauville in summer, we journeyed to Hollywood and the company worked on the beach at Santa Monica. The lifeguard, a tall, bronzed young fellow crossed the sand to my side.

"Mr. Chevalier?"

"Yes?"

"I just wanted to say hello." He grinned. "I'm Baby Leroy."

Baby Leroy! Suddenly in my brain there was what in the films we call a "blur pan." It's when the image on the screen moves so swiftly to the next image that everything blurs for an instant, and it's often used to flash one backwards through time from one event to another. It was happening to me now, for this good-looking boy was no longer twenty-five and tall, but ten months old and very small.

I was standing in a foundling home in Hollywood with Norman Taurog, my director, and we were choosing a baby from this nursery of abandoned youngsters for my latest film, *Bedtime Story*. In a crib an appealing infant was laughing, laughing with a wonderful toothless grin. He was marvelous, this little Baby Leroy, and Norman and I said practically together, "That's the one." And what a lovable child we had selected! The cast, the crew, everyone adored him as he laughed his way through scene after scene for the three months of shooting.

But, alas, retakes were necessary at the end for vital scenes to be inserted in the film, and Baby Leroy's tiny, empty gums were now proudly displaying two obvious teeth! What does one do in a case like this but shrug and go ahead? As a result, when *Bedtime Story* was shown around the world, baffled audiences saw my baby with no teeth, two seconds later with two teeth, and in the next two seconds toothless once more!

421

He was a great success, however, and Baby Leroy starred in ten films in the season that followed till inevitably he grew too big and a New York newspaper headlined its front page when my little protégé became a has-been at the age of two, "Is Baby Leroy Washed Up?"

The blur pan was reversing now and I was in the present again, grinning back at the strapping lifeguard. "What can I say, monsieur," I said helplessly, "but 'Come bounce on my knee'?"

THE muted roar of the giant plane's motors filled the darkened cabin as each minute brought us nearer to Paris. Far ahead in the east a hint of dawn had softened the black horizon to a kind of pale gray. Below through breaks in the snowfield of clouds was the sea, and above me was the limitless sky with the stars remote and cold.

I sleep little in airplanes. When the night surrounds me and reading becomes a trial, I flick off the light and sit in silent awareness of the smallness of humans and the vastness of the universe. And I think of time, the chain which links everything and governs all that befalls us. Time had been good to me, I was thinking now, for so much had happened to me and I was on my way to celebrating seven decades of living.

And, God willing, there was more to come. America was behind me for the present, but I would surely be back again and again. *Gigi* was completed and the reports were glowing. Of course, I had no oracle to tell me at that moment that the film would endear itself to millions and win nine Academy Awards in the year to come. The unpredictable workings of time. Nor was there a prediction for me that with *Gigi* I would be returning strongly to Hollywood's world in films with Deborah Kerr and Sophia Loren and Frank Sinatra and to work for the first time with my old friend Charles Boyer in *Fanny*.

422

This I could not know then, but I could at least relish the future for it seemed that good work was going to come my way. *Work and love.* These had been from the beginning the two great forces of my life. The first was strong and vital still and happiness was surging in me because of it. The second was only memory now, I was thinking, but I would be forever grateful that love had touched me, for it had given me perhaps its greatest gift: It had left me richer than it had found me.

If you have not loved at all, it's pretty sad because you have had nothing. But with love even when its pain brings suffering you become richer, because it leaves its mark in your heart and in your way of living after that. It can teach you to be more humble, to be less pretentious and to understand more deeply. And in love, just as in work, to learn truly you must try to go through failures in the best possible way. I think that what makes people great is not to have only moments of success — it is to have moments of failure and to survive them in as beautiful a way as you can.

But there is more to the wealth of love than that. For me at least it had left a tender and separate souvenir from each of the women with whom I had shared it. And though fate had not chosen to bestow on me the gift of that marvelous love with one woman for a whole lifetime, I had nonetheless been blessed, for though love had gone now, its rewards would be with me always.

Suddenly I was aware that we had reached the dawn and passed through it and day was around us, alive and gleaming with promise. The ocean was below us no longer. Now it was the familiar green and brown landscape of France. In less than an hour we would be on the ground at Orly.

And Nicole had written she would be waiting there. Her warm and sensitive letters had brought an extra brightness to so many hours for me, and I found myself eager now to be with her again and share our experiences since we had parted. That farewell had been only a few weeks ago, but I missed her. This was one of the qualities of a loving friendship, I was thinking, that as in love itself, separation could be bitter and reunion sweet.

It was still on my mind when the plane landed and taxied to the apron and we moved through the sparkling, cold morning toward the terminal. Why had it happened, I asked myself, this rare spiritual relationship I would guard unchanged for the rest of my days, this emotional understanding I called a "loving friendship"? Why had two people who had chosen to banish love from their lives slowly been drawn together in a sentiment that had so many of love's aspects?

The thought caused me to stop short at the door for an instant. This loving friendship offered the richness of devotion, the unselfishness of a deep affection, generosity and sympathy and faith. *In a way, was all this not a kind of love?* Had our hearts' unconscious search gone on and on even after love had been denied, and was this wonderful responsiveness between us truly another face of love?

Suddenly, as I entered the terminal to pass through customs, a special kind of happiness was singing in me, for it seemed that surely I had made an astonishing discovery this morning.

"Maurice?"

I looked beyond the barrier to the voice, and there was Nicole entering the room, her eyes alight with a look of joy and welcome that told me what I had just learned for myself: That there is no remedy for love but to love more.

FIN

424